A Promise Kept

A Tribute to a Mother's Love

ANDRIY J. SEMOTIUK

ISBN: 1483997669
ISBN 13: 9781483997667
Library of Congress Control Number: 2013906577
Create Space Independent Publishing Platform
North Charleston, South Carolina

"To the world you may be one person,

but to one person you may be the world."

William Griffith Wilson

Vancouver   March 30/2014

Для Лесі Куз —

" На пам'ятку "

з нашої зустрічі

з Повагою
—
Андрій Семотюк

Introduction

AS I WAS growing up, and later in my adulthood, I sensed that I should keep a record of my mother's life. It was not because she was some sort of celebrity, enjoyed any particular social status, or held any great wealth. On the contrary, what made her so remarkable to me was how she dealt with her normal daily life, especially given her difficult and limited circumstances.

I could not bear the thought that my mother's life would pass from this world without any record or at least some mention left of all the hardships she endured, the setbacks she faced, and the contributions she made to her family, her community, and the world at large. I therefore made it a point to remember many conversations we had together as well as with our relatives and friends. I recorded audio interviews with her, stored her letters and documents, and kept a journal of our lives together. To me this was sacred material. Many years after my mother's death, I was able to reconstruct her life story, as well as my life with her, from these sources.

Introduction

To distinguish my mother's actual reflections, and those of our other family members and friends included in this text, I placed her words in italics. While these inclusions may not be exact quotes, I have recounted them as closely to what was said as I could, reconstructing them a few decades later. What follows is the true story that emerged.

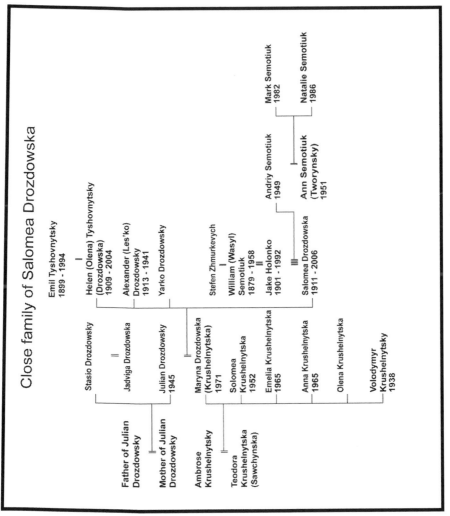

Close family of Salomea Drozdowska

Salomea Drozdowska's family tree

Close family of William (Wasyl) Semotiuk

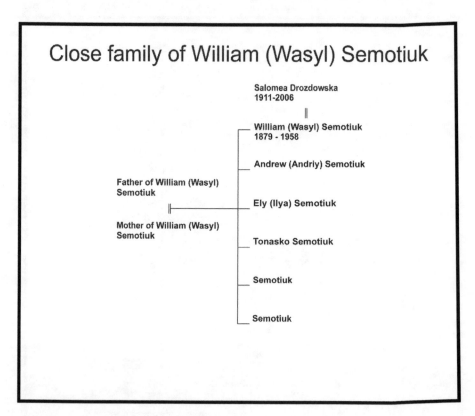

William Semotiuk's family tree

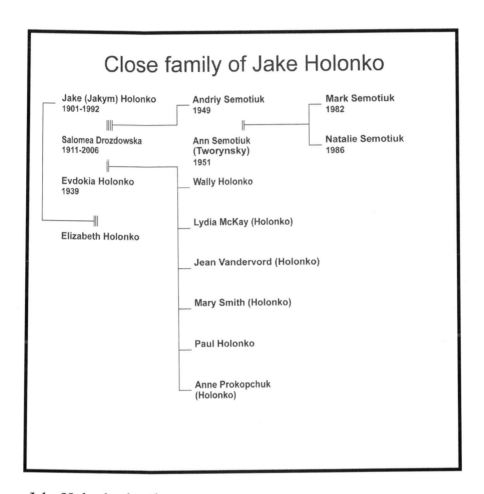

Close family of Jake Holonko

Jake (Jakym) Holonko
1901-1992

Salomea Drozdowska
1911-2006

Evdokia Holonko
1939

Elizabeth Holonko

Andriy Semotiuk
1949

Ann Semotiuk
(Tworynsky)
1951

Wally Holonko

Lydia McKay (Holonko)

Jean Vandervord (Holonko)

Mary Smith (Holonko)

Paul Holonko

Anne Prokopchuk
(Holonko)

Mark Semotiuk
1982

Natalie Semotiuk
1986

Jake Holonko family tree

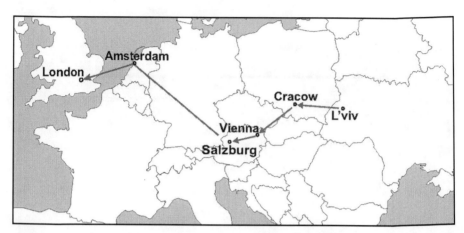

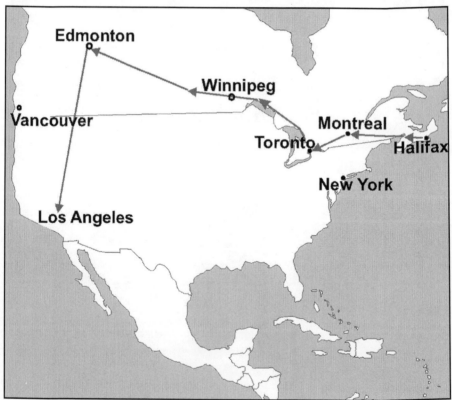

Salomea Drozdowska's life journey

Table of Contents

Chapter 1
The Early Years

1

First Memories

WHEN MY MOTHER was only two years old and playing outside with some other children one late summer afternoon in 1913, she fell ill and ran home. Her mother, Maryna Drozdowska, met my mother at the doorstep of their house in the Galician town of Drohobych in Eastern Europe.

My mother's complaints were unusual. Her neck hurt. She was listless. Her eyes were sensitive to light. Twisting and fidgeting after being seated on a kitchen chair, she resisted her mother's attempts to take a good look at her. When she eventually came down with a high fever, Maryna called out to her husband Julian to take a look at the child. After one look Julian declared he was going to find a doctor. Many years later my mother described what happened next according to what she was told by her parents later in her life.

After the doctor examined me, he concluded that I probably had caught a cold from a child next door. He left us some medicine and told my parents to keep me home and in bed. If all went well, he said, the illness would clear up after a few days. If not they were to call him again.

It took about a week for the illness to go away. I was happy to get outside again. My parents were relieved to see that I was feeling better. A few weeks later, however, while I was playing in my backyard, a neighbor called out to me, "Solomka." I didn't reply. After several further attempts, the neighbor noticed that I finally stuck out my right ear to hear her calling and reported this to my parents. They decided to call the doctor again.

After examining me this time, the doctor was shocked. He concluded I had been afflicted by spinal meningitis, and it had rendered my left ear totally deaf. I did not know then what a far-reaching impact that fact would have on my life in the years to come.

Without a doubt this was a major setback for my mother in her tender, early years. The illness had destroyed the nerve cell in her ear, but apart from the hearing loss, she was spared from any learning disability or brain damage. More important, the illness had spared her life. My mother and her parents were very thankful for that.

When these incidents occurred, my mother's family had just moved from the Ukrainian town of Pidhaitsi, in Galicia, where she was born, to the predominantly Jewish town of Drohobych. This town also was located in Galicia, amid grassy lands and rolling hills, near the strategically important Boryslaw oil and gas region, then under the control of the Austro-Hungarian Empire. When my mother's father, Julian Drozdowsky, got his first important posting as a judge in the key developing area

Julian and Maryna Drozdowsky, Salomea's parents in Galicia in 1908

of oil and gas law there, he packed up the whole family and moved them with him—the hundred miles or so—to the new town. Apart from my mother, there were two other children in the family, Helen (Olena), my aunt, who was two years older, and Alexander (Les'ko), my uncle, who would come along later and was two-and-a-half years younger than my mother.[1]

My mother, Salomea, was an energetic, limber child, with dark-brown hair, lightly tanned skin, clear brown eyes, and arched eyebrows. Alex was a freckled, fair-skinned, curly-haired boy. Apart from meningitis, my mother invariably came down with other childhood illnesses, as did her little brother. These were always a source of concern for their parents but served to bond the two children together. Once, when they were still small and came down with whooping cough, their mother placed both of them in bed and wrapped a blanket tightly around them. Then, under the blanket, she added some heated bricks covered with an aromatic medication at their feet to keep the children warm while helping them breathe at night. Overcoming such illnesses and sharing their early years together provided my mother and Alex with many stories to reminisce about later in life. Walking together to school, spending summers hiking in the Carpathian Mountains, swimming in their backyard creek, and camping and sitting around late-night

5

bonfires were all happy moments they shared. They were not only close friends but also allies, as well as mutual protectors and mentors.

Unlike her relationship with her brother, however, an early sibling rivalry developed between my mother and her older sister. Helen was a thin, agile brunette with a sandy complexion and a few freckles lightly sprinkled across her nose and face. As they competed for the attention of their parents, my mother felt that her parents favored her older sister. In part this was because her sister was born on April 23, 1909, while my mother was born on April 24, 1911. Since Helen's birthday came first, the family always marked her milestone before my mother's, thus eclipsing my mother's birthday, as if it was a sideshow to the main event. For this, or whatever other reasons—no doubt including my mother's hearing disability—their differences emerged early but didn't become pronounced until later in their lives. In the meantime they enjoyed various aspects of their childhoods.

I enjoyed school, although not everything. For example I found French a difficult language to learn. But I enjoyed the social aspects of being in school, sometimes staying after hours to the point that when I finally came home my father was waiting for me, wondering why I had not shown up for dinner. As he sat across the kitchen table from me, watching as I ate my late dinner, he would ask where I was. Since I didn't like him watching me, I didn't always tell him that I remained in school from four until six p.m. but instead just said I was playing with friends. He would sit with me quietly, deep in thought.

While my mother did not always welcome her father's company at dinnertime, she especially loved him, even though he was the disciplinarian of the family. When she misbehaved he would say, *"Marshiren do kutyka"* ("March to the corner") while pointing to the corner of the room. "While I had my turn standing in the corner for my punishment," my mother recalled, "he was gentle and fair to me and the other children."

Her father often said to her, "Solomka, tell me what time it is." Since she was still too small to tell time, she would say, "The big hand is on the one, and the little hand is on the four." He would chuckle to himself and later delight in sharing the story with his wife.

Julian earned a reasonable salary as a judge, but even so, money was tight, especially with three young children to look after. He hated any form of debt and kept a close rein on household spending. He passed on that mindset to his daughters, my mother and Helen, who both lived frugally and made a point of paying their bills on time, or even early, throughout their lives. Julian's wife, Maryna, who wanted to provide the family with little extras and small indulgences, often took part-time jobs writing articles for a newspaper or helping to cook for large gatherings for spending money.

Julian was a prominent figure in the community and so well respected that my mother could go to a store for the family and buy things on credit. She would say, *"Tatko zaplatyt"* ("Father will pay"), and the storeowner would allow her to take the goods because he trusted Julian to pay.

My mother's best friend during her childhood years was a girl named Sabina Springer. Sabina's family was quite large, with five children. Her father was a tailor, but a stroke had debilitated him. His arm paralyzed, he became a secondhand merchant, walking through the streets shouting, *"Handel, handel,"* which signaled to the townspeople that, for a few pennies, he would buy any goods they no longer wanted. He then sold the goods at a local market to eke out a living. To help put food on the table, Sabina's mother ran a laundry shop.

Sabina was the same age as my mother. One time my mother told me how they played together. "We studied history together. Sabina would pretend to be the teacher and dictate a history lesson to me while I pretended to be a pupil writing it down."

Apart from playing with the Springers, my mother and Helen liked to tease a neighborhood child, Myron Gawrychinsky, a small boy who played in the same courtyard with them. They would sneak up when he wasn't looking and pinch him, then run away in laughter as he turned around to chase after them. When there was no one else to play with, my mother would sit on a round wooden crossbar held up from the ground by two end fence posts, tilt backward while holding on with her legs, and swing completely around the crossbar, looping without falling. On other occasions, while at home, she liked to jump four steps at a time while going downstairs and also could leap from a top bunk bed down to a shelf, then down to the floor without any difficulty because she was so limber.

My mother once recalled the time she had gone sledding with her friends down the main street near the Drohobych prison, where they held political prisoners, mostly anti-monarchist revolutionaries, communists, and nationalists of the Serbian, Czech, Slovakian, and Ukrainian variety.

> *There was a long hill nearby. Kids would slide for quite a distance, and I overdid it one day. I distinctly recall coming home that evening, after sledding all afternoon, with back pain so bad that several times on the way home I had to lie down on my sled to rest. I was eight or nine years old at the time.*

A Mother Imprisoned

Around 1920, Maryna Drozdowska, my grandmother, was arrested for having been a cook in Drohobych for the anti-Polish Ukrainian military during the First World War.[2] My mother recalled the story as follows.

While Mama was in jail, she came down with typhoid fever and became deathly ill. As the days passed, our father could not bear the stress of it all. Trying to cope with Mama's dire situation while taking care of three small children—ages nine, seven, and four—without her was just too much for him. He had an emotional breakdown. Finally his oldest brother, Stasio, got his Polish wife to speak to her brother, who was a high-ranking Polish army officer, to gain Mama's release.

When we learned of her release, we waited impatiently for her arrival. But she didn't come straight home. Instead Mama went out to the countryside, took off all her clothes, and washed in the river. She didn't want to bring home the typhoid bacteria from the jail that could have infected our whole family. She then came walking home, passionately embracing our father and us on her arrival. We were overjoyed with Mama's release and safe return home. That was certainly one of the most joyous days of our lives.

If anything, being jailed for several months made Maryna an even more ardent Ukrainian patriot. She became the editor of one of the Ukrainian language journals in Drohobych, and she refused to speak Polish in public as a form of protest against the state's Polonization campaign. In fact she "Ukrainianized" her husband, whose family in earlier generations had assimilated into Polish society. She taught her husband and her children to love all things Ukrainian and to aspire to create a free, sovereign, independent Ukraine. She also became quite active in a wide variety of Ukrainian community organizations. Maryna was so involved in these activities that her children tried to pre-vent her from leaving home, according to Helen, who told me the following story.

> Our mother told us she needed to go to a meeting. Hearing this, Salomea, Alex, and I went outside in front of the house to block the doorway so she could not leave. To get around this, our mother sent out our babysitter, Hanka, a local girl with the capacity to enchant us with her storytelling skills, to distract us while our mother slipped out through the back window. Later, as we sat there absorbed by Hanka's stories, we looked up and were surprised to see our mother coming back down the road from her meeting.

The Challenge

A few years later, when my mother was twelve, she fell ill again. This time she came down with a dangerously high fever.

> As my temperature climbed, my parents bathed me in cold water to counteract the illness. My mother kept vigil at my bedside, holding cold compresses to my forehead. That was such great comfort for me. Finally, since the fever would not break, they called in the doctor.

Embarrassed by her inability to hear, my mother squirmed in her chair and resisted the doctor's examination. Her parents insisted that she stay put, and finally my mother relented. What they then discovered came as a total shock. She was now almost completely deaf. Scarlet Fever had almost totally robbed her of what was left of her hearing in her good ear.

From that pivotal moment on, she was plunged into a world of silence, as if forever separated from everyone by a window that allowed her to see—but prevented her from hearing—what was happening around her. Many years later she described her clarion resolve to deal with her setback.

> I resisted any efforts to acknowledge or draw attention to my hearing disability. I refused to be treated differently than other kids. I vowed then and there, at that early age, that I would lead the rest of my life without depending on anyone, and as if I was without a hearing impairment. I would find joy and happiness in the life I was given. I would find someone to love and who would love me, and I would raise children. I determined that I would contribute to the life of my community and the world around me, just like everyone else. I would learn to cope with this disability, no matter what it took, and I would pray to God, and especially to the Blessed Virgin Mary, to help me.

My mother's steadfast resolution was made possible, at least in part, by two advantages. First, she wasn't born deaf and was therefore able to hear her own speech until age twelve. She was thus spared the telltale "deaf voice," evidenced by the imprecise diction of someone who never has heard herself speak. This, when added to her second advantage of learning how to lip-read, made it possible for her to disguise her disability throughout her life and face life's challenges largely in the same way others did. Rather than identify with others who were deaf like her, she resolved to identify with the hearing world, even if it meant she might be somewhat socially isolated.

I have a picture of my mother from this time period that somehow survived. She's in school with her classmates posing for a group photograph, her long brown hair woven into a silk scarf at the back. She's sitting in a loose, long dress, and exhibiting good, attentive posture. Even though she isn't smiling, her face is warm and friendly. There's a hint of sincerity and kindness in her look. Viewing that picture, you could not detect the staggering loss she had just encountered. She was thirteen years old at the time.

Galicia, 1924. Salomea Drozdowska, thirteen years old, with her eighth grade class. She is sitting on the far right in the second row.

Vacations in the Carpathian Mountains

When passengers got off the train in Hrybeniw, a popular resort village in the heart of the scenic Carpathian Mountains, exactly 100 kilometers west of Lviv, they could smell the sap from the pine trees, almost like a perfume filling the air. Hrybeniw's wooded hills and snowy mountains were a magnet for hikers, cyclists, and skiers. Some of Galicia's most rewarding walking trails were located there. Because of its remoteness and relative inaccessibility, this "forgotten corner" offered travelers an opportunity to unwind while leisurely ambling through some of the country's most stunning scenery.

In 1925, with money they managed to scrape together, the Drozdowsky family, together with one of Maryna's sisters,

Aunt (Tsiotsia) Miltsia, bought some land and built a cottage near a stream in Hrybeniw. From that year on, every summer the Drozdowskys stayed at that cottage from the end of June until the first of September. Since Julian was a judge in Drohobych and later in Lviv, the Drozdowsky family was spared much of the hardship of the nearly global economic crisis in the 1930s. Despite his position, however, even he had to do other work on the side by helping charitable organizations deal with estate matters to make ends meet. To escape the day-to-day battle of survival, the family spent their summers in Hrybeniw.

It was there that my mother, then age fourteen, began to mature physically. Until then she had been very thin, in part as a result of her Aunt (Tsiotia) Yusia's strict nutritional regimen that involved locking up food and portioning it out in miserly amounts at suppertime while my mother was boarding with her in Lviv and going to school there. Although my mother was turning into a curvaceous, bosomy brunette with nice legs, clear dark-brown eyes, and a tanned complexion, she was still somewhat reserved in dealing with boys. She was more intuitive, discerning, and sensitive than many other girls. Helen, on the other hand, now sixteen years old, was an attractive young woman with a sandy, freckled complexion; clear brown eyes; and bright-white teeth. She was more congenial than my mother, at times even flippant and outgoing.

Their parents had built a veranda where the family sat in the evenings. They ate vegetables from their garden and delicious crisp apples from their apple trees. They hiked in the mountains to collect mushrooms, red currants, wild strawberries, and other berries. Occasionally they celebrated with homemade ice cream. A creek ran beside that cottage, called Black Creek (*Chornij Potik*), where they swam and played.

A shrewd entrepreneur, Aunt Miltsia bought some land nearby, where she decided to build a lodge to rent rooms to people from Lviv who wanted to spend the summer in the mountains. About two kilometers from the Drozdowsky cottage, the lodge was run so well that people from all over Galicia began to vacation there, praising it for its cleanliness, good food, and hospitality. Visitors went on mountain hikes and swam in the creek. They played soccer, volleyball, chess, and cards. Every night they sang and danced.

The Drozdowsky family on vacation at the Dubyna cottage in Galicia, circa 1930. Salomea is on the far left-hand side, standing in the second row. Her father is standing to her left, behind her. Salomea's brother Alex is sitting in the second row and is second from the right. Helen is sitting behind him, to Alex's left. Solomea Krushelnytska, the world-famous opera singer and Salomea Drozdowska's aunt, is standing in the back row on the right.

Helen Meets Her Future Husband

After a danger-filled career as a teenage recruit in the Austrian army in World War I—as well as his later service in the Ukrainian Galician Army fighting for Ukrainian independence towards the end of that war and a brave escape from a Polish prisoner of war camp after hostilities ceased—in 1925 Emil (Omelian) Tyshovnytsky found himself living in Czechoslovakia. With Western Ukraine under Polish control, Emil had to live in Czechoslovakia, because, given his wartime experiences, there was no way for him to return to his home near Lviv. At least now, holding a Czech passport, he could visit Galicia, which was how he had come to Hrybeniw in the summer of 1925 for a vacation.

While Emil and his friends talked, played, and sang around the lodge where they stayed, the housekeeper would chase them off, imploring the boys to be quiet because Reverend Joseph Slipyj was sleeping. The reverend was a close friend of my mother's parents, and they often swam in the local creek together. The unassuming man later inspired generations of Ukrainians worldwide by surviving eighteen years of brutal imprisonment in Soviet concentration camps before emerging to become a Cardinal and the Patriarch of the Ukrainian Catholic Church. Slipyj became a link between the Drozdowsky family and Emil, in that the Drozdowskys would come by the lodge where the priest stayed; this was how Emil noticed Helen.

Emil was looking for a young woman to court. He tried to impress Helen, but she detested him and hid in the attic when he came calling at the Drozdowsky cottage. She later recalled that he was so fat back then that she didn't want anything to do with him. Twenty years later her attitude towards him would change.

Emil Tyshovnytsky in his early 20s in Ukrainian Galician Army uniform circa 1915 in Galicia.

As the two sisters aged, their differences became more evident in their lifestyles. Practical and tidy, my mother led an orderly, planned lifestyle. Helen, on the other hand, was artistic and creative and led a more chaotic, bohemian lifestyle. As they matured further, their rivalry manifested itself in a more sophisticated way. My mother sought out ways to fit in and be like everyone else, copying their behavior in public situations; Helen searched for ways to stand out—to be unique and break free from outdated social restraints. My mother remained nearer to home, staying true to her close childhood friends, while Helen socialized more broadly and built bonds with a wider range of new friends.

Part of growing up in the Ukrainian Greek Catholic tradition was attending church services on Sundays and important religious occasions. Children were encouraged to go to confession as part of those services. They would enter a dark cubicle, usually located near the altar, to confess their sins to a Ukrainian Catholic priest. The priest sat behind a wooden lattice divider to hear the confessions of the children and absolve them of their sins.

While my mother was quite religious and faithful, her first confession at around age eight, was an unmitigated disaster.

Because she couldn't hear what the priest was saying through the lattice divider—nor could she read his lips in the darkness— he came barreling out of the cubicle and confronted her. She was so embarrassed that she physically cringed as she endured his scolding in front of the other parishioners who waited for their turn at confession. From that day on, though she honored the religious traditions and attended church regularly, she declined to go to confession and did not partake in Holy Communion. She often recalled the incident and the terror she felt because of her showdown with the priest.

After the first world war, when Galicia fell under Polish control, all of the Drozdowsky children became members of Plast, a Ukrainian youth organization, where they participated in weekly activities. My mother loved taking part in Plast, as it afforded her an ideal way to fit in with others, make new friends, and keep in touch with old ones. Unlike other politically oriented youth organizations of those days—such as the Komsomol, which indoctrinated Soviet youth in the ideology of the Communist Party, or the Hitler Youth, which cultivated Nazi dogma—Plast modeled itself on the international scouting movement. The organization also tried to counteract foreign blows aimed at eradicating the Ukrainian identity of its youth. Plast taught young people to believe in the equality of the Ukrainian nation with all others in the community of nations and to respect the rights of all individuals. It cultivated a faith in God and a love for nature, advocating a lifestyle built on strength, beauty, caution, and courage.

After my mother had been a member for a few months, however, her participation came to an abrupt end. She explained it this way.

I was driven out of Plast because I was not following instructions.
I could not hear what they were. Being thrown out like that was a

terribly embarrassing experience for me. As word of my expulsion got out to all my friends and acquaintances, I was humiliated by it all, and it undermined my self-esteem.

The misunderstanding and impatience of Plast's leaders stung her, and she felt the shame of being driven out, while her parents were reluctant to come to her defense. As a result my mother ended up feeling socially isolated. It took time for her to reestablish her social connections, but she eventually recovered. The incident probably turned out to her advantage because in 1930 the Polish government, perceiving Plast as a threat to its rule, banned it and put its leaders under surveillance, considering them people of unreliable loyalty. Fortunately none of the Drozdowsky children were affected by this Polish maneuver.

Unable to take part in Plast, my mother turned to other activities, including learning how to skate.

During the winter, I once tried my hand at ice-skating. I can't tell you how much I wanted to learn how to skate. I had skate blades, but they were unattached and needed to be belted up to my boots. I remember trying to fasten the skate blades to my boots, but I just could never get them to hold on. Since they never held properly, much to my disappointment, I was never able to learn.

In her later years, she often cited this example when she lamented that her parents didn't pay enough attention to her.

Around this time, however, my mother's parents learned of a promising hearing device available in Austria. It was a rare, primitive hearing aid. Her parents purchased it at some expense, and when it arrived, my mother put it on her desk in her room. Just then her sister Helen bounced in, noticed the device, grabbed it, and asked, "What's this?" My mother replied, "It's not for you" and reached for its return. They tussled over it, and somehow the device broke.

My mother was devastated. In her mind the one chance she had to access the audible world was lost forever because of her impudent sister. How could she? She fumed at Helen, refusing to talk to her—or even acknowledge her presence—for days. Eventually, however, her anger subsided, and her bitterness lifted, even though the hearing aid never was replaced. My mother eventually forgave her sister, reasoning that it had been an accident.

In school, knowing my mother was hard of hearing, her teachers placed her at the front of the classroom. There she could hear, or at least decipher enough from her teachers' lips to follow what they were saying. But she couldn't hear what students were saying behind her. As a result she lost a lot of the value of her education and was unable to interact effectively in classroom settings. Despite this she was able to learn the Polish and German languages, as well as Polish literature, geography, and history. She graduated from high school with little difficulty but wasn't able to continue with a university education—not because she was intellectually deficient but because attending university required more classroom participation than her disability permitted her to undertake.

It was my friend Sabina Springer who suggested I should go to vocational school to learn how to sew. I decided that is what I would do. So I went both to the vocational part of the school as well as the regular school. I attended vocational school for three years, studying the so-called "needle trades" to become a seamstress, and then in the fourth year, I transferred to Lviv.

Salomea Drozdowska as a teenager, circa 1928 in Lviv, Galicia

Sabina and her family stayed behind in Drohobych. That was the last time she and my mother saw each other. Although my mother never had any indication regarding what happened to Sabina, she surmised that her best friend, along with her family, most likely perished in a Nazi concentration camp.

The Move to Lviv

In 1928, when Julian was promoted as a judge to the District Court, the Drozdowskys left Drohobych for the city of Lviv. They moved into a three-story building, with a hidden inner courtyard, in the center of the city. Solomea Krushelnytska, one of Maryna Drozdowska's sisters, owned the building.

Krushelnytska had been a world-famous opera singer at the turn of the twentieth century. She was a rare spinto soprano who was able to sing all the notes from middle C to high D. In addition to speaking seven languages, including English, she knew the lyrics and music to more than fifty operas by memory. Krushelnytska had mentored the Italian tenor Enrico Caruso when they had performed in St. Petersburg together. She also had helped Giacomo Puccini rescue his opera *Madame Butterfly* from disaster by playing the lead role of Cio-Cio San, when, after a failed performance by others at the La Scala Theatre in Milan, they successfully restaged it in Brescia, Italy, a few months later. She toured the opera theaters of Europe, the Middle East, and even North and South America, where she made appearances in New York, Toronto, and Montreal. Through her career she amassed significant wealth, which allowed her to purchase the building in downtown Lviv, not far from St. George's Cathedral and what today is Ivan Franko National University, where the Drozdowskys were now to live.

Over time my mother's relationship to her famous aunt grew stronger and became a source of great pride and honor for her. Despite their forty-year age difference, the opera star and my mother were drawn together not only because they shared the same first name but also because they were both Ukrainian patriots and were linked by frequent family gatherings. Perhaps what drew them together even closer was the cruel irony—which both of them sensed—that, due to her hearing disability, my mother was never fully able to appreciate her aunt's great vocal talent, which the rest of the world admired and applauded.

My mother's relationship to Krushelnytska also served to lift her standing in the eyes of others, and in that way, the opera star's legacy helped my mother overcome some of her social isolation, particularly in her later years.

While the Drozdowskys were happy to be living with Krushelnytska in the building downtown, not everything about it was welcome. Across the street from where they lived was a large park called Jesuit Park (Jesujitskyj Park). Every spring and into the summer, thousands of black crows (vorony) came to make their nests and lay eggs there. The Drozdowskys could hear them crowing throughout the park. Along with the crows, the park attracted a cross-section of the population: old people going for a walk, young lovers peering into each other's eyes, students doing their reading assignments, mothers strolling with children in strollers, and occasionally a disturbed character.

One day, when my mother was in her late teens, she came out from her building and noticed a man standing in the park in a raincoat. As she looked up at him, he quickly opened his coat to reveal his naked body. She was shocked and fled in horror as the flasher watched his bewildered victim disappear. My mother quickly learned that this was just another part of "life in the big city." She was growing up.

The rivalry between my mother and Helen intensified around this time as well, eventually playing itself out with boys. Reserved and not always confident, though perhaps more curvaceous and attractive, my mother competed for their attentions with Helen. As someone who was more worldly and open to new adventures, my aunt wasn't as restrained as my mother in relating to the opposite sex. While the rivalry wasn't quite fair because of Helen's two-year seniority, there were times when some boys in whom my mother took an interest ended up twisted around Helen's finger as my mother observed in confused amazement and probably even resentment. Nonetheless my mother did establish her own set of friends, including boys with whom she had good romantic relationships.

Their younger brother Alex was very well balanced. In fact he was the only member of the Drozdowsky family who truly understood my mother and her hearing impairment. He had a gentle, sensitive nature, and as he and my mother matured, he became her closest friend and confidant. They even developed their own sign language, using physical gestures to secretly communicate with each other. He understood how stressful she found it to be in a group of people where it was difficult for her to hear the conversations. Their sign language was particularly helpful to my mother in social situations, as Alex would signal her to be alert when someone spoke to her or when she needed to say something in response.

Solomea Krushelnytska's building in Lviv, where Salomea Drozdowska and her family moved to in 1928

Solomea Krushelnytska performing as Cio-Cio San in the opera *Madame Butterfly* in Brescia, Italy, in 1904

And the Boys Would Kiss Your Hand

In Galicia, ballroom dancing was an intrigue—an intrigue of romance.

This was the philosophy that schools of ballroom dancing promoted at the time. These schools took their craft very seriously. Through dance one could say what no words could convey. Men were told, "You must look deeply into the eyes of your partner. Lead your partner, who must become yours, and only yours, during the course of a dance. Remember that there is no woman who does not like to dance. Women like men who are strong but who also have humility." They were taught, "Even if you never see each other again, after a dance your partner should remember that she was held in the arms of a real man. Strive to have her think only about you while you dance." In short, "Dancing was a form of romance, hidden in music and movement."[3] While not in step with today's standards or view of the sexes, this dancing philosophy found many adherents in Galicia.

Like many other young people at the time, both my mother and aunt took these courses in ballroom dancing in their free time. By 1929 my mother was attending vocational school to learn sewing, while Helen was studying botany at John Casimir University. On weekends and holidays, however, they attended various dances held in the city. These dances, organized by engineers, doctors, and other professionals, were formal affairs not to be missed.

The girls sat on one side of the dance floor and the boys on the other. A boy would walk over to a girl, bow, and ask her to dance. Then, following the dance, he would escort her to her seat, bow again, thank her for the dance, sometimes kiss her hand, and then return to his place. There was no mingling or holding hands.

At such events, parents and teachers sat and watched like hawks to make sure the girls were held at a proper distance during the dances; they also ensured the safe return of the girls to their homes afterward. This formality loosened up a bit as the women came of age, but nonetheless constraints were placed on the conduct of young men and women even then.

After the dances the young people rushed home to avoid being locked out. It was quite common for the building doormen to lock the gates to their buildings punctually at ten p.m. If the young people were late, they paid a fine to the doorman, who had to be awakened. The fine was twenty-five cents (*hroshiw*) until midnight and fifty cents afterward. That was serious money back then, and the young people tried to avoid paying it. My mother recalled more than once that she had to awaken the doorman to her building to get in late at night. Rather than call for the doorman, however, there were those who tried to lift their friends over the gate but weren't always successful. Try as they might, sooner or later they would call the doorman to the rescue.

During these years in Lviv, my mother enjoyed going to the luxurious Hotel George for ice cream, where she could peruse various illustrated European magazines, including those published in German, French, and English. Julian was fond of the Vienna Café, where Ukrainian intellectuals frequently gathered and read Ukrainian newspapers such as *Dilo* and *Novyj Chas*.

The opera house, which still stands today in a plaza in the center of the city and is now named after Solomea Krushelnytska, was the focal point of community life. Cafés, boutiques, newspaper kiosks, candy stores, and tobacco shops were sprinkled around it, and a favorite pastime of the population, including the Drozdowskys, was to stroll through the plaza on Sunday afternoons and other leisurely days. The Bistro and Café de la Paix were two popular nightclubs for evenings on the town that the wealthy populace frequented. My mother particularly loved to go to movies that featured Marlene Dietrich; the actress's early silent films were her favorites since they did not require her to be able to hear the words.

There were also banquets, weddings, and nights out with other young people, as well as special events, such as the bewitching Andriyivsky Vechir - an evening of fortune telling and rituals that my mother loved. During this evening young women poured melted wax into water to divine their future by interpreting the formations that emerged. They also floated rings of flowers down a stream of water, each ring holding a lit candle, to determine which ring would float the farthest and thus indicate who was to marry next.

Young Adulthood

By the 1930s my mother had become a very good seamstress and was earning a decent living in Lviv, designing coats and dresses for fashion-conscious women who came to her due to her elegant designs and evident skills. With the purchase of a sewing machine, she was able to do even better work and expand her client base. By then the rivalry between her and Helen was less pronounced but still present. Because of my mother's profession, she was able to dress elegantly, and she also was well manicured. Helen, on the other hand, who always was looking to stand out, tended to dress more colorfully but not always tastefully. Sometimes my mother scolded Helen, urging her to "do something with your hair" and to dress more appropriately, describing what she was wearing as being "dressed like a fruitcake."

While my mother was making inroads in her career as a seamstress, Helen played the piano and dedicated herself to music. Her parents nurtured that love in her, and by the early 1930s, she had been taking private piano lessons for about ten years. Helen applied to the New Vienna Conservatory in Austria, where she passed an entrance exam, no doubt in part due to her ten years of piano lessons. She became a student of the conservatory, leaving her Lviv botany university studies on hold at the end of her second year in order to travel to Vienna.

Living in Vienna, the music lover in Helen was ecstatic. An Old World city, Vienna was then considered the capital of music. After two years of piano studies, she received a certificate of graduation that entitled her to work as a piano teacher. For the next three years, she taught piano. She lived and breathed music, spending her evenings and weekends in the cafés and bistros in the Ring that surrounded the inner city. She remained in Vienna until 1934, when she returned to Lviv just before Hitler's invasion and the unification of Austria with Germany.

Around this time Alex graduated from law school and was striking out on his own by opening a law office. Bright, thin, and tall, he was a fair-skinned, good-looking young man with wavy brown hair combed straight back over his head. Alex had all the makings of a good lawyer: character, a propensity for hard work, and a dedication to the law. The fact that his father was a prominent judge in Lviv also helped open doors for him in the legal community.

The family gathered during major holidays such as Christmas and Easter. During Christmas they attended Mass at St. George's Cathedral and, along with other parishioners, greeted their bishop, Metropolitan Andrey Sheptytsky. They'd buy a fresh-cut pine tree to take home to prepare for Christmas and hang ornaments and candles on it, which they'd light in the evening, always watchful to make sure the tree didn't catch on fire. They'd cook and serve the traditional twelve meatless dishes that represented the twelve apostles of Christ. Then they'd await the Christmas carolers, who came to sing songs and raise funds for various charitable causes.

During Easter the family baked Christmas bread (*paska*) and prepared an Easter basket with freshly painted Easter eggs, mainly done by Helen, who had more of an artistic flair than the others. The basket included sausage, eggs, horseradish, beets, butter, and ham, and the family attended church to have it blessed by the priest before sitting down to an Easter meal.

Since both parents had many siblings, these family events were large gatherings. While the relatives sat together around the large dining room table, my mother enjoyed helping her mother and others set the table with special silverware that displayed their family crest, in which they took pride, as well as prepare and serve the tasty foods, refreshing drinks, and delicious tortes, cookies, and other pastries.

Bracing for the Coming Storm

In 1933, while the West was distracted by Adolf Hitler's rise to power in Germany, the U.S.S.R. sealed Ukraine's borders to prevent escape and then sent in soldiers to requisition all grain and feedstock from farming communities, thus unleashing a devastating man-made famine on Soviet Ukraine. When the extent of the starvation became more apparent to the Ukrainian Catholic leadership in Lviv, they published an urgent appeal to their parishioners that called upon them to come to the aid of those who were without food. Mortified by the shocking news of hunger stalking Soviet Ukraine, the Drozdowsky family and others urgently collected food to send by train to the other side of the Polish-Soviet border. Soviet border guards, however, blocked the shipments in an attempt to cover up the extent of the human tragedy unfolding there.[4]

The artificial famine, imposed on Ukraine to break its resistance to Soviet rule, was more brutal than anyone imagined. Even those who are most skeptical concede the death toll was between 2.5 to 3 million.[5] Some estimates place the number as high as ten million victims; though more likely some six to seven million people perished. [6] Those who survived did so only through extreme measures, some even through cannibalism. This development served as a stark reminder to the Drozdowskys of the ruthlessness of the Soviet

In this, one of the few pictures from the period, people walk by victims of the artificial famine lying emaciated in the streets. While millions starved in Soviet Ukraine in 1933 authorities refused food supplies shipped there from Lviv

regime that had oppressed and sought to Russify Ukrainians from the U.S.S.R.'s inception—a lesson that would be critical to the family's survival in the years ahead.

It was also during this inter-war period, in August 1939, following the recent death of her husband in Italy, that Solomea Krushelnytska, the opera star, decided to move from Via di Reggio, where she was living in a villa on the Italian Riviera, back to her home in Lviv. The rise to power of Benito Mussolini was a troubling development for her future in Italy. As growing international danger mounted, she made her way back to Ukraine and into her building with her sisters and their families. She did not know then that she never would return to the West again.

During a family get-together around this time, Krushelnytska pulled out a ring that Tsar Nicholas II had given her as a memento of her performance in St. Petersburg years earlier. The ring was studded with diamonds, and in its center, it held a pearl the size of a small marble. Krushelnytska related how she had defied the advice of those who had helped stage her concert and had sung Ukrainian folk songs as a subtle protest of the Tsar's Russification of—and rule over—Ukraine. Despite her evident defiance, Nicholas II, taken by her performance, had visited her backstage and given her the ring. Krushelnytska then passed the ring on to the Drozdowskys to keep as a family heirloom. That ring would later help the family during a time of great hardship.

Ring given to Krushelnytska by Tsar Nicholas II. The pearl was sold by my mother to buy food for her ailing father during World War II.

Chapter 2
The War Years

2

Surprise Attack

*I*N THE EARLY hours of September 1, 1939, rumors spread through Hrybeniw where my mother was vacationing with Helen and my grandmother—that the country was at war. The Germans had struck Poland without warning at four forty-five that morning. In the predawn darkness, some one-and-a-half million German troops, spearheaded by hundreds of planes and tanks, had smashed into the country from the north, south, and west. By midday armored panzers were slicing through the heart of the Polish countryside, not in support of infantry but preceding it. This blitzkrieg "lightning war" was leading to the complete and utter collapse of Polish resistance.[7]

My mother recalled that day when she returned to Lviv from Hrybeniw.

Trains were not running because German bombers had blown out all the bridges on the railroad. Helen and I, along with our mother, hurriedly made our way back to Lviv by horse and buggy. It took us most of that late-summer day to get home. Along the way, we could see the first German bombers, dozens of little cross-shaped planes, flying thousands of feet above in formation in the clear-blue sky above us.

Meanwhile our father and everyone else who had a radio in Lviv were listening to Moscow, Berlin, or Polish news. They learned scattered details about the German invasion. Polish stations began playing military marches to psychologically prepare the population for the rigors of war.

By the time we reached Lviv in the evening, the streets were in utter chaos. The central railway station had been hit, and a plume of smoke and debris rose up into the sky. People were running around dazed and confused, looking for family members, while yelling and screaming. Vehicles everywhere were beeping their horns, turning and stopping to avoid accidents.

That night, large areas of the city burned. The sky was aglow with a reddish color, and an eye-burning smoke filled the air. The smell of burned wood, material, and corpses was everywhere. Everything was upside down. There was mass confusion. Parts of the Lviv had no electricity, gas, or hot water, since the city's electrical power station was hit and numerous gas lines had ruptured. All of Poland, it seemed, was on fire.

By the end of that second day of fighting, most of the city's factories were bombed and going up in smoke. The Luftwaffe had established complete air supremacy over Poland and was attacking cities, railways, road junctions, military convoys, and troop concentrations at will. Outgunned and outmaneuvered, the Polish army was in retreat.

Meanwhile the people adapted quickly and shed their naïveté. My mother and her family learned to seek shelter in the basements of buildings and in bomb shelters built for that purpose. As soon as they heard planes coming overhead, people shouted, "Go to the shelter! Go to the shelter!" My mother scrambled down the stairs, almost falling over others in her haste. For the next two weeks, there were air raids every night.

The basements were overcrowded, and the shelters were oppressively hot and humid from so many bodies being in such close contact. The air was foul from bad breath and body odor. Although there could have been serious political debate in those basements, people restrained themselves; in fact they rarely spoke while the raids were underway. They sat there trying not to think about the dangers, not to listen for planes passing overhead or the anti-aircraft fire outside, not to strain to hear the whistling of falling bombs. With each explosion the ground shook, and bits of dirt and plaster sprinkled down on them from the ceiling.

The raids seemed to last for hours, until finally the explosions ceased and the anti-aircraft guns stopped.[8] Since my mother didn't hear well, she didn't suffer the mounting anxiety of those shrieking moments. Instead she would be jolted by the sudden unexpected impacts. She resolved it would be wiser for her to avoid the shelters and instead use her eyesight to protect her. Somehow this worked for her. She remained above ground and braced against the walls instead.

As German planes raided Lviv day after day and the Polish anti-aircraft batteries remained unable to stop them, chaos reigned. Such events tested the mettle of each person, sharpened their survival instincts, and left behind a lifelong legacy from those days. To help deal with the chaos, the population made efforts to aid and comfort one another. Strangers and neighbors became friends. Over time, however, fear and dread set in, and people became depressed. A dark, heavy cloud of uncertainty hung over everyone. There were complete black-outs at night. For days Lviv Polish radio played sad music, every so often announcing updates about the course of the battle and the state of the Polish soldiers.

The fighting in the western region of the country, the conges-tion on the roads, and the destruction of all forms of transpor-tation interrupted the transport of food from the farms to the cities. Thus, food shortages appeared. There was a run on all stores. Shelves and market stalls were quickly cleared of anything that was edible. As soon as the air raids ceased, people ran to the nearest stores then back to their homes before the next assaults came. Within a few days, most of the food shops were closed. The daily hunt for food and supplies became the dominant pre-occupation of everyone. Barefooted ragged figures wandered the streets; crying mothers tried to find their children; and children who had lost their parents searched aimlessly for them.

The possibility of a German attack had been debated heat-edly for a long time at the Drozdowsky home and many other places in Poland. Generally speaking, while Ukrainians knew the Germans weren't exactly bringing them liberation, they welcomed the invasion nonetheless, because it would free them from Polish oppression. They didn't give much thought, how-ever, to what the Germans would bring with them.

Poland Devastated

By the second week of the war, the magnitude of the Polish defeat was clear to everyone living in Lviv and certainly to the

Drozdowskys. By then the city was witnessing a flood of refugees from the western region of Poland pouring into its streets. The stream of newcomers started with the wives and girlfriends of high-ranking military and administrative officials, as well as their children. Fleeing the capital city of Warsaw and other cities where the front was now approaching, these bewildered women and children couldn't believe that Poland was failing and that life as they knew it was about to end. Driven by chauffeurs, they left in such a hurry that they often were not appropriately dressed, and they stopped in Lviv to buy something to wear from the local stores.

Following them—hour by hour, day by day, week by week—in the lulls between bombings, more people filled the streets. Their clothes were wrinkled and dirty. Their faces were unwashed and drawn with fatigue and fear. Their eyes were glassy and filled with confusion. Some carried suitcases, bags, or knapsacks packed with their belongings; others pushed carts, carriages, or wheelbarrows. The luckier ones were in automobiles, while others arrived in horse-drawn wagons. All headed eastward. Barely audible—except for an occasional shout, a cry of a child, the grinding of a car's gears, the honking of a horn, or the gunning of an engine—they came in a never-ending human stream, trudging in exhaustion, wending their way through the streets of Lviv, as they headed east, away from the oncoming Germans.[9]

Since the city had lost its electrical power, it was impossible to hear the news reports from the front. There were no newspapers to find out what was going on. The mere presence of the refugees, however, told the local population everything they needed to know about the course of the war.

The bombing, lack of food, and desperate conditions made everyone anxious and despondent. In time, however, the residents of Lviv grew more accustomed to war conditions, and life returned to the city. Even so, they were perplexed by the failure of the Americans to get involved in the war and wondered what had happened to Poland's allies, the British and the French.

What Should We Do?

On September 17, 1939, after having watched Germany attack Poland for more than two weeks, the Soviet Union launched its attack on Poland from the east at six a.m. Earlier that morning, the Soviet government had communicated a request to Berlin for the German air force not to operate in the area of Lviv, as the Russian air force would begin bombing that morning. As German forces withdrew from Lviv, the Soviets began to occupy it.

Helen, now thirty years old, opened up a discussion with her father, contrasting the various options now open to them, especially given the difference between the invading armies.

"There is no doubt about it, Father. The Germans are going to win this war," she asserted.

Her father was not convinced. "I'm not so sure, my dear," he replied. "The Allies have declared themselves to be on Poland's side. It is not over yet."

With the entry of the Red Army into Lviv, discussions such as the one between Helen and her father took place across the city, and serious questions arose in every household—life-and-death questions that had to be faced and answered. "Should I escape to the West, or should I stay under Soviet occupation? Will we be better off here, or should we flee?" These were certainly questions that troubled the Drozdowsky household and were not easily answered. And the options chosen, while not so evident to the people then, had far-reaching, lifelong consequences.

Many believed that the clash of Nazi Germany and the Soviet Union ultimately would result in a situation in which the titans would be so weakened that Ukraine and other subjugated nations would be able to reassert their independence and freedom. According to this view, citizens needed to be ready to help these new nations when they sought to get up on their feet.[10] Others weren't so sure this would happen and fled.

By September 29, 1939, a majority of Polish army troops had surrendered. On October 1, German troops entered Warsaw, and by then the two foreign powers had completely occupied Poland. On October 6, the last of the Polish forces surrendered. On October 19, German-occupied Poland was incorporated into the Third Reich. The U.S.S.R. incorporated the Soviet-occupied part of Poland shortly thereafter.

The Germans meet their Soviet allies in Lviv, Ukraine, in September 1939.

Last Chance to Escape

My mother described her decision to escape from Soviet-occupied Lviv as follows.

In the months before the outbreak of the war, I traveled to Warsaw and worked there on my sewing machine, designing dresses for prominent women. Now twenty-seven years old and back in Lviv, I watched Soviet propaganda declare that in the new Western Ukraine everything would be free. I reasoned that, in my circumstances, I would not be able to make a living and that I would be better off in Warsaw. Having left my sewing machine there previously, I had an argument with my mother about returning to Warsaw because of the machine and in view of the change in circumstances in Lviv following the outbreak of war.

Despite this fact, when she reflected on these moments later, she could not forgive her parents for allowing her to return to Warsaw on her own in this time of war. But they did, probably because there was no way to stop her. She was now an adult, and when my mother made up her mind to do something, it was difficult to get her to change it.

I decided to leave Lviv in late October 1939. Just before I left, I went into my bedroom, which I shared with my brother Alex. Standing at the foot of his bed where he was lying, I grabbed the end of his blanket to get his attention. Shaking it, I implored him to cross the Soviet-German border with me. He declined, saying that his fiancé, Iryna Chojnatska, would not go because she would not leave her family behind, and he would not leave without her. Though I tried, I could not change his mind.

This would turn out to be a fateful moment for both Alex and my mother.

On November 1, 1939, I crossed the German-Soviet border by myself. In Peremyshl there was a steel bridge where displaced persons could cross. Announcements indicated that those people, largely Poles, who had escaped to Galicia to avoid the advancing German front could return back to their homes in Poland at that border crossing. Many Ukrainians slipped across the border at that time, and I slipped across with them. It was the last day on which it could be done.

The border was now sealed.

I spent that winter in Warsaw. I slept on the floor of a house and worked in the oldest part of the city, in Stare Miasto. I made ends meet by sewing. It was a bitter, cold winter and one that was especially difficult due to hunger. The entire city was famished. Ultimately I ended up in the Ilnycky family household, helping them with cleaning the house and sewing. It was while living there that I witnessed the Nazi regime's requirement that all Jews wear the Star of David on their sleeve and saw the announcements concerning the creation of the Jewish ghetto.

While reflecting on those days, my mother recalled watching Nazi German soldiers march Jews through the streets in rows of four, unimpeded by the local population.

Sometime in the spring of 1940, my mother moved to Cracow, where she lived with Bohdan Sterniuk and his family, to whom she was related through the Krushelnytsky link. Bohdan and his wife had a daughter, Marta, who was a young child at that time. My mother took on the role of caregiver, helping the Sterniuk family with tasks such as taking the child to appointments, as well as other household chores, including looking after her when the parents were away.

A Perilous Moment

My mother described an incident in Nazi-occupied Cracow that involved her.

One day in the spring of 1941 [probably during the early evacuation of Jews and others from the city], as I was returning to my home not far from the Wavel Cathedral in a central part of Cracow, I took a shortcut through the train station. As I ran up the steps to the platform and jumped on to it, I suddenly realized I was in the wrong place.

There in front of me was a row of armed German soldiers, approximately twenty meters apart from one to the next, all the way down the length of the platform, guarding a train with boxcars full of people waiting to leave the station. I instantly had to make a life-or-death decision. I could turn around and try to flee, but I knew that the guards had spotted me. They looked at me with surprise and may have chased me and put me on the train. The other alternative was to go ahead in the direction I was planning, walking in between the train and the guards, hoping that I would be allowed to pass without hindrance. I decided to go ahead.

There was no doubt in my mind that the train was full of marked people headed for an unknown but surely unhappy destination—in hindsight probably a concentration camp. As I slowly proceeded, I carefully looked down on the platform in front of me, hoping not to draw too much attention in this way. I knew any false move could result in my arrest and joining the people in the train. Conscious of the moans and sighs coming from the people on the train from a lack of food and water, I walked the entire length of the platform without daring to look up either to the left or to the right, for fear of being stopped, questioned, arrested, and put on the train. Somehow I carefully managed to navigate the entire length of the platform past the series of German guards without incident and then in great relief ran off to my home.

My mother remained in Cracow until the Nazis attacked the Soviet Union in June 1941, when she returned to Lviv.

Paris of the East

Now that the front had settled, life had started to return to "normal" for the rest of my mother's family in Soviet-occupied Lviv. Russian-speaking soldiers inundated shops. Hundreds of Russian-speaking civil servants and administrators and their families began to pour into Lviv to manage the factories and businesses the Soviets had seized. The new arrivals commandeered the nicest city quarters, with running water and toilets, even if they didn't always know how to use them.

Soviet housing authorities made an all-out effort to find quarters for hundreds of thousands of refugees, while declaring that each person was entitled to seven square meters of floor space. Everyone who owned housing was obliged to report it to Soviet authorities so that the surplus could be allotted to those in need. One day they announced that all the buildings of Lviv, whether they were government buildings or privately owned, were to be turned over to the housing department; they were de facto nationalized. Krushelnytska was called into the building administration with Julian at the end of November 1939 and forced to sign papers to surrender her rightful claim as owner.

Everyone living in the apartment houses had to be registered, and no outsider was allowed to stay overnight without permission and registration at the nearest militia post. Nightly inspections now took place.

Meanwhile, in Italy, Mussolini nationalized Krushelnytska's villa in Via di Reggio on the Italian Riviera. Now she was left to lead the rest of her life behind the Iron Curtain with nothing, having lost her buildings and everything else except her talent, intellect, and wits.

By the late autumn of 1939, stores had run short of products, especially sugar. Lines grew to more than one hundred meters in length. This was ironic in view of an incident the Drozdowsky sisters had experienced earlier. A day or so just after the war had broken out in September 1939 and before Salomea had left Lviv, Salomea and Helen were sitting on the curb out in front of their building. A man pulling a cart filled with sugar stopped to ask if they wanted to buy some. They looked at each other, thinking this was odd, and said no. Now the Drozdowskys longed for it.

In addition there was now a shortage of flour, which had a catastrophic impact on the supply of bread. Meat, butter, and milk shortages followed. Food became so scarce that long queues formed in front of grocery and butcher shops, and people had to barter for butter, eggs, cheese or chickens with farmers who came to market. They would stand there for two or three hours for a single loaf of bread. For two pounds of sugar, the wait could be five hours. Dry goods and shoes were even in shorter supply.

Under the new regime, Julian Drozdowsky was told that he would not be allowed to remain in the city, so he and Maryna traveled to their cottage in Hrybeniw. When they arrived, they found the place completely demolished. All that was left was the outer walls of the building and the roof. All the furniture and all the utensils had been cleaned out. The outhouse was overflowing with human waste. Evidently the Red Army had come through and used not only the outhouse but also the entire garden surrounding the cottage as a waste field. There was such a foul smell that it took them several weeks to dig out the human waste and clean up the lot.

Arrests, Disappearances, and Deportations

If the Drozdowsky family had watched events unfolding in Lviv under the Soviets with dispassionate concern and preoccupation with their own family matters, that all changed on April 10, 1940. On that day the NKVD, the Soviet secret police, organized massive overnight deportations of the Ukrainian intelligentsia. What Jews were for the Nazis, nationally conscious Ukrainians were for the Soviets. From a Soviet ideological perspective, previous arrests in Galicia were a sideshow to this, the main event. Ukrainian patriots had to be cleared out at all costs.[11] That night's deportations were the beginning of a wave of terror that spread throughout society—one that eventually would find its way to the Drozdowskys' doorstep.

To see uniformed Bolsheviks in front of a house was to know absolute horror. Always operating at night so fewer people would see them, the NKVD secret police knew the likelihood of capturing their targets was better at that time, since they likely would be sleeping. Their targets' resistance would be lower since they would be awakened suddenly and unable to react quickly. After such a nocturnal visit, these individuals could end up in the local cemetery, in a concentration camp in the Gulag, wandering in the Siberian hinterland, or sitting in prison with one wall separating them from their unknowing family members.

The uncertainty of whether they would survive the night— or whether the NKVD would stop them on the road to work or school, or whether they may be called out from the office due to a search of workers in the area, or whether they would be accused of being "Ukrainian nationalists," or whether their family would be arrested in their homes while they were away— was overwhelming. The terrorized population was unable to have a peaceful night's sleep. Thousands suffered from insomnia, lost weight, turned yellow from jaundice, or aged quickly. Others stayed constantly on the move, changing their place of sleep every night to avoid being arrested and also taking menial jobs to have a "proletarian face." It got to the point where visitors to an apartment would ring the doorbell very briefly and quietly so as not to frighten the residents inside. Some packed their bags, preparing for a possible nighttime arrest and deportation to Siberia.

Helen recalled those days as follows.

> *I was always extraordinarily courageous and never feared anyone, neither in Ukraine, nor later in the United States. Nevertheless the one group that I feared was the NKVD. These people were ruthless. I sat in terror at times in my home, fearing that there would be a knock on the door, with the NKVD coming to arrest me.*

By April 1940 the arrests and deportations reached the Ukrainians, starting with their intelligentsia. These arrests started small and grew ever wider in waves. As the circle widened over time, at a moment's notice, anyone could become the object of deportation. For the Bolsheviks, lawyers were among the worst enemies because they knew the laws and prosecuted communists. This was a problem for the Drozdowsky family, as Alex was a lawyer, and Julian was a judge.

There was another reason to be afraid. The Bolsheviks also viewed as enemies any families who had a relative, particularly someone close, outside the territory of the USSR. This was the first step to being regarded by the NKVD as a foreign spy, a saboteur, or a terrorist. A question on government forms asked, "Do you have any family members or friends beyond the territories of the USSR, and where?" This made it possible for the state to identify suspects. Those who had the courage to write letters abroad were especially in danger. In the case of the Drozdowsky family, Krushelnytska had lived abroad, and they corresponded with her close friends, which made them targets. Moreover, my mother was now in Cracow under Nazi rule.

In addition anyone who, for any reason, had found themselves labeled "bourgeois" also had difficulties sleeping. To own a furnished, respectable home now bought one a ticket down a road to disappearance. People hid their paintings, their carpets, their silver, and any kind of special ornaments. Since Krushelnytska was an opera star and was considered wealthy, the family had another reason for concern.

There was one further reason for the Krushelnytsky family to be nervous. Ever since Krushelnytska's building in Lviv had been nationalized, the Krushelnytsky family had been in conflict with the new owners. At any moment they could report the Krushelnysky family as "troublemakers" to get rid of them and then take over their furniture and personal effects.

Pure Terror

On St. Nicholas Day, December 6, 1940, the NKVD came to the Drozdowsky home in Lviv. By then only Helen and Alex were living there, since their parents were in Hrybeniw, and my mother was in Cracow. Other members of the extended family, however, including Krushelnytska, were all living in that same building. The NKVD was after Alex. Helen later described the events to me.

> As soon as we heard the sound of a car in the street beside our building [at those times there were very few private cars], all the families living in it turned off all their lights and looked out cautiously through their windows to try to determine to which building the car had come. The terror that gripped us on that night permeated every cell of our bodies.

The War Years

While awaiting the knock on the door, we gave each other advice about what should happen in the event that we were taken. Not to worry. Not to cry. Keep a level head. Such scenes took place in almost every apartment. All people—urban dwellers and rural dwellers alike—were consumed by fear.

My brother Alex was a hardworking person who was punctilious in his work. In 1937, after studying law at the university, he earned a master's degree and then established his own office. Alex loved his profession, even though in those times it was hard to make a living running a law practice. In addition to being a member of the bar, he was also a member of many other community organizations. Politically, without reservation, he stood for the national independence of Ukraine. However, he never took part in—nor was he ever a member of—the Organization of Ukrainian Nationalists.

The occupation of Western Ukraine by the Soviet Red Army prompted three sisters from the Ivanchuk family to consult him regarding their fears about life under Soviet occupation. He told them that there was not much that they could do except to stay out of sight of those in power.

The NKVD came to the Ivanchuks' apartment and arrested the sisters. Before leaving, however, they kept the sisters in their home, awaiting others who might be associated with them. They lay in wait to capture Ukrainians who were anti-Bolshevik.

That's when I arrived. The NKVD asked me what I was doing there. Thinking quickly on my feet, I said that I had come because one of the Ivanchuk sisters was a seamstress and I wanted to pick up some sewing. I was arrested and taken in for interrogation. During the interrogation the NKVD asked me where I worked. I indicated I worked for a professor at the Ukrainian university. Eventually I was released. I later realized why.

The Bolsheviks launched a propaganda campaign purporting to advance Ukrainian in schools and in those portions of Galicia where Ukrainians made up the majority of the population. In the midst of this campaign, a very decent Polish university professor by the name of Cheminevski called me into his office and asked me to work for him as a teaching assistant because I was Ukrainian and spoke the language. This now turned out to be my salvation. The Soviet NKVD secret police were under strict orders not to bother anyone working at the university, since the university Ukrainianization was a showpiece of propaganda for the Bolsheviks. All three Ivanchuk sisters, however, were taken by the Bolsheviks and perished.

As a result of their consultation with Alex, his name came to the attention of Soviet authorities. The NKVD came to our home looking for Alex. I wanted to leave to warn Alex not to come home, but they made sure that nobody left the house to forewarn him. After a few hours of all of us—NKVD officers, family members, and me—waiting, Alex showed up. He was immediately put under arrest.

By that time a new phenomenon had appeared in Lviv; mass numbers of people were disappearing, usually at night. The general population of Lviv soon learned from cemetery workers that every night the Bolsheviks drove four large trucks filled with corpses to the cemetery. In this way the Soviets were systematically executing leaders of Polish, Ukrainian, and Jewish political, academic, professional, and industrial organizations. In total, over the course of their twenty-two-month-long occupation of Western Ukraine, according to a letter written by Metropolitan Andrey Sheptytsky to the Vatican, the

Soviets arrested, exiled, and killed nearly four hundred thousand Ukrainians in Galicia.[12] One never knew where arrested relatives would end up.

Salomea's brother Alex Drozdowsky before his arrest in Lviv 1940.

Frantic efforts by Helen to determine Alex's whereabouts revealed he had been taken to Brygitky Prison in Lviv. She let her parents, Julian and Maryna, know what happened, and they returned from Hrybeniw to Lviv to see what they could do to free their son. But endless appeals to Soviet officials on his behalf fell on deaf ears. Fear for his safety mounted with the passage of time, and the family felt helpless.

Then the unimaginable happened. The NKVD arrested Julian. Helen and her mother were paralyzed in fear. Luckily, however, as the van in which Julian was taken stopped on a city street so the police could gather some other suspects, a bomb went off. Everybody scattered. In the momentary confusion, the detainees, including Julian Drozdowsky, were able to escape.

The Germans Approach Lviv

By the summer of 1941 with Nazi Germany in control of most of Western Europe, the political atmosphere in Galicia was charged with anticipation of the outbreak of war between Nazi Germany and the Soviet Union. Following Hitler's declaration of war against the U.S.S.R. as the front moved eastward approaching Lviv, at 5:00 a.m. on June 22, the Drozdowskys heard the distant sound of droning airplanes and the rattling fire of anti-aircraft batteries. Rumors spread. Some thought it was the advancing front, while others thought it was just military maneuvers. No one knew for sure.

By 6:00 a.m. Red Army soldiers had filled the streets. Vehicles stood bumper to bumper, and tanks lined up behind tanks. For the Drozdowskys the outbreak of these hostilities was September 1, 1939 all over again. Again they were being awakened by the sound of droning aircraft, whistling bombs, and frightening explosions. Again they rushed into their cellars to protect themselves.

By the next morning, Monday, June 23, 1941, it became evident that the Red Army already was starting to retreat. Some skirmishes had broken out between the Reds and Ukrainian partisans. On this, the second day of the war, the evacuation of Bolshevik civil servants and the administrators who previously had arrived in great numbers from the Soviet Union, was underway.

Meanwhile ordinary citizens of Lviv, including the Drozdowskys, watched quietly from the sidelines and expectantly awaited the change. Before the German army entered, would the Drozdowskys be able to find Alex and free him?

A Stunning Discovery

On Tuesday, June 24, 1941, the German onslaught on Lviv began. By Friday more and heavier German bombing began. Anti-aircraft guns no longer protected Lviv, and the entire city felt a sense of terror. As the Soviets continued to make their way out, the streets filled with tanks, along with trucks carrying soldiers with guns and armed NKVD officials. Danger mounted. Even a casual glance at a truck could result in death. Occasional sniper fire from nearby buildings prompted NKVD officers to enter in search of those shooting. Everyone in the building would be arrested, including old women and children, and taken in trucks to be exiled. The exodus continued.

As the warfront moved east towards Lviv, the biggest problem troubling the NKVD were the Ukrainian civilians, mainly the intelligentsia, in Lviv jails. There were 3,638 such inmates in prison number one on Lontsky Street, 801 in prison number two on Zamarstyniv Street, and 706 in Brygitky Prison, including Alex Drozdowsky. Furthermore, in all of Western Ukraine, there were some twenty thousand such prisoners.[13] At first, as the front advanced toward the city, the NKVD simply fled, leaving the prisoners behind.

In Brigitky, where Alex was imprisoned, it became evident to the prisoners that the prison guards had disappeared. The prisoners tried to make a run for it through the main gate. Just as they did, however, a Soviet military unit passing by opened fire on them, which drove the prisoners back inside. The Soviet unit paused long enough to post soldiers to guard the jail, forcing the prisoners to await their departure. Meanwhile the battlefront temporarily had stalled west of Lviv, so the NKVD returned.

The prisoners realized that the NKVD were still uncertain about which way the war would turn. After anxiously debating what to do, the prisoners decided it was best to stay where they were and remain quiet. This wasn't a time to anger the NKVD, especially in this tumultuous period. Just then, however, prisoners who were able to look out into the corridors from their cells noticed there were tables laden with alcohol and sausages prepared for the NKVD. It was obvious that the NKVD were being prepared to do something of great difficulty. The prisoners deduced that the guards were about to be called upon to annihilate the inmates.[14]

Unable to evacuate the prisoners in view of the newly advancing front, the NKVD began to slaughter them en masse, regardless of whether the inmates were incarcerated for major or minor offences.[15] According to eyewitnesses, as soon as the bombing of Lviv began again, NKVD officers led prisoners in front of a courtyard prison wall, where they shot them. The executions continued day and night. Prisoners in the cells heard a continual volley of gunshots as more and more inmates were taken out. Similar massacres took place in other cities in Galicia.

Ukrainian partisans sought to intervene to prevent the shootings, but they were unable to penetrate the prison on Lontsky Street as well as Brygitky.[16] Before the final Soviet evacuation, according to the National Memorial Museum of Victims of the Occupation Regimes (*Tyurma na Lonskoho*) in Lviv, some four thousand prisoners were shot and buried in the basements of Lviv prisons alone, and approximately twenty thousand perished in the prisons of Western Ukraine. In an effort to erase evidence of what they had done, NKVD officers set fire to Brigitky and the other prisons.[17] At night the red flames from the prisons illuminated the downtown area while dark-gray smoke spread throughout the city. Those prisoners who had survived the shootings burned to death.

The German Entry

On Monday, June 30, 1941, in the early-morning light, a dead silence descended upon Lviv. Then a German soldier appeared. He asked locals, "What is burning?" Lviv residents replied that it was the jails. Then more German soldiers appeared.[18]

There was no looting. There were no rapes or murders. The Soviets had fled. Order returned. The Red Terror was finally over. For most Ukrainians, and even some Jews, the German army represented relief from the bestiality of Soviet rule, as well as the impending return of European culture. Civilization would replace Asiatic barbarism, and the familiar Hapsburg liberalism would return. At last Ukrainians saw the arrival of a "liberating army," surely committed, they thought, to the establishment of the long awaited independent Ukrainian state. Since the Germans had not yet begun their deportations and repressions, their true intentions were still unknown to the local population.[19]

That morning word spread through the city that the Bolsheviks had killed all the inmates in the prisons. There were very few Ukrainian families in Lviv who did not have a relative in prison then. While the population was prepared for almost anything, the Drozdowskys among them, somehow they never anticipated and could not believe that the inmates would be the victims of such an insane slaughter.

Along with other terrified relatives, Julian, Maryna, and Helen rushed to the jails to find Alex. They broke down the doors, and as they entered, they were confronted by the putrid smell of decaying dead bodies. They were stunned. Hundreds, if not thousands, of corpses lay in prison cells and in the court-yards. A fire had been set in the prison area where inmate records were kept; there were no files and no one left to rescue.

Inside the prison the Drozdowskys found rows of black swollen bodies. All of the victims had been shot with a bullet to the scruff of the neck. As relatives made their way through the courtyards, fresh blood oozed out of the earth under their feet as steam rose from the still-warm corpses below. In total some 2,400 dead bodies, mainly Ukrainians, were discovered in Lviv alone.

In some prisons, rescuers found cells filled with mutilated body parts. Women broke down sobbing uncontrollably at the sight of the bodies of their loved ones among thousands of corpses. Men walked in stoic silence with clenched fists as they searched for lost relatives. Moved to the depths of their being, dazed, and traveling from one prison level to another, the Drozdowskys frantically looked for Alex with handkerchiefs held to their faces to shield them from the putrid smell.[20]

Rescuers were particularly struck by the fact that the prisoners often had faced sadistic, meticulously prepared torture, rapes, and mutilations before their executions. In Brigitky, for example, live prisoners were blocked in with a brick wall built around them so that they could not escape. Eventually they suffocated. Many of the cells were more than half full with stacked corpses, piled high—layer upon layer, with mounds of sand in between. According to a July 7, 1941, newspaper report, the Soviets had stacked the corpses of the murdered like piles of wood.

Initially the German army allowed family members to enter the prisons to collect the remains of their loved ones. It was early July 1941, the hottest time of year, and people waded around in human blood, as well as other organic liquids and bones from corpses in various states of human decay—a toxic danger. As the German army took better control of the city, however, they posted guards in front of the prisons and then refused to allow people to enter without first producing identification papers to establish a connection to those who had perished. According to Helen, while German soldiers supervised the work wearing gasmasks to protect themselves against the overwhelming stench, frenzied family members stricken with grief reviewed each body as it was brought out in order to see if it was their loved one.

Those who had come earlier had pulled bodies out by themselves to retrieve them from the prison. This work was soon assigned to Jews, some of whom were just walking by and who were ordered by the German army to dig up the improvised graves inside the prison, pull out the corpses, and then line them up for the local population to identify as family members.[21]

Some Ukrainian families approved of this German mistreatment of the Jews. Hysterical as they were in their grief about the deaths of their own loved ones, they were persuaded by the Gestapo's accusations that pointed blame in the direction of the Jews, identifying Jews as part of the "Bolshevik scourge." Most families, however, were not convinced, and neither were the Drozdowskys. Nonetheless, in the few days following the German arrival, some four thousand Jews were killed in the process of opening up the jails in Galicia.[22] Decisive measures in preventing the spread of this pogrom—which had been initiated by the Nazis with the help of local Ukrainian thugs—included an appeal for calm issued by Metropolitan Andrey Sheptytsky of the Ukrainian Catholic Church, the efforts of the Ukrainian militia in Lviv to stop it, and the arrival of the Forty-Ninth Army Corps of the German Wehrmacht—Emil Tyshovnytsky's unit.[23]

Emil in the German Army

Emil Tyshovnytsky later recalled how he ended up in Lviv as a *sonderführer* (lieutenant) in the German army at that time.

Early in June 1941, I received an official letter delivered by courier to my apartment in Cracow, where I was then living. I opened the envelope and found call-up papers ordering me to report to the local German commandant's office on June 12. At first I thought about ignoring the order but decided it was unwise to do so. So I complied. When I arrived at the office on the fixed day, there were a number of people waiting in the hall. Shortly afterwards we were collected into a military bus and driven to an old Austrian castle outside Cracow. There we were locked up in underground quarters. We slept on bunk beds. None of us knew what was going on. The uncertainty of our situation was very disconcerting.

The following day a German officer arrived and announced, "Germany will soon begin a war with the Bolsheviks. You will be assigned to different units of the German army as interpreters. Until then no one should learn of this, so you will have to stay here in isolation until you are needed. Service in the German army is a great honor for you, and I hope you will accept it voluntarily. If anybody wishes to refuse, he should say so now."

Nobody refused. None of us was exactly overjoyed about joining the German army. For example, why would I, a Ukrainian by nationality and now a Polish citizen, want to join the German army? But I spoke thirteen languages, and there were unknown, and likely unhappy, consequences awaiting anyone who refused. So we were imprisoned in the castle for several days until we were taken by the Germans, one by one, to various assigned destinations.

Emil was assigned to the headquarters of the Forty-Ninth Mountain Army Corps and was stationed in Łańcut. His job was to translate for some of the German staff who were leading the front from the San River through Western Ukraine and the entire right bank of Ukraine to the Dnieper River. He ended up providing endless translations of questions posed by German soldiers to captured Soviets and then translations of answers provided by the hapless prisoners.

Emil continued:

In the beginning I was just a private. Young non-commissioned officers taking advantage of their superior rank, and just for fun, would intentionally stop me, demanding that I salute them, or send me to fetch cigarettes for them. I found it hard to accept such treatment and decided to bring this matter to the attention of General Ludwig Kubler, the corps commander.

"Your Excellency," I said to the general, "I graduated from the Austrian officers' school and served in the capacity of an officer at the Italian front in World War I. I even received Austrian combat awards. Between 1918 and 1920, I fought at the front against the Bolsheviks as a lieutenant of the Ukrainian Galician Army. I am a certified engineer and forty-two years old. Moreover, since I am not a German, I am not obliged to serve in the German army. But now that you have drafted me, why should I be an errand boy for corporals and sergeants? I think I deserve an officer's rank, especially given that my work as a corps headquarters interpreter is very important and responsible."

The general turned out to be an understanding man. He issued an order promoting me to the rank of sonderführer. From that moment on, my personal situation improved significantly. I was given an officer's pay, ate at the officers' canteen, and was even assigned an orderly to help me with my belongings.

When our unit arrived in Lviv, we were stationed at the Georgia Hotel in the downtown area. Wearing my German army uniform as I walked in the streets, I met up with some of my old friends, and soon we were drinking coffee and talking about the prospects for Ukrainians under the new Nazi regime. My friends were disappointed when I warned them that they should expect no deliverance from Hitler. They hoped that Hitler would bring them freedom and independence from their Soviet nightmare. I cautioned them they were wrong, even as I knew it was dangerous for me to talk openly like this. I trusted my compatriots, and they did not let me down.

The Germans Gain Control

As part of the Nazi effort to create the most propaganda out of the atrocities committed by the Soviets, Emil and other translators were assigned to travel with foreign correspondents to view the prisons in Western Ukraine. Journalists from Switzerland, Sweden, Portugal, and the United States (which had not yet entered the war) and observers from the International Red Cross accompanied Emil and his colleagues as they toured through the burned remnants of Brygitky, as well as the other prisons in Lviv and other cities in Galicia. "We witnessed terrible scenes of human anguish and grief, disturbing incidents that bothered us greatly," Emil said. "But for me there was no escaping the German army and this assignment."

The journalists carefully recorded their observations. Many of the inmates had been murdered brutally and sadistically, with their eyes poked out, tongues removed, and hands, feet, or breasts cut off. One priest, Zynoviy Kovalyk, was found crucified with his stomach cut open and a dead human fetus placed inside. Another incident involved nuns who'd had crosses cut into their backs. The international press published articles and showed films in theaters about these atrocities; they chronicled and recounted these scenes in graphic detail. According to modern-day estimates, in the four prisons in Lviv at that time, 75 to 80 percent of those killed were Ukrainians. The rest were Poles and Jews.[24]

News from Lviv Arrives in Cracow

My mother was living in Cracow at the time of these events. Friends, she told me years later, brought her the news of Alex's death when she met them at a Ukrainian church.

Since the front had moved eastward beyond Lviv by then, I immediately made my way back home to my family. As soon as I arrived, we rushed to Brigitky to continue the search for the fate of Alex. I recall that both my parents went to the jail with me to see if we could identify Alex's body. But we could not find him. There was a swarm of flies buzzing around the dead bodies that lay on the street while the process of identification took place. The swarm was so heavy it was like a sea of the locusts swirling over that part of the city. The stench of the dead bodies rotting also was unimaginable. I could barely deal with it.

Probably Alex was smothered to death. He was sentenced to six years jail. If it hadn't been for the moving front, maybe he may have been exiled and could have survived. His birthday was November 18, 1913. But we don't know the date of his death, nor do we know much about the circumstances of it. However, according to Iryna Chojnatska, his fiancé at the time, who went and identified the body following the arrival of the German soldiers in Lviv, he was one of the dead found in that prison.

Once confirmed, Alex's death became a deep, lasting wound in the hearts of members of our family. For months following the identification of the body, my father sat alone, silently mourning the loss of his son.

Helen was so devastated by this loss that she refused to talk about it in any detail for the rest of her life.

Alex's death became a defining moment in my mother's life. His death seared right through to her soul. Like a deep scratch on a record album that causes the needle to recoil back to it again and again, my mother spent the rest of her life repeatedly lamenting his passing, vainly asking why it had to happen. Her loss was emotional, mental, physical, social, and spiritual.

Until he died, Alex was my greatest source of support. On various occasions he would help me, when, due to my deafness, I was unable to cope in social situations. Around the dining room table, for example, if someone began saying something to me, Alex secretly signaled me by mouthing words across the table so I would look up to see who was talking and pick up on the conversation. In this way, and in many others—such as escorting me to dances and being at my side when I needed him in social settings—Alex was a main pillar of comfort and strength for me.

Years later, my mother and I discovered, among the seemingly endless list of names of those who had died in those days in Brigitky, the following entry. "Mr. Alexander Drozdowsky, attorney candidate in Lviv, after being arrested in 1940 and sentenced to six years of hard labor in exile in the far reaches of the USSR."

First German Initiatives

On July 15, 1941, notices were posted on kiosks and building walls in Lviv ordering every Jew to wear a white armband (*opasky*) with a blue Jewish Star of David on his or her right sleeve when going outside. The penalty for the failure of a Jew to wear the band in public was death, which frequently occurred on the spot when the infraction was discovered.[25] The Germans began a system of registering locals at the city hall, where they issued identity documents that proved residence (*Kennkarten*), and then registered residents at local labor offices (*Arbeitsämter*), where they received work cards (*Arbeitskarten*), which became very valuable documents to have. These documents were a source of identification for frequent showdowns on the streets with SS troops who grilled anyone confronted and often collected those who were unemployed to be sent to labor camps. My mother and Helen recalled seeing the notice regarding Jews and observing the transformation in the streets of Lviv that followed as the Jewish population complied with the requirements.

Around this time, in July 1941, the Gestapo began to post signs calling on the local population to turn in partisans. In one village a Polish leader informed the German High Command that on a previous night partisans had visited and stayed in the village. The Gestapo immediately appeared in the village and called a meeting of the entire population. They asked all those villagers with whom the partisan units had stayed to step forward. Twenty-six such villagers volunteered. The Gestapo shot them on the spot.

That was the end of informants in Ukraine helping the Germans. Through events such as these, and hundreds of others, the meaning of the Nazi occupation was becoming crystal clear to the population of Galicia.[26]

German leaders strut through the streets of Lviv 1943.

The "Aktion" Against the Jews of Lviv

In October 1941, the Nazis posted multilingual posters all over Lviv and published ads in newspapers proclaiming the creation of a Jewish residential area, the Jewish ghetto, in the northern and northwestern parts of the city. The Shoa was beginning.

Jews across the city were given one month to move into the ghetto, while Aryans were ordered to move out of the area reserved for Jews. This was a matter of great importance to the entire population of Lviv, since it disrupted so many lives. A massive exchange of accommodations had to take place as Jews and non-Jews negotiated their new living arrangements.

Around this time, in August 1941, German military personnel requisitioned the Krushelnytsky building for their use. Only with great difficulty did Krushelnytska, with the help of Julian Drozdowsky, manage to get the Germans to agree to allow her family to move up to an apartment on the third floor where they could continue to live. All other residents on the first and second floors were removed. Many years later while, we were on a trip visiting Lviv, my mother mentioned something about this incident. I vaguely recall her telling me that she was troubled by a memory of her identifying a Jewish family that was cleared out of the building to make way for her family's resettlement.

This lingering memory also troubled me. I wanted a more exact explanation, even if it was painful and undermined my mother's standing. While digging into the question after her death, I began by asking myself how was it that there was a Jewish family living there in the first place? The answer was that such a family only could have taken over that residence at the expense of the Krushelnytsky family—the owners of the building—by being pro-Bolshevik and gaining the Bolsheviks' intervention under the previous Soviet rule. With the change in the regime, that family would have been vulnerable to removal due to their political affiliation and religion. Since it was a fact that the German army had taken over two stories in the building, it would have been virtually impossible for a pro-Soviet Jewish family to remain there in those circumstances. The only possible explanation for my mother's troubling memory could be that she identified the family as Jewish right at the time of the German army move-in.

Researchers who work in the Solomiya Krushelnytska Museum, which is now located in that building, pointed out to me that if there had been such a Jewish family living there during the war, their removal was inevitable and their demise assured, whether or not my mother had been involved. That was the best I could make out from my research regarding my mother's comment.[27] In the end, however, I believe my mother did identify such a family, and I fear they may have perished in the Holocaust.

A Hard Winter

While the winter of 1940–1941 was severe, the following winter was even worse. There was a shortage of fuel in Lviv. People froze in cold buildings, and the pipes carrying water cracked in the cold. What was even more difficult for residents to bear was the hunger.

The Germans fully understood that starving people were not capable of opposing the regime. Therefore they put Lviv's population of three hundred thousand on food-rationing cards (*Lebensmittelkarten*). Surviving on the *Lebensmittelkarten* was almost impossible, particularly when it came to sustaining a family.

To make matters worse, residents of the Jewish ghetto were provided half the standard allotment, which pushed them to the edge of starvation. Meanwhile all sorts of food products were exported to Germany to feed the leaders and also were sent to soldiers on the front. Soon people were selling almost everything in order to get food, including wedding rings, carpets, fur coats, winter coats, and watches. Illegal trade—including trade with German soldiers, as well as soldiers who were allies of the Germans in the city—became the norm.

By 1942 hunger was a fact of life for almost all Poles and Ukrainians, particularly for Jews in the ghetto, who by then were little more than walking skeletons. Older people on fixed incomes found it especially difficult to survive and were dying in great numbers.

The war also decreased the morale of the population. Alcohol was being consumed at work. Pornography flourished. Many young women became prostitutes. Theaters were filled with people seeking to relieve themselves of the day-to-day hardships. Despite these stark consequences of Nazi policy, however, the Germans had a problem that turned out to be a way for my mother and her family to break out of the cycle of hunger and despair.

There simply were not enough *Reichsdeutsche* (Germans from Germany) to occupy all the newly conquered territories. The Nazis, therefore, started to look for people of German origin and their assimilated descendents, who were given the name *Volksdeutsche*, to help them rule. The *Volksdeutsche* were acknowledged as people of German descent if at least one of their ancestors up to three generations in the past had some sort of German blood. This acknowledgment gave the *Volksdeutsche* access to special German stores that were filled with bread, butter, meat products, sausages, cheese from Holland, French wines, fish products, preserves, and the like. These individuals also received access to clothing, shoes, and other privileges, including a new or appropriate residence.

At least initially, registration on the so-called Volkslist— that is to say, being registered as *Volksdeutsche*—was voluntary. Since life circumstances were so intolerable, a long line formed in front of the building occupied by the German commission in Lviv that collected names. People stood outside the German commission headquarters day after day. In Lviv alone the total number of *Volksdeutsche* ended up being about nine thousand, the vast majority of whom were Poles.[28] Some of these *Volksdeutsche* were called upon to capture Jews who lived beyond the ghetto and to perform other unsavory duties.

Probably for such reasons, obtaining a *Volksdeutsche* card was viewed as a becoming a "sellout" by the Ukrainian leadership in Lviv and was regarded with disdain. Despite what others thought, however, my mother wasn't prepared to tolerate savage German food restrictions and decided to do something about it. Even though she had no German ancestry, somehow she obtained a *Volksdeutsche* card. How she obtained it—and whether she compromised herself physically, spiritually, culturally, or emotionally to get it—only she knew. Family members speculated it was probably related to some sort of student status she claimed. No matter how she had obtained it, however, the card helped save the lives of all her family members by easing the food crisis they faced.

German Victory or Defeat?

By the summer of 1942, the Germans had occupied almost all of Europe and were marching eastward, deep into Soviet territory. By then Galicia had become so much a part of the interior of the German empire that the nightly prohibition against lighting was abolished in Lviv. As the city darkened at twilight, a lamplighter would appear. He carried a long pole with a device for lighting streetlamps on the end of it. The man would reach up with the pole, open the door to a lantern, and with the aid of his lamplight, set fire to a little tongue in the lamp. The tongue would begin to glow through the colored glass, reflecting a bluish green light on the sidewalk. As the street lanterns lit up on the edge of the sidewalks, reaching all the way from Academia Street to the opera house, they left a stirring impression on those who walked by. The whole quarter changed character, as if packaged in a light-blue serpentine ribbon. The street seemed to come alive, as if from some strange world. Even the pedestrians seemed different, almost saintly, as if they'd forgotten all their problems, which, as a rule, had been created by the war.[29]

Academia Street was a meeting place for friends and lovers. Students gathered there to stroll along the clean, well-kept sidewalks; there were no discarded cigarette packages or cigarette butts under the pedestrians' feet. As my mother or Helen, or sometimes their parents, strolled up this street, they were drawn by the streetlamps to the display at the end of the street that had been erected to remind the population of the massacres of the Bolsheviks. Specially equipped cases presenting graphic pictures from the prisons of Lviv served as a silent memorial to the loss of thousands, including Alex Drozdowsky. *Did they all die in vain?* the Drozdowskys and others wondered.

The Final Solution for the Jews

As the summer yielded to fall of 1942, it was time for the Germans to implement their Final Solution by sending six million Jews to their deaths in concentration camps and elsewhere, among them four million Jews from Poland and Ukraine. In the process, the Nazis also would kill some five million non-Jews: Romas, homosexuals, communists, Soviet prisoners of war, and others, including Ukrainians.

As part of this new thrust in late August 1942, announcements were posted all over the city, signed by *SS-Gruppenführer* Fritz Katzmann, warning Aryan residents of Lviv against sheltering Jews outside of the Jewish ghetto. "It is forbidden to accept

Jews into buildings and residences in the non-Jewish areas," the posters stated. "Whoever consciously or knowingly gives Jews a place to stay, including residence, feeds them, or hides them will be punished by death."[30] The goal of this campaign was to terrorize the Ukrainian and Polish population of Lviv into turning in Jews. New regulations concerning employment also were promulgated. They required all businesses that employed Jewish workers to furnish the *Arbeitsamt-Judeneinsatz* (Jewish employment office) information about these workers.[31]

Despite these explicit warnings and the severe consequences for disobedience, around this time in June 1943, a Jewish girl appeared in my mother's seamstress shop. While cautiously looking out the window, she turned to my mother and asked her if she would take her in for work. For my mother this posed an obvious risk, one that involved the whole family if it was discovered.[32]

My mother had a good sense of character and knew how to read people; it was probably a skill she had developed due to her hearing impairment. She sensed the girl's desperation, her willingness to work hard, and her gratitude for any help she might receive.[33] Since my mother had grown up in the company of Sabina and her family, as well as other Jewish families, the idea of giving this girl a chance seemed right. She later described the girl's emotional state to me.

> While working with me sewing women's dresses together, the girl's nerves were as raw as they could be. She lived on pins and needles and recoiled at any unexpected sound. She was literally eating her heart out in terror of the Gestapo. Despite the risks for both of us, however, I continued employing the girl for as long as I could. Finally, one day the girl just didn't show up. Inquiries led nowhere. She was gone—probably another victim of the Holocaust.

In hindsight I regret that I never asked my mother for the name of the girl, even though in later years Aunt Helen and my mother talked about her with me on several occasions.

What Now?

From early April through June 1944, Lviv experienced increasing Soviet bombardment as the war front moved westward. By June, as a steady stream of military transports and increasingly gloomy German faces headed westward daily, the evacuation of the German administration and population commenced. The city was placed under strict nightly curfews. The population of Lviv could see that the Germans were retreating. The front was moving in on Lviv. Again the immediate threat for most Ukrainians was the Soviet Union.

For this reason Ukrainians began to make a mass exodus westward—not to support the Germans, since it was increasingly evident that they were no better than the Bolsheviks, but simply to escape. It is estimated that some one hundred thousand people escaped from Galicia at this time. After experiencing the barbaric deeds of the NKVD secret police, the Drozdowsky family also decided to move westward. It was time to save their own lives, even if it meant the loss of valuables acquired through hard work, as well the abandonment of heirlooms handed down over the course of many generations. It was time to start over from scratch, continue their lives amid the unknown circumstances of a war-torn Europe, and if they were lucky, find a future in peace. The Germans occupying Lviv now displayed a sense of hopelessness. Even the Nazis no longer believed in their ultimate victory, although they didn't acknowledge this, except reluctantly in private conversations.

My mother related to me how she and Helen took one of the last trains leaving Lviv westward before the Soviet front approached in mid-July 1944.

> The trains for Ukrainian residents of Galicia seeking to escape the Red Army were arranged with the German High Command in Cracow through the intercession of Volodymyr Kubijovych, the head of the Ukrainian Central Committee. Our parents left Lviv earlier, in March of 1944, and then tried to find accommodations in Novy Sacz in Poland. Because it was full of displaced persons and others, they ended up staying with a priest who was a family friend in Zhegestovy, a little town just outside of Novy Sacz. We, on the other hand, left Lviv on one of the last trains traveling to Peremyshl.

Then, following a brief reunion with their parents after their arrival in Novy Sacz, my mother went on to Cracow, where she had developed work-related ties before the war, while Helen headed to Slovakia, where she joined a forestry group headed for Vienna.

Meanwhile, as the Red Army moved westward into Lviv, Emil also tried to escape. Earlier, he had been relieved of his duties as a German soldier. In his memoirs he related how this had happened. He had developed a plan to leave the army as the front moved eastward, in the direction of Stalingrad, beyond Ukrainian territory.

> I decided, now that we were approaching the eastern border of Ukraine, I no longer wanted to serve in the German army. I approached my commanding officer and decided to level with him. I explained my circumstances, telling him I was Ukrainian and that, so long as the German army was fighting the Bolsheviks and clearing them out of Ukraine, I was happy to help them. Now, however, we were about to enter territory that was beyond Ukraine, and I no longer felt the drive

to continue, particularly in view of the atrocities I had witnessed firsthand. I asked to be discharged and be allowed to return to my home.

General Kubler said there was no such thing as a discharge to be allowed to return home from the German army. However, having sympathy for my story, the general said to me, "You know, as I look at you, I see you look ill. I had better have you examined by our doctor." He then picked up the phone and called the doctor. Over the phone he said, "I am sending you a man named Tyshovnytsky who is sick! You understand?" Then he hung up.

I went to the doctor's office and that same day received a medical discharge as no longer fit to serve in the German army. I was allowed to collect my things and board a train headed back from the front to Poland. I returned home to Western Ukraine, and that is where I stayed for the rest of the war until the arrival of the Red Army moving westward toward Germany.

Despite his earlier medical discharge from the German army, Emil was now arrested by the Germans and sent to Dresden to work under the guard of SS troopers as an engineer in an underground German airplane factory with thousands of other military and civilian prisoners from various European nations. The German war machine was getting desperate and forced them to work under very harsh conditions with little food.

Emil's camp was not seriously affected by the bombings of Dresden, but as the Red Army approached that city in the weeks that followed, his group was transferred to the Province of Wuerttemberg, near Stuttgart. There the US Armed Forces finally liberated them in April 1945, and Emil was placed in a displaced persons camp.

As for my mother, she remained close to her parents and, from time to time, traveled from Cracow to help them.

> Earlier, while on route to Zhegestovy, our father caught a cold and in time the cold developed into a full-fledged case of pneumonia. Our parents struggled with their situation. There was no penicillin available in those war conditions. Since there was no medicine, our mother sought to make up for it by providing our father the best possible foods so his immune system could gain the strength needed to ward off the disease. But where was this food to come from?

My mother did what she could. To help her parents, she took the ring they'd received as a family heirloom from Solomea Krushelnytska and sold the large pearl to a jeweler. She asked him to replace the pearl with a plausible fake so no one could tell it was missing. Combining the proceeds with her earnings from sewing while living with the Ilnytsky family in Cracow from July 1944 to January 1945, my mother traveled back and forth to Zhegestovy, bringing fresh food, including hard-to-obtain eggs, meat, and milk. Even fresh food was not enough, however. Julian eventually had to be hospitalized in Novy Sacz.

As the warfront moved in from the east, my mother faced a heart-wrenching decision. Should she stay with her parents in Poland or leave them behind? When she spoke to her mother about it, her mother said that a wife's duty was to be with her husband. My mother, on the other hand, had an obligation to do what was best for her. She decided to flee, reasoning that she could help her parents join her later. She described how she left.

> When it was time for me to say goodbye, in view of his illness, I did not know if I would ever see my father again. This made our goodbyes especially tender. My father was such a decent man. He led such a

good life. There were never any intrigues, embarrassments, or wanton revelations. Above all he dealt with me honestly. That was my fondest memory of him and his most precious gift to me.

In January 1945 my mother made her way westward, criss-crossing war-torn Europe as a displaced person. When she left, she could not have known that she would not see her mother for another fifteen years. Nor did she realize that during that time her mother would remain trapped in Novy Sacz, unable either to go home to Lviv or to make much of a living where she was.

By then most of the railroad system in formerly German-occupied Europe was in chaos. Every major train station had been bombed, particularly those standing at major crossroads. In every station, on the platforms and on the rails, there were crowds of people with suitcases, boxes, knapsacks, bags, and children's wagons waiting for—and trying to get onto—a train. Theft was rampant. Among the refugees there were now increasing numbers of recently released prisoners from Nazi concentration camps.

Finding Each Other

By this time Helen's group had arrived in Vienna, where the Germans, who were skilled at exploiting people with technical skills, quickly determined that Helen and her friends had forestry expertise. Helen recounted what happened.

Our group was forcibly put to work in a forestry academy research center. The German military needed sap from pine trees in the Alps to grease certain guns used at the front. Our group was required to collect this sap and deliver it to the military. This was not always safe.

One day while we were collecting sap, American airplanes bombed the forest. We were lucky to escape alive. But the next day, we were back in the forest continuing our work. What else could we do? We had to earn money to eat. The entire city was on food-rationing cards. People were hungry. I starved. We all struggled to survive.

While in Vienna, Helen met a Lithuanian boy named Peter who was several years younger than her. Their relationship deepened over time, and eventually they moved in together. But the Germans soon drafted him to go to work in Dresden.

On the night of February 13, 1945, hundreds of Royal Air Force bombers, directed by Air Marshal Arthur Harris, dropped thousands of tons of incendiaries and high explosives on Dresden. Within a few short hours, at least 35,000 civilians lost their lives in an inferno that was visible more than a hundred miles away. Yet Peter managed to escape. However, instead of returning to Helen, Peter, evidently shaken to the core by the Dresden experience, found refuge in the arms of another woman. Helen was devastated and never spoke of it again. I only learned about it from my mother years later.

When my mother reached Austria, a friend of hers, Lydia Burachynska, who later would become the president of the Association of Ukrainian Women in the United States and who worked at the post office in Gratz, intercepted a letter addressed to my mother and brought it to her; it was from Novy Sacz. As my mother's eyes intensely scanned the text, tears welled up and then streamed down her cheeks. She read that her dear father, the person she had become closest to following her brother's death, had passed away on February 18, 1945.

I decided to leave Gratz and make my way to Vienna, where I knew Helen was living. In Vienna I searched for my sister but could not

*find her. However, on a Sunday we both attended the same church
service and found each other there. I was overjoyed to reunite with
Helen. After all I was deaf and had to face all these hardships on my
own. She could help me, and I could now also help her.*

While reflecting on the dark moments before reuniting
with Helen, more than once my mother professed that it was
the Blessed Virgin Mary who had saved her. She spoke of riding
trains at night, purposefully made dark for security reasons. She
admitted that not being able to see what was happening was her
greatest fear, since she could not hear instructions being barked
out by officials. In those moments of terror, she directed her
prayers to Mother Mary, asking for her help, and attributed her
survival to heavenly intervention.

Helen Drozdowska in Western
Europe, 1947

My mother joined Helen
in her living quarters. As the
war drew to a close, they ended
up living in the British zone.
Somehow they paid the rent;
my mother sewed clothes,
while Helen worked odd jobs
and taught piano. For the time
being, they were able to make
due.

On April 30, as the Soviet
Army overran Berlin, Adolf
Hitler committed suicide.
Soon after, on May 8, 1945,
Germany surrendered uncon-
ditionally. That day Europe
and the Allies celebrated V-E
Day.

On August 14, 1945, having finally grasped the magnitude of their loss after two atomic bombs, Japan agreed to the terms of surrender set at the Potsdam Conference and surrendered unconditionally to the US and the Allies.

While the Western world celebrated, they could not deny that war had left a toll. Millions of people had been uprooted from their homes. Estimates of the total number of displaced persons vary from eleven million to as many as twenty million, not including several million ethnic Germans from Eastern Europe who were expelled and repatriated to Germany.

Life in a Displaced Persons Camp

As happy as my mother was to be reunited with Helen, it was not long afterward that she was on the move again. Driven by a search for food and better living conditions, she left her sister in Vienna and made her way to the Lehener Kaserne displaced persons camp in Salzburg, Austria, located at 4 Franz Josef Kai. There were 1,200 people living at that camp, many of them Ukrainian. This is where she spent her remaining time in Europe as she awaited the decision of the Western Allies regarding what to do with these displaced persons and all these "Galileans," as the Galicians were sometimes mistakenly called.[34]

Back in Vienna, Helen had applied for a forestry course through the Forestry Experimental Research Academy in Mariabrunn, Germany, where she had worked as a forced laborer during the war. The Nazis in the academy had been cleared out, which left spaces open for students such as her to complete their studies. She completed her diploma there but soon realized there was really no place for her in this land. Austrians sought to employ Austrians, not foreigners. Disappointed, she moved on, eventually joining my mother in the camps.

Displaced persons consisted of not only refugees fleeing Stalin and the Bolsheviks but also former inmates of German concentration camps, labor camps, and prisoner-of-war camps, as well as the Ostarbeiter slave laborers taken to Germany from Eastern Europe and the Soviet Union. Psychologically, physically, and spiritually scarred, these people now found themselves in alien lands facing an uncertain future.

By May 1945 there were more than two million Ukrainian refugees, including my mother, Helen, and Emil. More than five years of war with continual bloodshed, bombings, executions, air raids, and scarcity of food weighed heavily on their minds. Nearly all of the refugees were malnourished, and a great number were ill or dying. Shelter often was improvised. Fortunately there were many instances of military personnel sharing their own supplies of food, medicine, and clothing to help these refugees until more stable circumstances could be found.

In his displaced persons camp, Emil had nothing but time on his hands. He devoted himself to learning English and related what happened next.

> To survive in war-torn Europe, I realized I had to learn English fast, since going back to Ukraine, now under communist rule, was not an option. I never had to study English before. At age forty-six, learning a totally different tongue was not easy. But I applied myself to the task. Using a German-English dictionary, page by page I read as many English books as I could and listened to U.S. Army radio newsreels broadcast hourly to capture English pronunciation. Within four months, my concentrated efforts won great results—I had mastered the language.

In August 1945, Emil made his way to one of the high-ranking American officers in Vienna.

I asked the officer in English if that officer could use an interpreter. The officer asked what languages I spoke. I replied, "What languages do you need?" When the officer realized I spoke thirteen languages, I was immediately put to work. I joined the U.S Army and served in the position of interpreter.

A Ray of Hope

Although stark, the Leherne Kaserne camp provided my mother with her basic needs. The hordes of bed bugs that nestled comfortably in the cracks of walls and elsewhere, however, so tormented her nightly that she was unable to sleep. She would end up walking around all night—much to the wonder of others living there. She bitterly complained about the bed bugs, and she became very anxious to leave.

While she was there, discussions went through the camp as to where the displaced persons should go. One day, in the course of such a discussion, one of my mother's friends in the camp, a younger daughter of a priest of the Eastern Rite of the Catholic Church who are able to marry, received a letter from a Canadian-Ukrainian named Jake (Jakym) Holonko who lived in Alberta, about sixty miles west of Edmonton. He wanted to find someone he could sponsor to marry him and to take care of his children. Upon reading the letter, the younger girl felt that he was a little old for her but suggested that maybe my mother would be interested. My mother later said:

At that moment I did not know what would come of my life, and frankly I didn't know where to turn. I decided to write to Holonko, and ultimately, through correspondence, I agreed to come to him in Park Court, Alberta. Shortly after that, I received an affidavit of support and money for passage, which was necessary for me to immigrate. Based on that affidavit of support, I became one of the first immigrants to arrive in Canada following the war.

Canada was the first country to open its doors for displaced persons. In discussions between my mother and Helen in the camps, my mother argued that Helen should take up the opportunity to go to Canada with her. Helen had heard from other people that America would soon open its doors, however, and that it was better to go to there. The result was that my mother chose Canada while Helen immigrated to the United States about a year later.

My mother described her trip to Canada as follows.

Once everything was ready, I caught a train through Germany to Amsterdam. From Amsterdam my group, which consisted mainly of lumberjacks headed for work in Canada, ended up traveling together to Southampton, U.K. While there, I was able to visit London on a side trip. Then, on a one-week voyage, I traveled by ship to Halifax.

While on board the ship to Canada, all the passengers were given a carton of American cigarettes as a gift. This was a phenomenal novelty for us. I immediately went down to my bunk, tossed the cigarettes on my bed, and then went to wash for dinner. When I came back, the cigarettes were gone. I can't tell you how demoralized I was by the theft. I had hoped to send the cigarettes back to my mother to help her survive. They would have been a lucrative currency for buying whatever she needed back home. Europe was full of thieves, and evidently one ended up on our ship. Yet most of the people on board were good people, refugees escaping persecution.

More often than not, the vessels that carried refugees across the Atlantic were converted troop carriers with Spartan amenities. During their voyages many passengers became seasick. My mother was no exception. She got very sick on the trip and threw up often. Passengers received a daily bulletin that updated their geographic location and gave the speed at which they were making progress. These bulletins also updated them regarding news events from around the world that had been received by radio. My mother tracked her progress across the ocean on a map, along with the others.

On the last night before their arrival, few people—including my mother—slept as they stood on the decks awaiting the first sight of land in North America. She marveled at seeing land on the other side of the Atlantic for the first time and wondered what life would bring her there.

Chapter 3
Starting Over

3

Arrival in Canada

MY MOTHER ARRIVED in Halifax, on the eastern coast of Canada, in the summer of 1947. She was thirty-six years old. An English-speaking customs official accidentally replaced the letter "o" in her name with the letter "a" on her papers; "S<u>o</u>lomea" thus became "S<u>a</u>lomea."

Upon emerging from customs, she rushed to a store to buy oranges and bananas, items that were not available in Europe or on board the ship. My mother had sixteen dollars with her when she arrived. Later, when she arrived in Montreal—about a two days' train ride westward from Halifax—she bought an expensive pair of shoes from a shopkeeper who tried to dissuade her and indicated she could buy something more appropriate on sale elsewhere. She wanted the shoes, however, and was prepared to buy them at a high price, even if it meant some financial discomfort to her. She paid ten dollars for them and also bought some lipstick. Someone would later steal that lipstick after she arrived at Jake Holonko's farm. For now, however, she had her New World possessions and treasured them.

In those days a trip from Halifax to Edmonton took four days and five nights by train. It was, after all, a trip across almost the entire width of the continent. The coaches were jammed, and people had to sleep sitting upright in their seats. The stops at the major cities across Canada were the only breaks that passengers had where they could breathe fresh air for an hour or two.

When my mother arrived, Jake Holonko, who would later become my father, picked her up at the train station in Edmonton, and then, on horse and carriage, drove with her the sixty miles west to Park Court. As she looked out at the landscape and the horizon, the flatlands of Alberta stretched as far as the eye could see. The trip took several hours; farm followed farm on the landscape, and my mother must have wondered what she had gotten herself into. There was not a soul in sight for miles. Park Court was in the middle of nowhere; it wasn't the end of the earth, but she could almost see the end of the earth from Park Court.

When they arrived, my father showed her his farm. He owned a quarter section of land, 160 acres, with a creek running through it. He had started with two large grain bins, each eight by ten feet, together with the land. He had nailed boards connecting these two-grain bins, creating walls for what became his first house. The inner room was divided into two sections—one half where the kids slept and the other serving as the kitchen and dining room. To provide insulation, he had poured sawdust between the boards, and in the middle of the house, there was a wood stove to keep the house warm. He also had a chicken coop and a barn for the cattle. Later Jake built a new house consisting of a kitchen and dining area and two bedrooms—about 1,500 square feet altogether.

In their correspondence, my mother had said that she knew how to cook, sew, and farm. All this was true, but not entirely. While she knew how to cook on a gas stove, she was ill prepared to cook on the wood-burning ones on the farm. Yes, she sewed, but she sewed clothing for women of high society, not everyday apparel. While her family once had a cow and a few chickens, she was basically a city girl. Still she felt the livestock they'd owned "qualified" her as being able to live on a farm, and she was ready to learn.

My father had written her that on his farm, which was not far from Edmonton, he had built a two-bedroom house with a stove and that there was water nearby. He had said that more than anything he was lonely and in need of a woman who could work alongside him and look after his children. He said that he was a widower and that he promised to take good care of my mother. All this was true, but not entirely. Park Court wasn't exactly in the midst of civilization, and he may not have revealed just how many children he had—just "a few," he had said. In actuality he had six.

Whether they wrote of marriage isn't clear, but it was certainly at least implied in their correspondence. My mother needed someone to look after her. She wanted to leave the displaced persons camp. My father's letters opened that possibility up to her. Cooking, sewing, and farming seemed like a fair trade for escaping her misery. While my father realized the conditions at Park Court were rather stark, he imagined that a woman from the old country, seasoned by the hardships of war, would soon adapt, be able to cope, and help make his life easier.

Whatever they wrote didn't much matter. They were together now and had to make the best of things. And so they did.

Jake Discusses His Past

I don't know when, but I'm certain that at some point after my mother arrived on the farm, Jake related his story about how he had come to Canada with his family and how his wife had died.

Although they were relatively wealthy by local standards, at the urging of his two brothers-in-law who were already in Canada in 1937, when he was twenty-seven years old, my father and his wife Evdokia and five children (Jean, Lydia, Mary, Wally, and Paul; Anne, their sixth child was not yet born) resolved to sell everything and emigrate from Hutvyn, a Ukrainian village near Rivne, then under Polish rule.

Foreign exchange controls in Poland at that time limited the amount of money one could take out of the country. My father converted the proceeds he received from the sale of his land and personal property into American dollars, knowing full well that the amount surpassed what he would be allowed to take out of Poland. He had a plan, however. To hide the money, he rolled up the bills and wrapped some rope around them; he then tied his suitcases with the rope. In this way he hoped to smuggle the money out of Poland so he could use it to buy a farm in Canada.

The family took a train across Europe then caught a boat across the English Channel on their way to Liverpool. There they caught the *Antonia*, a Cunard Line ship that sailed from Liverpool to Montreal in 1938.

When their suitcases were unloaded off the ship, my father noticed that the ropes were loose and, in some cases, broken and frayed. As soon as he saw that, he dashed out to buy new ropes and started to tie the suitcases together again, leaving the old ropes on the luggage. The men who were helping him wondered why he didn't get rid of the old ropes and simply tie the suitcases with the new ones. But knowing that his money was hidden in these old ropes, he insisted that he would need the ropes when he arrived in Alberta and refused to leave them behind.

Just then their youngest daughter, Mary, came down with the measles and was quarantined in a hospital. Alone in the hospital, she was afraid that she would be left behind while her family made their way to Edmonton. Jake went to the hospital with some Salvation Army workers, who brought Mary some clothes. He then arranged for Evdokia to stay behind with Mary while he took the rest of the children on to Alberta. On the way there, the other kids also broke out with measles, but my father hid that fact by bundling them up in blankets so no one would notice until they finally made it to Edmonton.

When they arrived in Edmonton, they stayed with one of my father's brothers-in-law near Park Court, Alberta. A few days later, Mary and Evdokia arrived. My father met them and took them out to the farm as well. Soon afterward he purchased a quarter section near the land his brothers-in-law owned.

Almost immediately following the family's arrival, my father received letters from back home asking him to sponsor other families to Canada. He did what he could. Over the course of the next two years, four immigrant families arrived to live with the Holonkos. Each had children. One of these families had purchased the Holonko homestead back in Ukraine, but now they came to Alberta. To accommodate everyone, the Holonkos built a new house and other buildings.

By the summer of 1939, there were five families living on the Holonko homestead, all from Ukraine—eight adults and more than twenty children. The place was inundated with adults and children. People slept all over the place, in the house, in the barn, in the granaries, and anywhere else they could find.

Jake's Wife Falls Ill

One Sunday morning, while Evdokia was baking bread and making pancakes, she suddenly buckled over with intense pain in her stomach. She was nauseous, began to run a fever, and vomited. The people on the farm went off to look for the neighboring farmer who owned the only car in the area to take Evdokia to the doctor. Jean, the oldest child, ran out to look for Wally and Paul and found them swimming in the creek. There was no time to waste. They hitched up the horses to the wagon, made a bed for their mother, laid her down, and started off in the direction of Evansburg, some ten miles away.

While Jake and the kids raced to Evansburg with Evdokia lying in the wagon, the people on the farm continued the frantic search for their neighbor with the car. Finally they found him, and he managed to catch up to the wagon about five miles down the road. They transferred Evdokia to the car and sped away to find the doctor in Evansburg. The doctor took one look at her and immediately told her to get to the hospital in Edmonton. He said he couldn't do the necessary surgery there. They raced down the highway to Edmonton, about an hour away.

Upon their arrival at the University Hospital in Edmonton, Evdokia was taken in for surgery. Her appendix had burst. Penicillin wasn't yet available, and there was no way to contain the infection. Ten days later she died. Her autopsy listed the cause of death as appendicitis, which was common to die that way back then. It was July 1939, just before the outbreak of World War II, and she was only thirty-six years old. My father could not pay the doctors. He had spent whatever money he had helping those he had sponsored to settle in this new land.

Back on the farm, the families were praying that everything would turn out OK. No one knew exactly what had happened in Edmonton. Then one evening the dogs started howling. Lydia, the second-oldest Holonko child, who was sleeping in one of the granaries, got the shakes and cried out, "The dogs are howling. Mama died. Mama must have died." Despondent, she jerked so wildly in bed that the other children had a hard time restraining her.

About an hour later, late in the evening, the children were awakened and told to get up. A wagon with Evdokia's casket had arrived. It had been transported to Evansburg by train and then loaded onto Jake's horse-drawn wagon so he could drive it back to the farm. Everyone was in shock. When Lydia came into the house where the casket had been brought, she took one look and fainted. When the adults brought her back to consciousness, she started to scream uncontrollably. Finally she was calmed down. Then the women began to wash the body for the funeral and dress Evdokia in some new clothes that my father had managed to find for her.

Paul was five years old and had slept through the arrival of his mother's casket. The next morning, when he heard the news, he was so overcome with grief and terror that he ran away into the wheat fields and hid there all day. No one could find him until nightfall, when he finally returned.

The funeral attracted hundreds of people from all the farms in the surrounding area. There were dozens of wagons; literally everyone came. The procession was so long that it stretched all the way from the Holonko farm to the cemetery a full mile away.

Just after the funeral, little Anne, the youngest Holonko child, who was only fourteen months old, cried in her crib and called out, "Mama, Mama, Mama."

Annie Charytoniuk, an aunt on my father's side of the family, asked, "Why is that baby crying?"

Jean answered, "I don't know why. She's probably crying for her mama."

"Well, when was the last time that baby was fed?" Annie asked.

"I don't know."

In their concern for themselves and feeding their own children, the other families had overlooked the Holonko children. So Annie fed and changed the baby and decided right then and there that she would take care of her for the rest of her life.

My father was now a widower at age thirty-seven. For the second time in his life, he had lost someone close to him; his brother Paul had drowned at age five. Feelings of abandonment, isolation, and loneliness grew within him. He turned to face his new life with six children. At fifteen years old, Jean was the oldest, and Anne was the youngest, at only fourteen months. He looked around him and saw primitive accommodations, harsh surroundings, and so many people to look after, with almost no money or food. Who would cook for them now? Who would help him take care of the kids? How would they survive, living in the middle of nowhere? There were no social welfare agencies to turn to, no government support. Even though Annie Charytoniuk had proposed to take care of Anne and my father had agreed, there were still five young children left with him.

In the years that followed, gripped by fear, loss, and sheer frustration, my father tried to cope by becoming a stern, authoritarian parent. At times he would take out his anger, or perhaps fear, on the children by hitting them. The family was dirt poor—one step away from total despair. Yet despite the fear and poverty, they endured. They had milk, eggs, and chickens and even made their own bread—albeit not always successfully, since they didn't exactly know how.

No doubt my mother and father visited Evdokia's grave. She's buried in a corner spot in a cemetery of perhaps a dozen graves in Park Court. The cemetery is next to a small church that today stands empty, half torn down and abandoned. Few visitors, if any, ever pass by that cemetery these days or are even aware of it. All you can hear is the rustle of the trees nearby as the wind blows through them.

I have no doubt that this story moved my mother greatly and that she would have wanted to do all she could to help Jake and his children. After all, he had paid for her trip to Canada and brought her to the farm to help him and his children. She was more than ready to give it a try.

Life Together

No stranger to hardships, my mother did her best, even if farm life was difficult. Soon her life fell into a routine. When she arose in the morning, she pulled on her clothes to go out to the outdoor bathroom. Then it was time to milk the cows. The family would go down to the creek at the foot of the hill behind the house to get water to bring back in pails for cooking, washing, and bathing. Jake didn't know how to cook anything, so my mother cooked with the help of the children. She'd light the wooden logs in the stove and the heater so she could make breakfast for the family, often Sunny Boy Cereal—a porridge made of wheat, rye, and flax—and other times eggs with toast. Then it was time to wash and dress the children for school. Lunch for school was always bread and honey since Jake was a beekeeper and traded his honey for other staples they needed. Once the children were off to school, my mother helped feed the farm animals and gather eggs from the henhouse. After the cows had been milked, the milk had to be separated from the cream. Bread had to be baked. The laundry had to be washed on a washboard in the creek, and the beds needed to be changed.

In the summer they grew a garden and collected the vegetables for their meals and for canning. They ate fresh lettuce, radishes, and onions picked from the garden, with dressing made from sour cream and vinegar. At the end of each day, the firewood had to be brought in for the next day. The house had to be kept clean, and once a week on Saturdays, my mother washed the floors with a brush and water. The children had to have their clothes sewed and kept tidy. Occasionally they had to butcher a chicken or a pig to eat. Jake had to plough the fields, attend to farm animals, and look after the supply of feedstock.

They picked wild raspberries, strawberries, gooseberries, and saskatoons to make jams and jellies as a source of fruit for the long winter months. Preparing for winter and storing up provisions was almost a full-time job. Besides berries, they could count on fish from the creeks and rivers nearby, as well as rabbits, grouse, squirrels, and bigger game such as deer and moose. These animals provided the necessary protein in their diets. Jake traded his grain, honey, and eggs for staples such as coffee, flour, and sugar.

Winters on the farm were brutal. As the days grew shorter, the snowfall came. Initially, when nature's white petticoat covered the landscape, it brought a sense of silence, cleanliness, and serenity with it. But as the temperature continued to drop and winds picked up, a bitter cold gripped the farm. When the water froze, cooking and maintaining the household and animals became harder. Heating the stove became a full-time necessity. Life increasingly became isolated and centered on the house, the storage bins, and the barn. From late October until the April spring, snow and ice covered the farm. Nearly all winter long the temperature remained below freezing. Sometimes the temperature remained at twenty degrees below zero for weeks on end. At times the temperature even dipped to below sixty degrees or colder, and when the wind chill was factored in, it felt more like minus ninety. During those times all they could do was sit inside the small, desolate house.

Fierce winds blew snow across the Canadian prairie fields, often smothering the land, bushes, and roads. No amount of clothing was enough to keep warm for long. Walking outside, they could hear the sound of snow crunching beneath their feet, see their breath as they exhaled, hear the sap in trees freezing up, and feel their cheeks get so cold that they'd become numb. Their toes felt frostbite nipping at them through their boots. When the children woke up on a winter's morning for a drink of water, they had to chop through the ice that had formed in the pail. Then they'd huddle around the woodstove to keep warm and eat breakfast.

Snow piled up high against the buildings, and howling winds carried it across the vacant prairie fields. Snow banks, several feet tall, surrounded the farm buildings so that mobility was severely restricted by cold, ice, and snow. Traveling, even to Evansburg, some ten miles away, became almost impossible. While the children attended the one-room school located diagonally across Jake's farm at the southeast corner of the property, my mother and Jake took care of the day-to-day winter chores that needed to be done on the northwest corner. The animals had to be fed and looked after. Cleaning and cooking had to be done. Month after month the winter kept the farm in its grip. On a big battery-powered radio, the family listened to the news, music, and programs such as *Procter & Gamble Hour* radio shows, *The Shadow*, *Fibber McGee and Molly*, and *Blondie*. My mother, of course, could not hear these programs and was therefore that much further socially detached from everyone else.

Time to Leave

When my mother first had arrived, my father was eager to marry her. He wanted her to step into the role of farmwife and mother to his children. My mother, however, balked at the idea. She saw herself as a seamstress and women's fashion designer—not someone who milked cows. She was a skilled worker, not just a future wife of a farmer.

Over time it became apparent that Jake and my mother weren't cut from the same cloth. My father was a farm boy and couldn't imagine how he could survive and feed his children while living in the city. My mother, on the other hand, was a city girl and couldn't see herself living the rest of her life in these do-or-die farming conditions.

If the farming challenges, social isolation, and interpersonal differences weren't enough, my mother faced other serious problems. For one thing, local communists in Canada had targeted her for criticism based on her heritage. Local Bolshevik Ukrainians had accused her father of prosecuting Ukrainian communists while he had been a judge in Poland. Their accusations terrified my mother. She was a simple woman, not capable of defending herself against a major intellectual challenge with respect to the merits or disadvantages of Bolshevism and their accusations concerning her father.

Then there were my father's three children who were still on the farm with them, Mary, Wally, and Paul. The other children already had left the farm before my mother had arrived. As children sometimes do, they took advantage of her poor hearing by making fun of her behind her back. They didn't realize, however, that she was astute enough to catch on to what was going on.

The cumulative effect of all these circumstances, especially Jake's not-always-gentle treatment of her, led my mother to start to think about moving to the city.

She began to travel to Edmonton by bus from Evansburg. First she did so to buy things or just to visit. My father would come out after her and bring her back to the farm. They began to argue about moving to the city; my mother encouraged him to consider city life, but he couldn't do it. After all he had a farm. What would he do in the city?

Their relationship became increasingly embittered and hostile. Just as it started to dissolve, however, my mother realized she was pregnant. In the hopes that a new child might draw them together, she proposed marriage. But now it was my father who balked, and an argument broke out. Accusations about failed expectations flew back and forth. Soon afterward the relationship fractured. My mother could see it was time to leave.

The parting was traumatic. My father treated her "brutally"—at least that was the word used by Alexandra Jendyk, one of my mother's friends, in whom my mother later confided. As my father had meted out beatings to his own daughters— beatings that had prompted them to also leave the farm—my mother must have been beaten as well. That was the impression I was left with from Dora Potsentelo, another of my mother's friends. If there was anything my mother never would accept, it was to be purposefully mistreated.

One day, in the late fall of 1948, my mother asked Paul, then thirteen years old, to get the horse and carriage and take her to Evansburg. When they arrived, her plan was to catch the bus to Edmonton, but she had missed it for that day. So she stayed there overnight, sleeping at the foot of the bed of a couple that had agreed to put her up until the bus arrived the following morning.

Salomea Drozdowska with Jake Holonko and two of his children, Paul and Mary, in Park Court, Alberta, in the summer of 1948

Chapter 4

Her Darkest Hour

Starting from Scratch

*L*EAVING THE FARM obviously wasn't easy. My mother told me the details many years later.

Pregnant, hard of hearing, penniless, alone, and unable to speak English, in the fall of that year, I left Park Court, and came to Edmonton. Although I did not know anyone, I did know that the sponsorship papers that brought me to Canada as an immigrant earlier in 1947 were prepared in the law office of Peter Lazarowich. So that is where I headed. Maybe he could give me some advice on what to do.

As I waited in the reception area, another woman came in. Her name was Maria Hnatiuk, but she had anglicized it, calling herself Maria Henick. While we waited, Maria started asking me questions. Was I new in the city? Where was I from? How did I come here? Where was I going? I acknowledged that I was new, but not knowing anything about this woman, I tried to deflect the other questions *away. Eventually Maria gave up. Tired of waiting for Lazarowych's return, she decided to leave.*

Later I also gave up waiting for Lazarowich and left. But just as I came out of the building, Maria called out, "Salomea" and approached me again. She asked me where I was going. Again I tried to be evasive. Sensing I was short on alternatives, Maria invited me to come to her house. As we spoke I learned that Maria was a widow. She had four children at home and lived somewhere in the north end of the city. Maria ultimately talked me into taking the bus with her to her house.

Frankly, I doubted Maria's intentions. I suspected Maria was after money. But I didn't exactly have much in the way of alternatives. We caught a bus, paying ten cents each to ride to the end of the line on the northern periphery of the city near a hotel on Fort Road around 129th Avenue. Maria then led me down sidewalks and then, at the far end, on wooden planks over mud in the direction of her house. Since I was clearly expecting, I was afraid of falling on the slippery, wet wooden planks. Somehow, slowly maneuvering our way along, we made it.

Then, after settling in and making some tea, Maria told me about her ugly marriage. Her husband would come home drunk every night, start yelling at Maria, and pretty soon he started to beat her. She had to hide under her bed to avoid him. Then one night, as her husband was coming home, a truck accidentally killed him. Maria and her four children were left living in that house and dependent on charity.

They say, "It takes one to know one," and that may be why, living through such hardships, Maria understood my situation. It was obvious I was in trouble. Maria offered to help in whatever way she could. Her decency, understanding, and sincerity ultimately won me over, and we became close friends.

Whenever my mother spoke of Maria, even years later, she referred to her simply as "the widow" (*vdovytsia*). She stayed with Maria that night and for a few nights afterward. She sewed some clothes for Maria and helped her with the vegetable garden from which they ate and with which Maria fed her family. In reflecting upon those days in her later years, my mother confessed the following.

> While I was healthy, I was in a tragic situation and just did not have a clue what to do. I did not want to be a burden on anyone and was only too well aware that there were others back in the refugee camps of Europe depending on my exemplary conduct in the New World. Before I left the refugee camps of Europe, I was warned to be on my best behavior since my conduct would be judged and could very well decide whether it would be possible for others to follow me to Canada.

Whenever my mother spoke of these times, she broke into sobs while her high-pitched voice recounted her very private pain and revealed how she was unable to hear herself, due to her being deaf.

In the early stages of her pregnancy, she pondered her limited options. There were no social service agencies to turn to, no government programs to help an unwed mother. At first she contemplated having an abortion but was dissuaded by my father. They had argued about the pregnancy, and he threatened to turn her over to the police, since he had sponsored her but she was no longer living with him. Though she knew it was an empty threat, it was enough of a threat to make her pause as she recalled the others who were depending on her good behavior back in the camps of Europe. She considered giving me up for adoption, but ultimately she couldn't bear the thought of completely severing her ties with her baby.

Maria took my mother to Misericordia Hospital for a checkup because she was complaining about morning sickness. The hospital sent my mother to see Dr. Harry Weinlos. He examined her, said that there was nothing seriously wrong, and informed her that she would deliver on approximately December 7, 1948. Then he told her to go home.

As an afterthought, he asked her whether she had anywhere to go. She said no. So he suggested she go see the Sisters of Service, an organization that had a residence for young women on 105th Street, south of Jasper Avenue, in Edmonton. She never had been to that part of town before and didn't exactly know how to get there. So Dr. Weinlos called the organization to send over a Polish-speaking woman to take her. My mother related:

> When I arrived at the Sisters of Service women's residence, I looked around, could not see myself staying, and decided to leave. I made my way back to the widow's home in north Edmonton. But after spending the night there, I realized that was no place for me either. So despite my initial reservations, I returned to the Sisters of Service. Fatefully this turned out to be a good choice because eventually I learned to enjoy living there. It was a good life for me. The French Roman Catholic sisters showed kindness and understanding to me.

My mother also got to know a few people at the Ukrainian Catholic church in Edmonton. Since she was one of the first refugees to come from Europe to Canada, a lady named Anna Preyma immediately recognized my mother as new and approached her after the church service. My mother wasn't bold enough to say she needed help, but Anna talked with people, asking them to help her, and did what she could. Organizations in the community hadn't yet been set up to help refugees.

A Promise Kept

In early December 1948, my mother moved to Misericordia Hospital, where she worked part time for the French Roman Catholic sisters who ran the institution. My mother told me later:

Some time before the birth, one of the nuns came up to me and asked me to sign over papers, effectively giving up my child after birth. An argument ensued. I yelled out that the nun had no right to do this. The nun contended that if I did not sign the papers I would be deported. Angry that they would do this, I declared I was leaving the hospital immediately.

It was late at night, and the sisters got upset by the fact that I wanted to leave in what they knew were borderline-desperate circumstances in the middle of a cold winter night. But I would not relent. So finally they called me a taxi. I left the hospital, taking the taxi back to the Sisters of Service a few blocks away. Since I realized I was no longer staying there, I paid one dollar, got out of the taxi, and took a bus out to Maria's house in north Edmonton. The widow was amazed to see me at the doorstep so late that night, but I explained I had no other place to go.

A few days later, on December 7, 1948, I returned to Misericordia Hospital to give birth, but in a different part of the hospital. After examining me, the doctors announced I had arrived too early and that they had to send me back home. They asked me if I had a place. I answered, "Not really." So they arranged for me to go to the Beulah Home, which was on 98th Street and 137th Avenue in Edmonton.

The Beulah Home was a charitable facility for unwed mothers, run by the Salvation Army. Life at the Beulah Home was very good. They treated me very well. I was in an environment with a lot of understanding and with other women also in my circumstances.

107

At Christmastime, to celebrate, they brought in a turkey. While normally they regulated the amount that each girl ate, since it was Christmastime they didn't pay too much attention. Having free reign to eat as much as I wanted left me full, which, when combined with the fact that I was very pregnant, left me gasping for air. I barely made it through that night.

I went into labor at the Beulah Home on Ukrainian Christmas Eve, Thursday, January 6, 1949. Across the street there was a medical clinic. That is where they took me. There was an elderly nurse that was fairly stern that looked after me in the early stages of my contractions. In fact I went through forty-two hours of labor before actually giving birth. I remained at the medical clinic overnight and through the following day until a doctor arrived. After examining me, he declared that I had to be taken immediately to the hospital. They took a number of blankets, put me into the doctor's car, and while I endured increasingly strong labor pains, he drove me down Princess Elizabeth Avenue to the Misericordia Hospital.

Following her arrival at the hospital, my mother was given a sedative and put on oxygen to help her relax and breathe more easily. Then she lost consciousness.

A New Life

On January 8, 1949, I was born. When my mother awoke, she was in a daze and asked the doctor what had happened. He told her she had given birth to a ten-pound baby. Not understanding, she pointed at him and at herself to ask whether it was a boy or a girl. The doctor pointed back at himself, and in this way, for the first time, my mother learned she had given birth to a baby boy. I was brought in the next morning so she could feed me. As I lay in my mother's arms in peaceful innocence in the days that followed, I could not know of the turmoil churning like a tornado around us. Here, protected temporarily in the eye of a storm, my mother pondered our fate. By all accounts the future looked bleak.

The coincidence that my mother had delivered her child in similar circumstances to those of the Blessed Virgin Mary drew her to the Virgin Mother. After all, both were displaced from their homes, both were poor, both had no place to give birth, and both had delivered at the same time of year. From that time on, my mother believed that the Blessed Virgin Mary was her patron who would intervene, with her son Jesus, on her behalf whenever she prayed for help. In the years that followed, there was more than one instance when I wondered whether this indeed was not true.

In Search of a Home

Calculating that they could capitalize on this moment of despair to break through my mother's resistance, the nurses at the hospital, (all of whom were nuns and took a very dim view of unwed mothers) again presented her with a document that would renounce all of her maternal rights and put me up for adoption. The document was accompanied with a threat—sign now, or you and your child will be deported back to war-torn Europe.

The nuns, however, had miscalculated. In a fit of anger and disdain, my mother hurled the document across the room, denouncing them and their scheme. She declared that she never would sign such a paper and that her baby was the son of a Canadian citizen who was protected by the laws of Canada. The sisters relented; the new immigrant mother had declared her rights. Some other arrangements would have to be made.

Following our release from the hospital, my mother and I were welcomed back at the Beulah Home. We were at the Salvation Army facility for about a month while she recovered from post-birth complications. She had lost a lot of blood and was weak from the protracted delivery.

Meanwhile my mother was faced with the difficulty of deciding what to do with me. With no support, little knowledge of the English language, and—though she was intelligent enough— no knowledge of how things worked in Canada, my mother had to learn fast. It was so different than life in Europe. Even simple things like sending a small package to her mother in Poland involved asking someone to show her how to do it. In later years, she'd often wistfully say that all the suffering she had endured would have been unnecessary if only she'd had contacts who could have shown her how to do the things she needed.

We moved to a room on the southern fringe of the city and stayed there for a while. In fact for the first year after my birth, my mother attempted to find some sort of stable arrangement that would enable her to live in a room, keep me, and work somewhere as a dishwasher or seamstress. But very few people were willing to rent a room to an unwed mother and her child. My mother searched around the city high and low, doing the best she could, moving us from one room to another. The fact that it was an especially bitterly cold winter didn't help the search.

One day Dora Potsentelo, a woman she had met at church one Sunday, invited her to attend a reception held at one of the Ukrainian halls. After that my mother and Dora became close friends, and from then on, we often visited her. She would leave my mother at home while she went shopping downtown, and her husband encouraged my mother to take whatever was in the fridge and to feel at home while he tended to their corner grocery store out front. She would open the fridge and greedily take whatever vegetables, fruits, or butter there was to feed me as a young child. Tragically, Dora's husband died early, leaving her a widow with her own son.

Following her husband's death, whenever we visited Dora, she and my mother commiserated, sharing their past suffering with each other. In the years that followed, whenever they recalled their early days in Edmonton—particularly the times when my mother had come to the widow's house, or the hospital where her husband had stayed—they broke into tears as they reflected on the hard times they had endured. Things had not turned out the way they were supposed to. Or had they?

Eventually my mother found a day-care center, run by Franciscan sisters, in a red-brick building on 110th Avenue and 96th Street. There I was put into a group with mostly older children who would play together, running in and out through a doorway that led to the outside. The running in and out intensified when the nuns went to pray. My mother speculated that I likely caught a cold while standing near that door as it was opened and closed in the winter weather. At first it seemed like a simple cold, but it became worse when my left ear became inflamed. I was two years old.

Paralyzed with fear that I would lose my hearing, as she had, my mother scrambled around looking for some way to find full-time care for me. The only accommodations she could find were in an orphanage in Mundare, Alberta, run by Ukrainian nuns, who assured my mother they would look after me and help me heal. There was a slight problem, however. The nuns saw orphans as potential recruits for the Catholic priesthood or sisterhood. This was a source of apprehension for my mother, since she perceived that it would lead to complications in getting me back from them. Not having any other alternatives, however, she decided to risk it.

Meanwhile she had moved to a rooming house run by Julia Kiniski, a Polish woman who favored left-wing politics. Kiniski would later unsuccessfully run for political office fourteen consecutive times. Eventually, however, she became one of Edmonton's most popular and famous alderwomen until she died in office in 1969.

While I was at the orphanage, my mother had no appetite. She was so profoundly worried about me that she cried constantly. She didn't know what to do. She harbored the dim hope that maybe her sister would somehow step in and help her. In her darkest hour, after having written Helen an SOS letter, finally she received a reply. The letter contained some words of encouragement and a one-dollar bill—enough to buy perhaps a week's worth of milk. My mother broke down and wept.

After leaving me in Mundare, my mother worked at a variety of jobs, including dishwashing, babysitting, and sewing clothes. All the while she continued her search for some sort of long-term resolution to our situation. Whenever she could, she came out to Mundare to visit me, which wasn't an easy matter, since no buses traveled there. She took the Edmonton bus up to the end of the city limits, and then from there she hitched a ride to Mundare. When she arrived she would call out "Andrijko" to me, and I'd look up, see her, and come crawling on my hands and knees to her as she wept and swept me up into her warm embrace. In later years she emotionally recalled those heart-wrenching moments.

One day, after visiting me in the orphanage, she was making her way back into Edmonton.

> *Standing on the side of the highway, I managed to wave down a car. As I got in, I recognized that the driver was former Chief Judge John Decore, a Canadian-born Ukrainian, who stopped to give me a lift. Through the whole trip, Decore tried to find out what I was doing there on the side of the highway. I was embarrassed and bobbed and weaved to avoid his questioning about why I had come out to Mundare. Eventually, not getting anywhere with his questions, Decore wound up warning me about the dangers of young women hitchhiking and dropped me off somewhere downtown.*
>
> *He must have later mentioned this trip to one of the Ukrainian lawyers in town, a guy named Shkwarko, who, bumping into me one day, bawled me out for even thinking about hitchhiking, because of the dangers involved. Nonetheless I continued coming out to Mundare.*

The nuns at Mundare were dedicated but there were limits to how much time and effort they could devote to me. While I don't remember the orphanage, it did leave an indelible unconscious impression on me. Years later, while reading an article about a child in an orphanage aching so for human contact that it rocked itself to sleep, I realized that my own rocking for comfort, even as an adult, is a legacy passed on to me from the Mundare orphanage and my darkest moments there.

Apart from rocking in bed, the only other thing I have from Mundare is a picture of myself in the orphanage. Sad, and with my hair sweaty and disheveled, I'm sitting in my crib in a dark room with a bandage wrapped around my head and under my chin. More recently I found a picture of the orphanage in a book about Mundare. It consists of a large main room filled with about two dozen cribs within reach of each other. Small children are standing or lying in the cribs while the nuns are looking on.

Me in the Mundare, Alberta, orphanage with an infected ear in 1950

Medical measures at the orphanage did not help my infection. My ear became worse as puss (*ropa*) ran down the left side of my face, infecting a large area. I developed scabs. Almost frantic at the sight, my mother transferred me into the Mundare Hospital next door. When that didn't do any good, out of desperation she took me to the Royal Alexandra Hospital in Edmonton, where finally my ear healed. This entire process took more than six months. Later my mother contended that the fact that I was able to heal without any long-term effects to my hearing was a miracle and the result of her persistent prayers to the Blessed Virgin Mary.

114

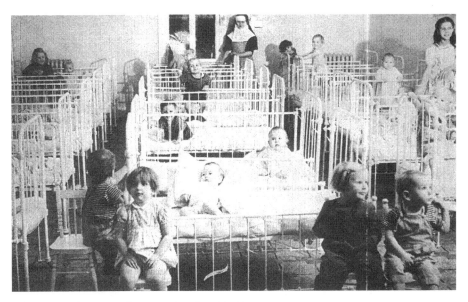

The Mundare orphanage in the 1950s

The Man with the Curled Mustache

My mother sensed that because she was an immigrant, she was neither liked by the traditional Ukrainian community of Edmonton—even though they themselves were earlier immigrants or their descendants were—nor by the broader Canadian society. People mistook her hearing impediment for low mental capacity. Wherever she took me, whether it was to church, meetings, or private homes, people felt sorry for me. When we were on a bus, people would speak to me, giving me a quarter or some other little gift to cheer me up. Later, when my mother reflected on those encounters, emotion would overcome her.

She considered the times she had endured belittling scrutiny to have been the hardest moments in her life, even harder than her experiences during World War II. Sometimes, just to

115

get away from it all, she'd take me to the park and pick saskatoon berries off the bushes to feed me. She told me later:

> I did not ask for help from anyone, including my sister, and sought to do everything on my own. The only help that I relied on was the help of the Blessed Virgin Mary, to whom I prayed often. I led a humble life and was somehow able to cope with all the difficulties because of that.

In general these experiences led her to develop a deep attachment to her independence and her freedom, which she would protect with fierce determination from that time on.

> In the spring of 1950, I put an ad in the Edmonton Journal, looking for a position as a housekeeper. Among some thirty responses I received, there was a letter from a man who invited me to visit him at his house in Edmonton. When I came he physically attacked me. I barely escaped. That taught me to be more cautious!

> But there was one other letter from a man named William (Vasyl Semotiuk) that stood out. It was on a yellow piece of paper, and he promised me that if I came to help him that I would never regret it. Now more cautious, I nonetheless decided to come see William in person. He lived alone in his own house on 100th Avenue and about 107th Street. The home was just north of the CNR railroad tracks.

William, as he signed his name in English in his books and documents, was seventy two years old when he met my mother and came to her rescue in Edmonton. By then he had been living and working in Canada for thirty five years.

He was a man of medium height and had tanned skin, dark eyes, and a mustache that curled up at the ends, in keeping with the Austrian fashion of those days. He arrived in Edmonton in

1913 just when the High Level Bridge was being completed. The bridge, which stretched across the whole river valley, cemented the union of the towns of Edmonton and Strathcona, creating a new provincial capital city with a combined population of 53,611. A collection of wooden and brick buildings on dirt roads, Edmonton was a raw settlement carved out of the trees and bush.

Brash and defiant, Edmonton was a far cry from the railway station in Chernivtsi, capital of the Austro-Hungarian province of Bukovyna William had left behind with tearful farewells in the spring of that year. William was from the village of Karliv, near Chernivtsi. Before leaving the village he had worked hard tending cornfields planted by his father, to support his family of ten.[35]

William showed academic promise in his youth and the local priests suggested that he be sent to school - even to university, but in view of the family's poor economic circumstances, this was impossible. The oldest of four brothers and four sisters, he had to drop out of school to take over the family farm after his father died when William was just 16 years old. He took over the role of head of the household and responsibility for looking after his mother and helping raise his younger siblings. He attended the local Prosvita cultural hall where he learned to read and even taught himself some English.

At the age of 21 in 1900, William was conscripted into the Austrian army where he served as a corporal in the 24th infantry division for three years. Following his release in 1903, over the course of the next nine years, he completed the task of looking after his family and ensuring that all his brothers and sisters finished their education.

His life moved on and in November of 1909 at the age of 30, William married Paraskevia Nikiforuk who was only 18 and an only child. Following their marriage, William moved in with his wife and her family as was customary. The two of them slept in a room with the wife's parents with only a curtain separating them.

Like others, William was attracted to Canada because of the lure of financial reward and the promise of free land—the promise of a homestead there. But when William asked his wife if she would go with him, she declined, since she couldn't bring herself to abandon her parents. Although her father was the village reeve, he was unable to read or write, so he relied on his daughter to help him. Her mother, who was blind, depended on her as well.

William pleaded with them while sharing his dream of earning enough money in Canada to return to his native village to live a prosperous life with the other members of his family. They all reluctantly agreed that William should go but only if he was prepared to go alone. He left, planning to be home in two years. He couldn't know when he was leaving that he never would see his wife or return to his native land again. This tragic dream of temporarily leaving behind close family members to pursue prosperity abroad with the intention of returning home and bringing back wealth later is part of a Ukrainian saga that continues with other immigrants to this very day.

William was one of the first immigrants to leave for Canada from his village. He traveled via Antwerp, to London where he boarded the 'Montezuma', a ship owned by the Canadian Pacific Railway (C.P.R.). The manifest shows that William Semotiuk was born in 1879, had $25 to his name- that he knew some English and was heading for Calgary.

The voyage was harsh. Apart from the danger inherent in traveling across the Atlantic made evident earlier that year when the Titanic sank with some 1500 passengers who perished, such voyages were also not very pleasant. Many passengers became seasick. Some suffered from other illnesses. The ship reeked from garlic they ate to ward off illness and the turpentine they rubbed on their bodies to ease aches and pains. After 14 days the Montezuma docked in St. John, New Brunswick on November 8th, 1912. He then took the seemingly never-ending five-day train ride across the expansive country to Calgary and eventually arrived in Edmonton.

Shortly after arriving, William had bad problems with his teeth. His mouth ballooned from infection, but he had no money to pay for tooth care. He had to put up with the pain until he found work and made enough money to get dental help. He did manage to find a job with the Canadian National Railroad in Stony Plain, Alberta. He started out at 15 cents an hour. That was good money in the beginning, and after fixing his teeth he began to cut unnecessary expenditures to save up for his wife. It was, however, hard work. Once he almost froze to death at his job in the bitter winter cold while doing repairs on a railroad bridge somewhere west of Stony Plain. He persevered. There was money to be earned and he knew his hardships would not last forever. As he toiled he dreamt that someday soon he would be going home.

William, having trimmed down his mustache somewhat but not completely, was now working on the Canadian Northern Railway living in bunkhouses with the rest of his gang laying ties and was able to earn three dollars for an eight-hour shift. From his first day in Canada he kept meticulous accounts of all his earnings. Life had taught him to be frugal and to also track his expenses. He was careful with money and spent it only on bare necessities. He regularly sent money back home to support his family, particularly his wife. By 1914 William had saved close to $500, which was well over a year's average salary in Canada. That was serious money for anyone returning to Bukovyna – it could buy a large acreage and still leave money for day-to-day needs. However, events in Europe were changing his plans.

As an English colony, Canada followed England into the First World War against Austro-Hungary. Having immigrated from Austro-Hungary and not yet a naturalized British subject William suddenly became an "enemy alien." Moreover, Austro-Hungarian authorities sent out letters ordering men, even those in Canada like William, to report for military service, threatening them with a court-martial in Austria if they failed to obey. In view of these developments, any plans for returning home had to be put on hold. After all, the last thing William wanted now was to return to fight for Austro-Hungary against Canada.

In Canada a national registration drive required everyone to carry an identity card with him at all times. However, only Canadian citizens and British subjects were issued such cards. From time to time mounted policemen would stop people on the streets and in hotels and stores, arresting those who could not produce identity cards, handcuffing them one to the other in a long chain and then lead them before a magistrate who would fine them for failure to produce registration cards. Soon there was a call for the Canadian government to use the War Measures Act to arrest Germans, Austrians and Ukrainians in Canada and send them to work in internment camps such as the one located in what is today Banff National Park, where some internees became forced laborers building the Lower Basin of Banff Hot Springs as "enemy aliens". Others were put to work building roads for five dollars a month under the watchful eyes of sentries who guarded them with rifles. Discipline in the camps was strict. Many succumbed to the hopelessness of their situation.

The only thing that saved William was his employment with the railroad. Rail transportation was regarded as a national priority. Since the war absorbed much of Canada's manpower, which created a shortage of workers, William avoided internment. He was secure but not without stigma. William was required to report regularly to the police, sometimes even two or three times a month. He had done nothing to precipitate it. He could work as hard as he wanted to, be as loyal a subject as humanly possible yet still Canada disdainfully considered him an alien from an enemy state.

The outbreak of World War I and news reports about mobilization were also sources of concern for William. For one thing he could no longer send financial support to his wife and family who were dependent on his help as this would be seen as "abetting the enemy". He knew this would cause them severe hardship. For another, since his brothers were of recruitment age and in good health, they would likely be recruited into the Austrian army and end up fighting on the wrong side of the war. All this put him in an extremely awkward situation. He simply had to cope with it all and see how things developed.

One day out of nowhere William's brother Ely showed up on his doorstep in Canada. Ely had deserted the Austrian Army while on a leave in Cracow and headed to Canada via Odessa while still in his army uniform. Before boarding the ship he managed to tear off the telltale insignias to convert it into an ordinary looking jacket and pants.

As a corporal in the Austrian army, Ely met another corporal who was Austrian, but who served in the German

Army during the war. Ely would later describe him as a well-organized, disciplined, "good soldier". This German Army corporal of Austrian descent was a man named "Adolf Hitler".

By 1939 William, still sporting his mustache somewhat curled up on the ends, had sworn allegiance to Canada and had become a Canadian citizen. He sponsored his brother Andrew (Andriy). Andrew was an educated man who had finished school and then joined the Austrian army. Before he was able to secure work on the railroad in Canada with a wage, however, Andrew worked for an entire year on a farm in Alberta making moonshine during the night and sleeping during the days. Andrew was no stranger to bizarre experiences, as I would later discover. Our paths would cross more than once in the future. In 1929, however, Andrew was looking for a way to secure his life in Canada.

Years later, while reflecting on this part of his life to a friend in his home in Edmonton, William related:

> In 1929, Ely and Andrew came to me and asked me to lend them some money so that they could start a farm. We discussed options – I suggested something close to Fort Saskatchewan, the other boys wanted to farm out in the Lavoy area, near Vegreville, Alberta. Finally I agreed. Just as they leased a farm one mile from Lavoy, Alberta, the market collapse led to the price of wheat falling below the cost of seeding and an unprecedented decade of drought set in. Since I had a job working on the railroad my livelihood was not on the line. I got involved with the farm however, to help my brothers. I was the one who put up all the money. The farm was a way to provide my brothers a livelihood.

That year the once-lush prairie fields dried up and the crops burned in the sun and most were destroyed. Many families simply abandoned their farms altogether to seek work in the city. But not my brothers - they had lost their first crop that year but were determined to stay on.

Year after year my brothers watched as either their crops failed or the market price of wheat made their efforts valueless. Year after year, their hearts broke. Finally, on the fourth year they were able to bring in a crop that paid. Eventually I ended up buying half the farm, while Ely bought the other.

While far away from the events in Europe, William had seen his share of hardships surviving the Great Depression on the Canadian Prairies. Men traveled across the country on railroad cars in search of work. Farmers lost their crops year after year to the dust bowl. Families lost their houses because they could not pay their property taxes. Fortunate to have work on the railroad when so many others did not, his job consisted of checking railroad tracks and crossings during the summer and driving a railroad track snowplow during the winters. With what money he earned he bought a few houses on tax sales and then rented them out to build up a retirement fund.

Though immersed in his life in Canada, his thoughts were never far from his family in Europe and the events unfolding there. This was particularly so because William's brother Ely knew Hitler from his service in the First World War. They therefore watched in amazement and apprehension as Hitler rose to power in Nazi Germany and then attacked the West.

By 1942 William had worked on the railroad for 30 years. Now he was a foreman in Stony Plain, Alberta, just west of Edmonton. Every day he took a crew out on one of those teeter-totter handcar wagons that traveled down the railway track to make repairs wherever they were needed. Usually he had a crew of about half a dozen men with him. He didn't know it then but his work in Stony Plain was coming to an end.

William was a hard worker. That is all he knew all his life. He expected the same kind of hard work from his men. He was a serious man and didn't suffer fools gladly. Not all his workers were cut from the same cloth. When he took a new crew out one time, immigrants who had just come in from Europe, he worked them hard. They were not used to the driving pace. By the end of a few days, they pretty much had enough of the work, and especially of him.

Just then they heard the sound of an oncoming train down the track where they had stopped and just completed some work. Seeing the train, William called out to the men to gather around their cart to lift it off the tracks so the train, now approaching down the track at full speed, could pass. Instead of listening to orders however, the men scattered into the ditch leaving William alone to deal with it. Try as he did, he could not lift the cart by himself. It was too late. The train came barreling down the track and annihilated the cart.

That was the end of William's career as a foreman. The CNR moved him to Edmonton where he became a flagman who sat in a booth at a railway crossing and lowered the gate to stop traffic so trains could pass by. That is where he spent the last few years of his railway career before he retired in 1945.

William Semotiuk in Canada in the 1950s

Loneliness and Forgiveness

One day in 1948, when Ukrainian Orthodox Bishop Basil Ladyka came from Winnipeg for a festival, William resolved to confess his sins and seek spiritual guidance from him. He was guilt-ridden about having left his wife behind. He had retired and lived off a retirement fund largely based on the money he made from buying distressed properties on tax sales during the Great Depression. Although he was a Ukrainian Greek Catholic, he had become a member of the Ukrainian Orthodox Church in Edmonton, along with a number of other prominent Ukrainian immigrants. The parishioners there, mostly from his generation of early pioneers to Canada, were better organized, and they were more affluent.

He confessed his guilt to the bishop, telling him how he had left his wife behind but had supported her by sending packages. The bishop approved of his efforts. When William confessed how isolated and lonely he was, now separated from her for some thirty years, the bishop asked, "So what? Is there a shortage of women in Canada?"

The good bishop clearly understood what it meant to be cut off from one's family in the Soviet Union, and he probably meant to suggest that William could find innocent company in Canada to soothe his loneliness. William, however, was perplexed by the bishop's comment.

A man named Prokop often came over to William's house to talk about the future. Questioning William about being alone in the house when he was now in his sixties, and possibly not having someone to give him so much as a cup of tea in his final moments, Prokop challenged William to find someone who would look after him in his older years. This had a big impact on William, and he started to look for someone who could fulfill that role.

No Lady's Man

To put it bluntly, William was no lady's man. Though not ugly, he wasn't the type that easily attracted women, especially due to his long solitary life. He was a very serious man and was self-educated. The result was that he didn't get along with just anyone. He needed someone who could not only help him around the house with cooking and cleaning but also someone who could deal with his Spartan views and with his disposition.

Although not immediately evident, loneliness troubled William all his life until he met my mother. Throughout his life in Canada, William sought somehow to redeem himself from the fact that he had left his wife Paraskevia behind in Ukraine. So long as he was alive he sent his wife parcels to help support her. He also would provide for her support in his will.[36]

It was later in the spring of 1950 that my mother first got to know William. At that time she and I were living with the Bodnar family in Redwater, Alberta. She described her first visit to his home.

> I came alone. It took me over an hour to find the place. I had come in from 107th Avenue down to 105th Street to near the CNR railroad tracks, where the house should have been. When I was unable to find it there, some men told me that the address was indeed on the other side. I then returned and finally noticed the garage, and behind the garage, the house where William lived.

I was a bit afraid, given my previous experience. After knocking and then entering the house, William looked at me as if he was seeing some sort of apparition. Nonetheless we had a conversation, and afterward William showed me where he kept an extra key to his house. He told me that whenever I came I could use the key to enter when he was away.

In the months that followed, while coming over from time to time, on one occasion I noticed William sitting on his front steps throwing up. He was sick. But he would hide this from me. His unhealthy cooking, lack of good hygiene, and use of dirty utensils would ultimately result in him getting stomach cancer. But nobody knew that back then. I did not know what circumstances William was in. All I knew was he had a house, with an outhouse in the back, and porches in the front and back.

It was an uncomfortable life for my mother and me in Redwater. The Bodnars were having disagreements with one another. We did not have access to water and needed to wash clothes, so my mother and I would come to Edmonton with the Bodnars in the morning to do laundry and go back to Redwater with them later in the day. During those visits to Edmonton, we would come to William's house, where my mother would lay me down on the bed and then spend the day helping clean and cook while visiting with him. In the evening she'd pack us up and return downtown to be picked up by the Bodnars and taken back to Redwater. This took place many times, every two weeks or so, from the spring until the fall of 1950.

According to my mother, William was at all times kind, respectful, and gentle, always asking her to come to spend more time there next time. While he was considerably older than her—in fact some thirty years older—and a few inches shorter than her, despite his stoic manner, she was attracted to him because he was responsible, trustworthy, and caring. He had learned about responsibility and trustworthiness at the age of sixteen after his father had died and he had to drop out of school to run the farm and look after his family. He developed a sense of compassion because he had seen so much suffering on the faces of thousands of unemployed men riding the trains in search of work during Canada's Great Depression. In short, as Dr. Peter Kurylo, who became a close friend of William's, once said, "to find another person like him would be as hard as searching for a treasure by the light of a candle in the darkness." It was this character that drew my mother to William's side.

In November 1950, after arriving at William's house with me and finding that he wasn't at home, my mother opened the door with the spare key. She lay me down on the bed and began to cook. It became late—too late to catch a ride back to Redwater. By then it had become clear to my mother that we needed to find another place to live. That night, for the first time, we stayed with William.

We lived with William from that day on. Life in his house, however, wasn't always easy. Unlike most other houses in Edmonton, William's house did not have gas heating. Instead he had a coal-burning stove. The smell of smoke permeated the entire household, including all of his clothing. The house had no indoor plumbing. Instead it had a detached outhouse that made things particularly challenging during the winter months.

Since he lived next to the railroad tracks, sometimes the piercing whistle of a railroad steam engine would break up a conversation. While others found this astonishing, to William it was quite normal. When trains passed by his house, he hardly noticed them, while his visitors observed how the windowpanes shook and pots and pans danced around on the kitchen stove. William had worked on the railroad for so long that he had grown accustomed to these incidents, and besides, he loved the sound of the whistles and the trains moving down the tracks.

We settled in with William in that house and at the Hollyburn Apartment on Jasper Avenue at 122 Street when he bought that building a few years later. He got to know my mother and started to take care of me. These were comforting times for all of us. But he also was apprehensive. He thought my mother would leave. He was concerned that some man would lure her away. In reality my mother had no place to go, and given what she had just lived through in Park Court and in her early days in Edmonton, leaving was the last thing on her mind.

One thought that evades my efforts at recollection is the sleeping arrangement between my mother and adopted father. I vaguely recall their sharing an old large brass bed. I'm unable to recall any perceptions related to their physical attraction to each other, although it must have been part of their joint lives. The elusiveness of this thought, at least in part, relates to my apprehension regarding the significant age difference between them and the propriety of their having a sexual relationship, given my father's marital status and their community social reputations. But no one ever brought up the propriety of their relationship with me until after William's death, when his brother, Andrew, questioned me about what my mother had done with his estate. He seemed deflated when I said she had done what William had told her to do.

William Semotiuk's railroad identity paper

William Semotiuk's house in Edmonton near the railroad tracks on 106th Street and 104th Avenue in the 1950s

William Semotiuk with his brothers, Ely (left) and Andrew (right), circa 1935 in Edmonton, Alberta

A Visitor from the Past

One day, when I was about two years old, my natural father came to our Hollyburn Apartment to visit us to persuade my mother to return to the farm. This was a very tense moment. William didn't take my father's intrusion kindly and was very hostile toward him. Everyone became very upset. I remember William saying to my father, "So this is how you treated your woman and child?" before my mother told me to go outside to play.

I went out the back door of the apartment building and sat down in a makeshift wading pool—a large bucket with warm water. I waited for the arguing to subside and for my father to leave. That was the one and only time in my memory that I saw my real father. I do not remember what he looked like. Although he never contacted us again, later I learned that he knew I was well looked after and had decided not to disturb us again.

From that day forward, for the next fifty years, no matter when or how I raised the subject, my mother refused to allow my father's name to even pass her lips. When, as I was growing up and even after I reached adulthood and married, I asked my mother about my father, her body would stiffen. Shifting in discomfort in her chair at her kitchen table, she would wave her hand to dismiss me. If I tried to press further, her voice would strain, and then, referring to my father as "that man," she would do whatever she could to steer the conversation away from the topic.

I recognized that part of the puzzle was that she was shielding me from a past not altogether happy. Still I wondered what dramatic events had made her turn her back on my father, separating us from him forever. Whenever I persisted in my questioning, however, the pain I saw in her eyes made me relent. I wondered where she found the strength of character to keep the truth of her ordeal locked away inside her all this time.

Years later my mother could not explain exactly what it was that led her to William's house or ultimately what made her stay. Perhaps it had been divine providence. Regardless, my mother came to see William as a true lifesaver.

Over time what had begun as a relationship of mutual help and affection turned into one of love. William could not marry my mother, since he was still married to a woman in Ukraine. He was, however, able to adopt me through a special court order. To make life easier for me, and because my mother and I were Catholics, despite the moral contradictions, he decided to revert to his own Ukrainian Catholic faith. Of particular concern for him was the fact that I would be attending Catholic schools, and he wanted the situation to be such that, when asked about the religion of my father, I would be able to say that he was also Catholic. This wasn't important to me, but for some reason, it appeared to be important to him. From the time of the adoption onward, William was my father.

The Bus to Nowhere

In Edmonton I started to travel all over the city on public buses for free by pretending to throw a ticket into the fare box. I was only five years old, so I really didn't have to pay. But I didn't know that. I thought I was fooling the bus drivers.

On one such trip, I took the bus west from our apartment on Jasper Avenue at 122nd Street to the end of the line. The bus driver then told everyone to get off since he was going to the garage. This was something new. Normally the bus would travel back to where I had come from. When I got off, I was lost.

It was early evening, and the sky was gray. As I walked along the street, my anxiety built, as I didn't know how I would get home. It felt as if suddenly I had shrunk in this world. The worst part was not knowing who to turn to and safely ask where I was.

As I walked down the street, I saw a dog carrying a paper bag. I followed it to the corner store. The dog barked, and the door opened. Then the dog entered. Soon the dog emerged, carrying the bag in its mouth back to the house where it had come from. I learned that an older couple had trained the dog to take money in the bag to the store and then return home with the purchase. I was fascinated. As I walked along in disbelief, a young couple came walking up behind me. The woman said, "Hi, Andy."

I turned around and asked how she knew my name. She said it was easy; it was sewn on the back of my jacket. My mother had done that so I wouldn't lose the jacket. The couple asked me if I was lost. I told them I was. They asked me if I would like to come to their house. I was reluctant to do that; even then I knew enough about the world to question such seemingly innocent offers. I had developed a kind of sixth sense about these things from the way I had been raised and from neighborhood kids and their parents. It could be summarized in the phrase "Don't trust strangers." But the couple convinced me to wait in front of their home for a few minutes. They emerged again with cookies and milk. They also had called the police.

The police arrived within a matter of minutes. When I saw the police car pull up beside me, I felt betrayed by the couple. I wasn't exactly elated about being found, as I still harbored the hope that I might find my way home, nor was I convinced just yet that it was time to call the police for help. Calling the police made the situation "serious." Now it was too late.

A police officer asked who I was, and I told him. He asked whether I was lost. I said yes. He asked if I knew where I lived. I told them no, but that it was near "the end of Jasper Avenue." They figured out where that was, and as we drove closer, I recognized the area and was able to guide them to my home. My parents were waiting anxiously, looking through the window as I entered.

Life With William

Strangely, apart from this incident, I don't have many clear childhood memories about interacting with William. My most vivid memory is a birthday party William organized for me when I was about three years old.

Even though I didn't really know many of them, my parents invited all the kids in the neighborhood over for birthday cake. I was aware that my friends spoke English, but ours was a Ukrainian-speaking home. I knew we usually would sing "*Mnohaya Lita*," but my friends didn't know that song. After I blew out all the candles with several efforts, William led the kids in singing "Happy Birthday" in his steady but soft tenor voice.

Happy beerday to you...
Happy beerday to you...
Happy beerday, dear Andrrrew...
Happy beerday to you!

It isn't William's pronunciation of "birthday" that marks this memory for me. Rather it's the act of pure love that he exhibited by singing in English for me and for my friends, although he knew and I knew that in our household English wasn't the language we used to express our best wishes.

How alien this party was for us, given where we had come from and our common history. But at the same time, William's effort to help me lead a normal Canadian life meant so much to me. Then my parents sang "*Mnohaya Lita*" ("Long Life") in Ukrainian, which went much more smoothly. My friends could only look on somewhat puzzled by what my parents were singing, but only for a moment. Then we cut the cake.

If there was any reluctance to play with me as a new "immigrant" kid in the neighborhood, from that day forward I was "one of the gang."

In 1953, while my friends and I were playing in front of our apartment building, however, a police van suddenly arrived. As we stopped to watch, the police entered our building. About five minutes later, they emerged with William in handcuffs. We were all in shock.

The officers placed him in the back of the police van. The other children turned to me and asked why he was being arrested. I had no idea. It was frightening, and I was humiliated.

I knew William was no criminal. Many people came to our home to seek William's advice and consolation. Sometimes they came to borrow money. He treated everyone with respect and kindness. William was a patriotic Ukrainian who held the best interests of the community at heart. He invested in Ukrainian companies to support their work. Among them were Independent Wholesalers and the Ukrainian Credit Union. My teachers realized that William was a prosperous man compared to other immigrant fathers. At the Christmas Ukrainian kindergarten concert, my teachers created a special part for me. I came out on stage to declare that when I grew up I wanted to be rich "so that I could donate to Ukrainian community charities." It was a big hit with the audience, who looked at William knowingly and enthusiastically applauded while he smiled back approvingly.

He took me to St. John's Ukrainian Orthodox Church with him on Sundays. Whenever we went to the Edmonton Exhibition, even though I didn't always want to go, he insisted that we eat at the Ukrainian booth. I remember attending the grandstand show with him and my mother, watching the fireworks and being scared of the loud explosions. I always wanted to leave while they wanted to see the end of the show. William would take us to concerts and various community meetings, usually at the Ukrainian National Hall on 98th Street. There he would buy me an Orange Crush in its distinctive ribbed, dark-brown bottle. I loved to watch the storekeeper as he popped the bottle open and to hear the burst of carbonated air escape. William would give me money to buy Old Dutch barbeque chips, grape chewing gum, or Lucky Elephant pink popcorn to eat while I waited impatiently with all the other children for the concerts to end so we could go home.

So the day William was arrested, I was at a loss to explain what we had just witnessed. While I was confused, I also knew this must be some sort of terrible mistake. I ran home to my mother, who was alone in the kitchen. She too was puzzled by what had happened and why. She reassured me and told me to wait at home while she went across the street to get our neighbor, Ivan Hamkalo, to help her. I realized this was serious; it was the first time she had left me alone at home. I recognized I needed to behave while I waited for her to return.

Mr. Hamkalo accompanied my mother downtown to the police station to see if they could get William out of jail. While they were unsuccessful, at least they found out why he had been apprehended.

We recently had moved from an apartment on the first floor in our building to a larger apartment immediately below. A single woman then rented the upstairs apartment we had vacated. A few weeks later, in the middle of the night, there was a commotion outside the building, so William went outside to investigate. When things settled down, he mistakenly went up the stairs instead of down. When he tried the door to the apartment, it was closed. He knocked, trying to get my mother to open it. The woman in the upstairs apartment was awakened by his knocking and was startled.

Opening the door slightly, she felt William press against the door to enter. Terrified, she held the door while William pushed on it, calling out "Salomea, it's me. Let me in." The woman held fast, but he kept pushing. Then William finally realized he was being denied entry not because my mother couldn't hear him but because he was trying to get into the wrong apartment. He apologized, went downstairs, and fell asleep. The next day, the woman called the police, complaining that William was "obviously some kind of lunatic."

My mother's efforts to bail him out were fruitless. William was taken to Alberta Hospital for a psychiatric examination. The woman told our neighbors about the attempted forced entry, and soon my friends became reluctant when it came time to play. I remember visiting William at Alberta Hospital with my mother. He wore a hospital gown and didn't look so good. While he was very happy to see us and tried to cheer me up, things looked grim.

Fortunately, William Hawrelak, then mayor of Edmonton, had a policy to allow anyone who wanted to see him to come to his office in the afternoon. Ivan Hamkalo and my mother went to see Hawrelak to seek his intervention. Hawrelak spoke fluent Ukrainian so my mother could clearly explain the circumstances. She told the mayor that she didn't hear well and that this was what had prompted William's loud and insistent behavior. A day or two later, William was released.

Hollyburn apartment, where we lived at 122nd Street and Jasper Avenue in Edmonton, Alberta, in the 1950s. This is where William was arrested for mistakenly going upstairs instead of downstairs after we moved.

My First Years at School

My parents both accompanied me on my first day of school at St. John's Catholic Elementary School in 1955. After introductions and registration, they went home and awaited my return at lunch. They offered to walk me back, but I said I would go by myself.

I understood that neither of my parents was good at speaking English, and the last thing I wanted was to put them into circumstances where they would have to deal with school officials. I sensed how apprehensive they were about dealing with any person in authority, especially my mother, whose hearing and listening skills would immediately be strained. I wanted to spare them any such burden; I would handle everything myself. That was the way it was for the rest of my educational life. I would do anything it took to spare my mother the apprehension of having to meet with teachers or school officials.

In the early years of my schooling, my mother and William spent time teaching me. They went through my assignments with me, helping me fill in the answers to written questions. In addition my mother read books with me after school. This not only helped me but also became a way for her to learn English. By the fourth grade, however, I realized my mother in particular was holding me back. For the first time in my life, I sensed the need to push back to give myself room to grow—a feeling that I would encounter again later in my life with my mother.

I told them I would study on my own from then on. My mother was disappointed but realized by then that I knew more than she did when it concerned school curriculum. Unfortunately my decision ended her formal English language training.

My mother with me on the east side of 101st Street, north of Jasper Avenue, Edmonton in the early 1950s. I was carrying a new toy in my right hand.

My mother actually was trying to evade the photographer who used a Polaroid Land camera to take the picture, but when he showed us the print, she decided to buy it.

Who's the Real Santa?

That Christmas, when my mother took me shopping, I asked her why there were two Santas. It was a snowy December evening. Although we were wearing winter jackets and boots, it was still quite warm, and the streets were slushy. Streetlamps lit up the sidewalks. The air was crisp and fresh. Big puffy snowflakes gently fell to the ground. I heard the sound of snow swishing beneath our feet as we walked along, as well as the distant jingle of a tambourine played by a Salvation Army representative collecting money down the street. There was no wind. We had just seen Santa Claus at the S.S. Kresge store, and following that visit, we had seen the Santa Claus at the Eaton's store.

My mother said that the Santas we were visiting weren't the real Santa Claus but only his representatives here in Edmonton. The explanation suited me fine; I was happy to visit them to collect the gifts both would give out that Christmas.

Some of my favorite times with my mother were on downtown trips such as this one. I loved going to a store called the Nut House on 101st Street near Jasper Avenue, where they served a wide variety of nut products, including my favorite, fresh peanuts. My mother would buy me a bag to munch on while we rode the bus home. The salty peanut-y taste of those freshly oiled nuts was heavenly. Another favorite activity was to visit the basement of Woodward's department store, where they served the best vanilla soft ice cream cones and where they also had a bakery. While I licked my ice cream cone, we'd wait in line for my mother to buy a fresh apple pie to take home to eat after supper. Life couldn't get any better than this!

One day early in 1955, shortly after I finished first grade we moved close to 109th Street, I was outside playing with a group of children in front of our building, next to a field covered with trees and bushes, and one of the children noticed a nest in a nook in a tree. He found an old broom handle and decided to poke at the nest while around a dozen of us watched with curiosity. As the hornets came buzzing out, furious at the disruption of their placid life, we had no idea what was coming. Suddenly I felt a terrible sting on my forearm and on my face and dashed into the building and up the stairs to our apartment.

William was home alone. I ran into the house shouting and crying. I cried out, "Bee, bee," which is what I'd heard one of the other children cry out when he had been stung. William was perplexed. What was a "Bee"? Again I cried out, "Bee!" and pointed to the sting. Still he was puzzled. Then I made a buzzing sound while moving my fingers in the air and pretending to land on his arm and then pinching him hard. "Ah," he said. "You mean *pchola*." "Yes, yes," I said.

He looked carefully at the swollen spot where I had been stung. Then he removed the stinger lodged there. Next he pulled out a knife and applied the cold metal to the wound, which remarkably helped soothe the pain. Then we both waited for my mother to come home to tell her about what happened and to see if there was anything else she could do. When she arrived, we were both relieved, although apart from the empathy she expressed for my pain, there was little more she could do.

Later that year, while still at the Queen Elizabeth Apartments, I recall seeing a television set for the first time. One of the other families in the building had bought one.

They invited me over one night to watch *Dragnet*, the program about Joe Friday, the no-nonsense police officer in Los Angeles who brought justice to the streets of that city. I was mesmerized.

We moved the following summer, in 1956, after William bought a four-suite apartment on 124th Street and 117th Avenue. Around this time we bought our first television set. It was a big box and sat prominently in the living room. On Saturdays I'd turn it on in the afternoon. There wouldn't be anything on yet—only the Sunwapta Broadcasting test signal, an American Indian chief with feather headdress in black-and-white on the screen. But that was enough for me, and even for my mother. We sat there watching the test screen, sometimes for an hour, waiting for the programming to begin.

William also liked to watch television, but he did not let on to that. As we sat in the living room watching TV programs, he'd sometimes look on from outside the room in the hallway, particularly when the news was on. Still he never joined us in the living room. My mother knew of his interest, and while his interest did not quite register with me, occasionally I'd catch him watching, and then he would turn and walk away. He just couldn't let himself admit to me that he was interested. I think it was because he was attached to reading books and considered the new technology as frivolous even though occasionally he got absorbed in the programming.

A Surprise Meeting

Around this time my mother took me on a long train trip to Los Angeles to meet her sister Helen. They had not seen each other in more than ten years.

We took a Yellow Taxi (my mother refused to take any other kind) from Union Station to the Echo Park Avenue address where Helen lived. After we disembarked from the taxi, my mother, wanting to heighten the surprise, stood by our four new cream-colored suitcases and sent me ahead to their door-step, telling me to knock and ask, "Is this the Tyshovnytsky residence?"

I remember this because I had trouble remembering and pronouncing the name. I knocked, and Emil came to the door. In Ukrainian I asked him if this was the Tyshovnytsky residence. He answered yes and opened the door to let me in but then asked me who I was. Just then Helen laid her eyes on me and blurted out, "That's Salomea's son."

She ran outside to find her sister, and they joyfully embraced. Emil and Helen then helped my mother bring the suitcases into the house. That night Helen prepared a nice dinner, and as we sat around the kitchen table, my mother recounted her life since she had last seen Helen in Europe, and Emil and Helen also told us their story.

After leaving Europe for Los Angeles in the United States on February 25, 1949, Helen eventually connected with Emil, whom she knew from Galicia. Emil, having left his displaced person's camp in Europe, had arrived in the United States on September 1, 1946 and joined the Texas State Highway Department in Beaumont, Texas, on November 1, 1948. Through correspondence, he and Helen got to know each other better and agreed to marry on December 24, 1951 in Beaumont.

It was the time of drive-ins, convertibles, crew cuts, and strapless gowns; when the comic strip *Dennis the Menace* began;

146

when Dean Martin and Jerry Lewis were in their heyday; and when General MacArthur gave his farewell speech, saying, "Old soldiers never die; they just fade away."

Emil was fifty-five years old, and Helen was forty-two. While they had known each other in Hrybeniw, Emil was overweight and not interesting enough for Helen back then. But now, in a new land things looked rather different. She decided she could take him under her wing, slim him down, and make it work. Emil once said that he wished he had found and married Helen much sooner in life and that God had made him wait fifty-five years before rewarding him with her.

Helen had studied at the University of Southern California to become a hospital laboratory technician. She worked in this field with Kaiser Permanente for some thirty years. Emil joined the US Army Corps of Engineers in Los Angeles and worked there until retirement. Theirs was a practical marriage, and it met their basic needs. They developed a strong relationship, even though they knew they were two very different people.

Emil was a well-organized, serious, and formal man. Helen had an artistic nature and a freeform approach to life. In fact she was very talented. She had a degree in music and played the piano very well. Gardening was another of her passions, and she spent a great deal of time cultivating her home garden. She painted, listened to classical music, pursued her literary interests, and took a keen interest in family affairs. She also loved animals and gave refuge to numerous homeless ones.

Though Emil and Helen had no children of their own, they treated extended members of the Tyshovnytsky family—many of whom also had migrated to the United States—as their own, never hesitating to help, even if doing so inconvenienced them.

Almost every day during our ten-day stay, Helen came home with a present for me. As she came into the house, she'd ask me what I had done that day, listen to my summary of the day's events, and then pull out her gift and give it to me. She bought me a pirate gun, a sword, a T-shirt, and various other delights. My favorite gift was a plastic squirt gun that looked like a camera. As soon as I got the camera, I loaded it up with water and could hardly wait to try it out. My victim would be Emil.

When Emil came home, he sat down in his room, waiting for supper. I came in and asked if I could take his picture. He said, "Of course." I had him pose and even got him to smile before I let him have it! His face drenched, he pulled out a handkerchief from his pocket while he angrily lectured me that this wasn't the way to behave. My glee turned into regret as I watched him scowl at me. I sensed it was too late. The damage was done. The incident got us off on the wrong foot and soured our relationship for years to come.

I liked Aunt Helen from the start, but she tried so hard to win my affection that she went overboard, which made me withdraw from her. She was just trying too hard. While I appreciated the gifts she brought me, and I wanted them, they weren't necessary. Although I have to admit I was disappointed when she didn't bring something home for me, my disappointment didn't influence my affection for her. Her attempts to "buy" my affection, however, made me resist her efforts. In this childish way, I punished her for not sensing the strong affectionate bond we already had. It was so obvious to me.

By the time Emil and Helen were seeing us off, I'd had enough of the visit and wanted to go home. Since there were no children in their house, there was little to keep me occupied. I spent a lot of time wandering around the neighborhood, trying to stave off boredom. I remember Emil kneeling next to me at the train station and asking, "So whom did you like best on your trip to Los Angeles?"—as if the answer wasn't obvious. I replied, "Uncle Emil of course?" The reply jolted my aunt, and she cried. But I thought, *That was a pretty stupid question to ask, wasn't it?* I felt she was smothering me, and I wanted her to back off a bit. What I felt was true, but I was cruel in saying what I did, and it clearly hurt her.

That trip became the first of dozens of trips we made south to visit them over the years to follow. Those trips in the late 1950s helped develop my affection for Los Angeles. Our visits to Disneyland and Santa Monica Beach were times we all enjoyed. Sometimes we'd drive to Hollywood Boulevard and then park so we could take a walk. I'd scout out the Hollywood stars on the Walk of Fame, recognizing some of the names of actors and singers forever memorialized there. We'd walk until we reached Mann's Chinese Theatre, where clusters of tourists searched out the handprints and footprints of their favorite stars imprinted in the cement pavement. The thrill of knowing that it was here where each year Hollywood recognized their best at the Academy Awards—and that those stars walked here on the red carpet—intoxicated me. The sight of the Hollywood sign up on the hillside as we drove home reminded me of the movies and television shows filmed in the studios nearby. I felt a sense of connection to that magical place quite apart from my relationship with Helen and Emil.

Salomea Drozdowska with me in Los Angeles when we visited Helen and Helen's husband Emil Tyshovnytsky in 1954.

William's Passing

For some time before William died, I knew that he was sick, but I didn't know any of the details. He had been sick for a long time. Even when my mother first had met William nine years earlier, she had seen him vomiting while he leaned against his house. Like most Ukrainians at that time, William had lived for forty years without the help of doctors and made no attempts to see any until he absolutely had to. Finally my mother took it upon herself to take him to various doctors to try to get some sort of diagnosis. When he was finally diagnosed, the doctor had a strange way of telling him he had stomach cancer. The doctor asked him, "How old are you?" ("*Skilky vam rokiv?*") He answered, "Seventy-four." The doctor then asked, "Isn't that enough for you?" ("*Vam vzhe ne dosta?*") What better way was there to tell a patient he had a terminal illness than by announcing it with some black humor? It was tough for William to take, however, and it hurt.

Over the course of the next two years, William suffered, going in and out of hospitals. Since I was often at school or out playing, I had no idea of the severity of his illness or how it might affect me. My mother looked after him throughout this entire period. By Christmas 1957, however, his long struggle with the disease was coming to an end. He was gaunt, and his skin had turned an off-yellow color. Always wearing pajamas, he appeared weak and unsteady on his feet. It was clear to everyone that he wouldn't survive much longer.

That year we celebrated Christmas together at our home in the apartment building on 124th Street. The mood was subdued and not very festive, although we were all home together. Sometimes William would sit on the floor with me, looking at new presents and just sharing time with me.

I have no doubt that he pondered what my fate would be following his death. I don't remember our conversations, what he told me, or what I said to him. All I remember is that we spent time together. Though it was unspoken, I sensed these would be the last days we shared together.

He returned to General Hospital at the beginning of January 1958. Then, on January 6, Ukrainian Christmas Eve, my mother took me to visit him. It was late in the evening, at least for me. It was dark, and freshly fallen snow covered the ground. Normally the hospital didn't allow young children to visit that ward. The staff, however, all knew this would be our final goodbye and that soon William would be gone. Previously, during the English Christmas period when William was still home, we had a photographer take a family portrait. By the time I came to the hospital, the portrait was ready, and he held it in his hands to show it to me as I entered his room.

The pale colors in the picture lacked crispness and intensity—a shortcoming of the early days of color photography. In the portrait William is sitting stiffly in his chair, while my mother is standing by him and I am sitting across from him. The muted colors seem to imply what was in store for us in the days ahead.

Family portrait taken in late 1957 that became the subject of an exchange between William Semotiuk and me on January 6, 1958, just before he died

I remember the hospital staff being especially moved by the event, particularly the nurses, as they looked at me with tears welling up in their eyes. But I didn't sense that my visit was as sad as they felt it was. Although I knew that some time soon William was going to die, at nine years of age, since I had not experienced the death of anyone before, I didn't quite appreciate the tenderness and finality of the moment. Perhaps to shield myself from the fear of being abandoned by him, I felt a sense of detachment from the emotions visibly affecting the others around me.

When I entered the hospital room, William was sitting in his pajamas on his bed. My mother sobbed gently to herself, on the other side of the room, as she looked on. William didn't have tears in his eyes but spoke to me in a subdued voice. As we looked at the portrait together, William jokingly said that I looked like a little monkey in the picture. I responded that he looked like some sort of a governor. He liked that, smiled, and patted me on the head.

I guess it was the right thing for me to say at that moment. We then said our goodbyes. The entire visit didn't take long. He told me to listen to my mother and to study hard. I don't remember any other details. That was it. Our conversation was over, and my mother took me home.

In the days that followed my visit to the hospital, my mother and William's brother, my Uncle Andrew, took turns staying with William next to his hospital bed while the other looked after me at home. My uncle took the day shift, while my mother spent her nights there. Every day, early in the morning, my mother would come home to get some sleep while my uncle went to the hospital.

Then, on January 12, 1958, early in the morning, my mother phoned home. My Uncle Andrew answered the call. I watched him across the table while I was eating breakfast. A somber look came across his face as he listened carefully. He didn't say much. He simply asked, "When?" Then he asked, "Are you coming home now?" My mother obviously answered, "Yes." He said, "Fine" and hung up. He looked at me for a long moment but didn't tell me what had happened. Instead he told me to go outside and play until my mother came home. He didn't need to tell me. I already knew. My father was dead.

Outside and in the backyard, while waiting for my mother to come home, I sat down beside an apple tree I had planted the previous summer. I wanted her to tell me the news and not Uncle Andrew.

The tree had grown considerably. It reminded me of a time in our lives when we were all still together. I sensed that those days were over. Now I wondered what would happen next. I felt a sense of loss, but I wasn't overwhelmed by it.

It was cloudy but not very cold. If there was any snow left on the ground, it was minimal. The ground was frozen, so I was able to sit on it without getting dirty. It was early in the morning, so there was no one else around. Dressed in my winter coat, I sat there quietly for about an hour as I waited for my mother to arrive. I already knew what she was going to say. I was already prepared for this moment. She finally came home and called me into the house. She gently told me that William had passed on and then embraced me. I tried to resist revealing the sorrow inside me, but her weeping moved me to tears as well.

The evening funeral service took place a few days later at the Ukrainian National Organization hall on 98th Street in

Edmonton. The hall was the size of a movie theater and had high ceilings. Gray neon lights created a cool atmosphere that evening. Uncle Andrew, as well as Aunt Helen, who had arrived from Los Angeles, accompanied us. Just their presence underlined the significance of what was happening to us.

About a hundred people attended the somber event, most of whom I didn't know. I was the only child there. I remember feeling somewhat detached from the occasion in a hall full of adults and not wanting anyone to pity my mother or me, as if we were outcasts who needed sympathy. The last thing I wanted was for people to add strain to our raw feelings with their weeping and wailing.

As the body lay there in the casket, mourners filed by to express their sympathy to us. Many of them offered condolences to my mother. She put on a brave face and showed great courage. The most moving part of the ceremony was the singing of "*Vichnaya Pamyat*" ("Eternal Memory") by the congregation. It was enough to melt even the coldest of hearts. At the end of the service, my uncle, my mother, and I went up to the casket. I wasn't tall enough to see the body from where we were sitting. But now, as we stood there for a final moment, I saw William's ash-colored, waxed face for the first time. I knew then for certain that he was gone.

The next day was the burial day. Only twenty people attended the service at St. George's Ukrainian Catholic Church, and again I was the only child. Since the church was almost empty, it reinforced the sense of aloneness we felt now that William was gone. In his eulogy Father Wolodymyr Tarnawsky, who had administered the last rites at the hospital and was familiar to our family, spoke about a man who sought to escape death by hiding in the desert. But the angel of death followed him

155

there and, having found him, told him it was preordained that it was his fate to die in the desert. We cannot escape death, the priest said. The story helped me understand that death is a natural part of our lives here on earth. With generous amounts of smoke from the burning incense, Father Tarnowsky blessed the coffin and helped us start up our own haunting version of "*Vichnaya Pamiat.*" Again I was moved to tears.

When the service was finished, Father Tarnowsky took a golden cross from the casket and gave it to me before it was closed for the last time. That cross would hang on the wall of our home from that day on.

We proceeded out to St. Michael's Cemetery in Edmonton and laid William's remains to rest forever. It was bitterly cold outside. The grave was one of the first in the new St. Michael's Cemetery, which was located on the far northern outskirts of the city. Our winter coats did not shield us from the penetrating wind. Mercifully the service was short. We clambered back into our cars to head for a post-funeral lunch, where various friends spoke about William's life and offered tributes to his memory.

Then finally we were able to go home. I was relieved that the funeral had come to an end. It was an emotional strain to be on my best behavior in the adult world of funerals and to be the focus of attention of people who felt sympathy for me. Finally I could just be a kid again.

William Semotiuk's funeral in Edmonton in January 1958

William Semotiuk, born in the village of Karliv, Western Ukraine, in 1879; died in Edmonton, Alberta, in 1958

Chapter 5
A New Life

5

Adjusting to Life Without William

*I*N THE DAYS that followed, as I prepared to return to school, my mother sewed a black ribbon around the left forearm of my jacket to signal that I was mourning William's death. I protested that I didn't want anyone to know about our loss, but she insisted I wear the ribbon to school.

I think my mother wanted to follow a tradition from the old country and also protect me from the emotional turbulence of probing questions from my classmates. As soon as I arrived, my classmates asked me about the ribbon, and I told them I was wearing it because my father had died. Soon I noticed they were avoiding me. Teachers realized my father had passed away and asked the children to leave me in peace. I hated being singled out that way, and the last thing I wanted was for anyone to feel sorry for me. By lunchtime I took the ribbon off. By the end of the day, things in the playground returned to normal, although my mother wasn't happy when I came home without it.

In the following days, my mother spent a lot of time with Walter Yanda, the lawyer who looked after William's estate. In his will William left the bulk of his estate, including the apartment house where we lived, to my mother so she could cover our financial needs and live from the rental income, leaving the rest to both the Ukrainian Catholic and Orthodox Churches, as well as to many other Ukrainian organizations.

William's wife, Paraskevia, in Ukraine launched a lawsuit. She wanted to overturn his will, since it assigned my mother to look after his affairs upon his death and left most of his estate to my mother. This litigation concluded in a settlement with my mother being granted the administration of the estate, provided she abide by the provisions in the will, which required her to send regular monthly packages to Ukraine to William's wife. She did this until Paraskevia died in 1963.

My mother and I spent the rest of that year adjusting to life without William, which wasn't easy. Part of it was the sense of grief and abandonment my mother felt. Another part was handling William's estate and looking after his legal and business affairs. I felt the impact of William's loss largely through my mother's preoccupation with his estate matters. We were beginning to grow apart.

Around this time I began to stay out late at night on weekends with my friends from school; we were planning to start a rock band. While our activities were pretty innocent and all we did was talk and hang out at restaurants and the A&W drive-in, I ran into trouble when I came home and found my mother waiting up for me. Arguments would ensue, and we wouldn't come to any resolution.

To help us along, during this rough time, my mother decided it was time for us to get away for a while. Almost a year after William's death, she decided to pack us up and take us on a train trip to New York City.

The Big Apple

The trip took three days and two nights. We traveled clear across Canada on the Canadian National Railroad to Toronto and caught the Amtrak train from Toronto to New York. It was tremendously exciting for me to see the big long train at the station. I loved the sight of porters standing with their freshly pressed white shirts and dark blue uniforms. I could hardly wait to hear the conductor shout out "All Aboard" and to see the porters scramble to get on board and close up the doors to their cars. Slowly the train made its way along the track. Then it fell into its natural rhythm as the wheels rolled down the rails – te-te-te-te...te-te-te-te...te-te-te-te....te-te-te-te.

When we arrived in Toronto we transferred over to the Amtrack Silver Liner. It was big, it was sleek, it was shiny, it was fast, it was clean, it was silver - and I loved it!

On that train I met two African American boys and we passed the time away playing games like Xs and Os, completing the squares, and my favorite: battleship. We loved watching the conductor go down the cars calling out "tickets please" Then he clipped each one with his hole puncher....chk-chk.....chk-chk.

We arrived in New York at Grand Central station. This was a huge building - so big that I remember the announcements echoed throughout the building. "Announcing ... announcing ...

announcing ... the arrival...arrival...arrival of the Amtrak train from Boston ... Boston ... Boston" - the deep voice booming.

We caught a taxi and went to one of the nearest hotels. The Tudor Hotel was on 42nd Street near 2nd Avenue. I remember my mother negotiating with the desk clerk over the price of our room, then the bellman closing the accordion gate as we entered the elevator and operating the manual control as he took us up to the 22nd floor. It was a huge building for a little boy from Edmonton, as were all the skyscrapers in New York.

Over the next few days, my mother and I walked all over New York City. We went to the top of the Empire State Building. We traveled by subway. We ate in restaurants. One of my favorites was the Horn & Hardart Automat. The food there was presented in little compartments with windows. One compartment might have a piece of apple pie on a plate. You'd choose the food you wanted, pay by inserting coins into the slot, and open the window while the tray with the dish on it would move forward for you to remove it. I was fascinated by all the food options and the mechanization. I regret that there are no longer any such restaurants in New York.

While staying in the hotel one day, I decided to try my new invention—a round cylinder made out of a piece of folded paper that could hold water and then serve as a water bomb. I filled the paper ball with water and opened the window at the stairway. I waited for the appropriate moment then dropped the water bomb twenty flights, just missing a passerby. Boy, was he mad! He looked up and caught me looking down at him. I ran to our room and closed the door. Then I heard the elevator come up to our floor. The bellman and my near victim were looking for me. Somehow I survived without being discovered. Of course my mother had no idea what I had been up to. I felt like the cat in a cartoon that had swallowed the canary while denying any knowledge of it to his master.

One of the highlights of our visit was seeing Broadway and Times Square. Anyone who has been on Broadway will know about the magnificent lights, all the traffic, all the people and the electronic stores there. I remember looking up on Broadway to see a man on a billboard blowing smoke rings into the air above the street from the Camel sign. I remember the commotion in the streets, the rush of people and cars driving by and honking day and night. I remember a man yelling out ,"Black or White – Five a Night" while handing out pamphlets promoting his hookers to passers-by. As my mother steered clear of him with me in tow the man bent over to give me one of his brochures. I remember looking at the brochure with curiosity, knowing it was something indecent and finally chucking it into a garbage bin before my mother could see it.

One day, as I looked at the store windows filled with transistor radios, I resolved right then and there to persuade my mother to buy me one. That Christmas, on December 24, 1958, after visiting about a dozen stores to do price comparisons, my mother finally bought me what I had been asking for—a brand-new powder-blue transistor radio. It cost

$9.95, and it was beautiful!

One of the happiest moments of my life came shortly after that purchase. It was New Year's Eve. I remember sitting in the hotel room. My mother was reading on her bed, while I was listening to my new radio on my bed. As we approached midnight, I tuned in to hear the host of the Times Square celebrations broadcasting live on my transistor radio while in the distance through our hotel window I faintly heard the excitement of the roaring crowd from that same Times Square welcoming the arrival of 1959. I was happy to be in New York, glad to be with my mother, fascinated by my new radio, and curious to know what was going on in Times Square somewhere in the distance.

Broadway, New York, 1959. My mother and I visited New York that year during the Christmas season through to the New Year.

Family Changes

Around this time my mother undertook an initiative with my Aunt Helen to sponsor their mother to move to Los Angeles from Novy Sacz in Poland. Emil prepared the paperwork and in time my grandmother moved to the United States. Shortly after that she came up for a visit to us in Edmonton.

She was a dignified woman with a strikingly kind face and blue eyes. By the time I met her, however, she was in the declining years of her life and following her return to Los Angeles, she led the rest of her life as someone looking on to the center stage of life from the sidelines.

I was too young and impetuous to care about asking her to relate any of the details of her life with me. Many years later I found an exchange of letters between her and Helen that spoke of her hardships in Novy Sacz and her desire to be reunified with Helen and my mother through immigration, but little else.

Was I Out of Control?

In seventh grade my school friend Mary Kryzynowski invited me to her birthday party. Mary planned for the two of us to break into the "hip scene" by inviting all the popular kids to her party. It worked, because from that day on, both Mary and I were invited to all kinds of parties held by our school friends, and we became part of the "in" crowd.

I started coming home after midnight and often in the early morning hours on weekends. I was drifting away from my mother's Ukrainian roots and joining kids from other ethnic backgrounds in the English-speaking world around us—at parties, school events, concerts, and sports gatherings. This development disturbed her. She didn't know where I was or what I was doing. While I was out with my friends, however, she wasn't exactly sitting home alone. She started seeing men, who would come by for coffee and sit around the house with her. This wasn't always to my liking, as I perceived these suitors to be a threat to my emotional stability. As these visits increased, at the high point I got so upset that I exploded, took a marble, and threw it against a window in the house, smashing it to pieces. That did little to help, however. So I began to make it a point to spend even more time away from the house.

Eventually my mother seemed to settle on a relationship with Stefan Zmurkevych.

Though I was reluctant to admit it at first, he was a good man for her. For example one of the special things my mother wanted to learn in her life was how to drive a car, and Stefan helped her do just that. With his help she also bought a car and for many years afterward drove around in Edmonton and later in Vancouver, dropping me off at school, helping her friends with rides, and taking them on excursions. Still the tension between my mother and me remained.

Ever since William had died four years earlier, she increasingly was having trouble raising me. She decided something serious had to be done to stop my descent into perdition. So she turned to Helen in Los Angeles, and they developed a plan for me—my aunt would step into my mother's shoes and adopt me as her child. For the time being, however, the plot would be kept secret from me.

In the summer of 1961, my mother and her now steady boyfriend Stefan announced they wanted to take a vacation and drive all the way from Edmonton to Los Angeles. They asked if I would like to go. That was a weeklong drive, and I was only too happy to go on such a huge adventure. I had no idea, however, what was in store for me in Los Angeles.

We stayed with my uncle and aunt in Los Angeles for about a week, and no one said anything to me. Behind the scenes, however, my mother and aunt worked out the arrangements for me to say there. Although difficult for her, I think my mother sincerely believed that my adoption in Los Angeles would be in my best interests. While we were very close, she perceived that I needed more guidance and discipline than she was able to provide.

Also, her evolving relationship with Stefan introduced an element of competition between him and me for a place in her life and raised new questions about where our lives were heading. In short, leaving me with my uncle and aunt seemed like a good solution to her current challenges.

Just for a Little While

Neither my mother nor my aunt could muster the courage to tell me exactly what they had in mind. They rightly feared that I wouldn't stand for it. Instead they portrayed their plan as a temporary measure, "just for a little while." Of course as soon as I learned that my mother was planning for me to stay, I begged her not to leave me behind. I had my school life up in Canada, I argued. I certainly didn't want to abandon all my Edmonton friends. Besides, apart from my aunt and uncle and the two children next door, I didn't know anyone in Los Angeles.

My mother and aunt, however, were determined. During the last few days of the vacation, they tried to reason with me, assuring me it would all work out for the best. Despite my protests, my mother finally insisted that I stay for a year to "give it a try." I didn't completely get it, but I sensed it would be best for her and me if I acquiesced. As much as I didn't want to stay, I perceived my mother needed time away from me. It was a bitter realization.

My mother knew that in time I would reach a point in my life when I would leave her behind and make my way out into the world. Since William's death she pretty much had devoted her life to taking care of me. For the first time in her life, now my mother was freely entering into a relationship outside of the confines of life's demands on her. She needed time away from me to allow her relationship with Stefan to flourish.

Despite what was happening, I knew my mother loved me, although I didn't know what the future would bring. Resigning myself to the inevitable, I turned to face my year in "exile," mustering all the courage I could manage.

As part of her encouragement, my mother promised to visit me several times that year, telling me the first visit would be at Christmas, which was "only three months away." She added that I could even go out to the airport to see her and Stefan off, since they had decided to ship the car back by rail and to fly to Canada. These promises helped ease the pain of her imminent departure somewhat, since I was thinking that three months wasn't that long after all and might be just long enough for it to dawn on my mother that what she was doing wasn't going to work. Besides, I loved going out to airports, where there was always something going on. To a thirteen-year-old boy at that time, that was a big deal.

I'll never forget going to the airport that day. My mother and aunt had prearranged that I would go out to the airport and return by bus after I saw my mother and Stefan off. My aunt would then pick me up at the Hilton Hotel downtown. I appreciated the gesture of their having me travel to the airport, since I felt vicariously like I was making the journey to Canada as well. As I saw them off, my mother promised me again that she would return at Christmastime. I have no doubt that saying goodbye was difficult for her, and it certainly was for me.

When she left, and while I was still at the United Airlines satellite terminal, I became conscious of a feeling of real abandonment for the first time in my life. While rationally I accepted my fate, emotionally I was apprehensive about what was to come. Was I being abandoned for good? I dreaded the idea of staying with my aunt and uncle; they were really "old school" and knew nothing about how to deal with kids like me. I yearned to return home to be with my friends and lead my life as I had before. Los Angeles wasn't my hometown; I was a foreign intruder here. While I wasn't afraid, I was deflated.

Wishing I too could catch one of those planes leaving for some northerly destination and ultimately connecting to Canada, I sat around for about an hour, watching passengers boarding aircraft and leaving. How happy they all seemed to be. I remember the occasional faint whiff of jet fuel and the occasional sounds of jet engines revving up as they left the gates. After a while I decided to go to the coffee shop and have breakfast with some of the money my mother had left me.

In a normal family, having breakfast at a coffee shop was no big deal. My mother was pretty flexible about this as well— but not my uncle or aunt. Except for formal occasions, such as weddings or church events, my uncle and aunt viewed restaurants as vile "slop houses" feeding substandard foods at obscene prices. I didn't dare let them see me enjoying myself in such a place or admit that I had gone to one. But they weren't at the airport, and I was.

I ordered my favorite breakfast, buttermilk pancakes (they called them "hotcakes") with a large glass of milk and some coffee. When the pancakes arrived, they looked like they had come straight off the cover of a box of Aunt Jemima pancake mix—only they tasted better than what I had grown up eating. They were made with some kind of different pancake mix. (I should know; I ate enough of them in my youth.)

I smothered the hot, buttery pancakes with plenty of maple syrup and washed them down with the cold milk. The sweet taste was incredible, especially since I was eating "forbidden fruit" in a forbidden place. I felt an instant sugar high, almost as if I had injected the maple syrup straight into my bloodstream. For a moment I forgot about my travails and simply enjoyed the meal. When I finished, to prolong the moment, I slowly sipped my coffee and pondered my future.

An Unwelcome Guest

At first it seemed everything would work out while I lived with my aunt and uncle at 1017 Waterloo Street, near Echo Park in Los Angeles.

Uncle Emil helped to register me at school and even took me on the bus one morning to show me how to get there. But as he saw my aunt spending more and more time with me, his initial support for my life with them waned quickly. I sensed that my uncle began to resent my presence. In time he began to feel that I had become a distraction to his wife, drawing her attention away from him. I suspect I was also an unpleasant visible reminder of his infertility and failure to have his own family.

Before long Emil made it clear to me that I was no longer welcome. In private discussions with me, he said he "detested my presence" and would do everything he could to have me "return to Canada as soon as possible." He made it clear to me that once I left I would never be welcome in his household again. Probably sensing there wasn't much he could do for the moment, he proposed a secret pact. He would allow me to stay until the end of the school term if I promised him that once I left I would never return. I was only too happy to comply. I had come to hate him. Now our feelings for each other were mutual.

My uncle was a very strict, inflexible man. He told me never to watch television and always to study or do something related to reading a book or helping around the household. Most days consisted of getting up around six thirty in the morning, eating breakfast, getting dressed, and going to school by bus. The bus usually took about an hour to get to Pater Noster High School on San Fernando Road near the Glendale Freeway. I'd arrive at the school early, around 8:00 a.m., and sometimes even earlier when my aunt drove me there.

Following school I often hitchhiked home. In hindsight I can't believe I was so careless, but back then hitchhiking was, in my experience, an acceptable option.

My weekends consisted of going to Ukrainian school on Saturday morning, followed by figure skating, and returning home for supper. Occasionally, after supper, we would go to a movie. On Sundays my uncle, who made me wash the car before we went to church, always would awaken me. We would get dressed, attend church, and sometimes go out for lunch to someone's house. I would study in the afternoon, and in the evening I would read. For me, this life was sheer drudgery.

On one occasion we were going somewhere for an evening outing. As I was getting into the car, my uncle peeled away while I was half in the car and half outside. I could have been seriously injured but somehow had the flexibility to scramble into the car and out of harm's way. Another time my uncle was driving up the driveway at the side of our house. He knew I was standing there. Speeding up the driveway, he narrowly missed me.

I was in his bedroom watching television one day when we had no school. He surprised me by coming home early and catching me with the television on. He warned me that I knew better and said I would be punished for this. Minutes passed. Then he pulled out a bamboo rod and ordered me to come into his room and lie facedown on his bed. He took the rod and whipped me twenty times across the rear end as I lay there.

During another school holiday, I decided I didn't want to stay at home, so I told Helen and Emil that we had a band practice at school. Instead I went to the local movie theater and watched movies all afternoon. Emil's experience during the war with interrogations obviously left him astute in deciphering such unsophisticated bluffs. My uncle became suspicious and called the band conductor, who confirmed that there was no band practice that day. That evening he called me into his room again and warned me not to lie to him again. We had a showdown, and I lost. Out came the rod, and he whipped me again.

The difficult home environment made me pine to leave. I spent my days dreaming about returning to Canada. On every occasion, I'd avoid going home for as long as possible. The result was that I spent a lot of time at school, or daydreaming at Union Station that I could catch the next train back to Canada.

My mother kept her promise and visited us on two occasions that year, and she allowed me to take her out to the airport to see her off each time. Following her departure, I would linger there, spending time in the coffee shop and dreaming about a day when I also would be able to take a plane and leave this cursed city.

Christmas, 1961

Instead of taking the bus home after figure skating on Saturday, Christmas Eve 1961, I walked to the entrance to Desilu Studios. Desilu, and neighboring Paramount Studios, were only a few blocks away from the ice arena where I took my figure-skating lessons. The studios fascinated me. I was attracted to them because they symbolized Hollywood and the life of entertainers and because they were the home of such television shows as *I Love Lucy, The Andy Griffith Show, The Danny Thomas Show* and *The Dick Van Dyke Show.*

For the next hour or so on that quiet evening, I stood outside Desilu Studios watching people drive in and out. I dreamed that one day I would be allowed inside as a director or actor or as some other person involved with the film industry. I struck up a conversation with the guard at the gate, but he soon began to wonder

I hung out at the entrance of Desilu Studio in Hollywood in 1961 hoping to meet celebrities coming in and out of the gate.

why I was there and asked me questions until I finally felt I had to leave.

I decided to walk home. As I walked along the streets that Christmas Eve, I looked into the windows of houses that lined the road. Inside, people were preparing for Christmas dinner with their families. Through those windows I saw the lights on Christmas trees, and the Christmas lights around the window-sills. I yearned to be with one of these families.

Eventually I made my way home. Surprisingly no one was upset about my late arrival. My aunt was working on her outdoor light display. Earlier that day she had dressed a Christmas tree. I hungered for the warmth of Christmas, the sharing of presents, and the company of family members close together. Instead we had the trappings of Christmas. What was missing was the Christmas spirit. We had lights and a Christmas tree. We had food. We were all there together, but the Christmas spirit was missing. It wasn't that we weren't trying; it was just that our home was filled with melancholy rather than happiness. I longed to go back to Canada, and Emil couldn't wait for me to leave. My aunt seemed to be going through the motions but fell short of the happiness she wanted.

In January 1963, Emil wrote my mother the following sharp letter.

Salomea,

I implore you once again for you, along with your son, to free me from your company and either move with him to another residence, of which there are thousands here for rent, or remove him and yourself back to Canada. You can see for yourself that our house is too small and too tight even for the three of us alone (Mother, Helen, and me).

Have at least enough dignity and honor not to keep your son in someone else's house against the will of the owner of that house. Were I brutal and uncivilized, I would forcefully throw both of you out, or with the help of the police. I am not doing this, primarily because of Helen and Mother, but also because generally I deplore violence and argument. Don't take advantage of this.

Your stubbornness, more specifically your keeping your son here against my will, is causing a rift between my wife and me and is poisoning my life to such an extent that I could lose my patience and control over myself and do something horrible.

For this reason I beg you—do not push me to extremes, and remove your son from me before it is too late.

Your brother-in-law

p.s. This letter is only to you and not to Helen, so do not show this letter or talk about it to Helen if you do not want Helen to again fall into such an emotional state, as she once already fell into, where Mother and I wanted to call an emergency ambulance.

The writing was on the wall. My mother would have to act soon. She decided I should remain in Los Angeles until the end of the school year that spring.

Return from L.A.

I had dreamed of escaping and going back to Canada on my own. In my more sober moments, however, I realized I was too young to really go on my own and that I would need the cooperation of my mother to make the trip home. I was fourteen at the time. I waited for the school year to end, and then

I boarded an airplane and arrived in Edmonton. Soon after I signed up for tenth grade at O'Leary High School. I was back!

When I returned to Edmonton, I soon realized that my mother had developed a much more serious relationship with Stefan Zmurkevych. Although I wasn't aware of it at the time, my return would complicate their relationship. It made it more difficult for them to be with each other. I had come from a house where I wasn't always wanted and had arrived at a home where I now felt somewhat like a stranger. It was like the feeling you get when you return to the house of your childhood and realize that, although it's familiar, it's no longer yours. While the place was the same, much of the sense of warmth and comfort was missing.

Lessons from the East

As we ate and drank our freezes on my birthday, Jerry said to me, "Hey, since it's your birthday, why don't you have your fortune told?" I agreed.

It was January 8, 1964, and I was celebrating my fifteenth birthday with my friends, Jerry Stelmaschuk and Mike Karpa, at Ciro's Restaurant below the old Strand Theatre in downtown Edmonton. The Strand was a *Phantom of the Opera*–type edifice, and Ciro's had great non-alcoholic freezes. The drinks made the restaurant a popular place for young people, but what made it especially exotic were the fortunetellers. So we invited a fortuneteller to join us.

The lady poured me some tea then poured my tea leaves out before her and began to tell my future. I don't remember everything she said that night, but one thing stood out. She indicated to us that I was about to take a long trip in an eastward direction. This was news to me, since I had no plans for any such trip.

After she left us, our discussion centered on how our lack of automotive transportation affected our lifestyles. Neither Jerry nor Mike had cars.

"I don't have a car either," I said, "but my mother does."

"Let's go for a ride," Mike suggested.

"Well, I'd like to," I said, "but I don't have a driver's license. All I have is a learner's permit."

"That's not a problem," said Jerry. "I have a driver's license, and as long as I'm with you in the car, you're legal."

As we talked about it, it became a better and better idea. We paid our bill, hailed a taxi, and went over to my place. We all make mistakes in life. It was time for me to make mine.

I went into the house. My mother was sleeping, but her car keys were on the kitchen table. I scooped them up, snuck outside, and opened the garage door. My friends were already waiting for me there. We jumped into the car and drove off. I remember that the roads were clear throughout the city on this particularly cold winter night. It began to snow.

We started wondering where we should go. Just then, Mike said, "Hey, the fortuneteller said you're going to take a trip eastward. Let's take a trip eastward."

I wondered aloud where that might take us.

"Well, the nearest city is Saskatoon, about six hours away. Let's go to there," Jerry said.

"What could we do there?" I asked.

Mike said, "I have a friend, Rosie Kozak. We could go visit Rosie."

"What about money?" I asked.

"No problem," Jerry said. "Let's pool our resources."

We discovered we had about $35 and, as luck would have it, a full tank of gas. "Let's go!" I told them

We started out with a "devilish idea." We would take a quick, late-night joyride in my mother's car. No one would even know. We would return it that night before sunrise. But that's not where it would end. Instead, in the face of their zeal for fun and lack of compunction, I willingly suspended my sense of what was right and wrong to join my friends in turning the momentary prank into an "exciting journey" to a neighboring city. Step by step we got into more trouble. The longer we were away from home and the farther we traveled, the less we wanted to turn back to face the trouble that awaited us, and the more reasonable it seemed to keep going. Like a woman on a diet who eats a few potato chips then decides that since she's broken her discipline anyway she might as well eat the whole bag, more and more we abandoned our sense of constraint for the sake of the adventure.

We drove all night. Early the next morning, about six hours later, we arrived in Saskatoon. Mike called Rosie and told her we had just arrived and that we'd like to visit her. She said,

"Well, I'm going to school right now, but why don't you come by around four this afternoon." He told her we would.

For the next few hours, we had breakfast, toured the city, had lunch, and kept ourselves busy. Around four o'clock we went to Rosie's house. She introduced us to her parents and to other family members. They probably wondered what we were doing there, but we were a gregarious bunch, and soon the parents invited us to stay for dinner. During dinner her parents asked us where we were going to spend the night. We said we hadn't decided yet. They invited us to stay overnight at their home and we "graciously" accepted.

The next morning Rosie went to school, and we discussed what we should do next. It became clear that we were running out of money. But I had a "brilliant" suggestion. I suggested that the boys give me $20 and take me to a local pool hall. I told them that I was pretty good at billiards and that I'd find someone to play and win some money. My friends believed me. Thinking that was a great idea, they gave me $20 and dropped me off at the nearest pool hall.

I spent that afternoon playing pool. It was hard to find someone to play with since there weren't that many patrons around. But I did find one farmer who agreed. He said he'd play for $5. It was a close game, but I lost. So then we played for another $5, and then another $5, and so on, until I lost all our money. When my friends returned to pick me up, I broke the bad news. We were crestfallen.

We needed money to go back home, but now we were broke. Then we came up with another "brilliant" idea. We'd go visit some of the priests in the city and tell them that we were good Catholic boys from a neighboring province visiting and that we had run out of money. We'd say that we wanted to borrow some money from the church—but only enough to get back to Edmonton—and that we'd pay them back. We found a church, told the priest our story, and he agreed to give us $40. It was that easy.

If it was that easy, we thought, why not try it again? So we went to another church with the same story and got the same result. Now we were flying pretty high. We were just full of "brilliant ideas."

Back in Edmonton things were becoming a little unsettled. We knew we had to let our families know we were OK. Jerry and Mike simply phoned home and informed their parents that they were in Saskatoon. In my case, however, I felt I needed a more "personal touch." I phoned my friend George Jendyk and asked him to go in person to see my mother to let her know I was in Saskatoon with our car and that everything was OK. He agreed. Needless to say, my mother wasn't impressed at all with either the emissary or his assurances.

With our newly acquired "bridge financing" in hand, we narrowed down our options. We could either return to Edmonton or continue traveling eastward to Winnipeg, a city approximately twelve hours away. Since we already had invested so heavily in our adventure and knew there was nothing but a growing storm of anger awaiting us back home, we decided to continue.

As we drove along, our first doubts about the wisdom of what we were doing started to surface. First Jerry said that Winnipeg was as far as he would go. That was where he would leave us. I stubbornly held my ground, arguing that now that we had crossed the line there was no turning back. It was too late now, as far as I was concerned. We had burned all our bridges to return. I contended we should continue on to New York and start up new lives there. But Mike also started to waver. My stomach tightened into a knot as I thought about what to do next. We rode for a long time in silence, deep in thought. Twelve hours later we arrived in Winnipeg.

Winnipeg was where Jerry was from and where his parents lived. His parents had sent him to school in Edmonton to get him away from bad company he was keeping in Winnipeg. In hindsight I suspect that he was homesick, and that's why agreed to continue on this adventure. He was pining to go home, just like I wanted to come home from Los Angeles a few years back. We first visited his girlfriend for a brief while and then went to Jerry's house.

His mother was "surprised" to see us. She served us breakfast then questioned Jerry about what we were doing so far away from Edmonton. In the course of that discussion, we discovered that Jerry's father had had an accident at work and was in the hospital. This now provided us a good pretext for the entire trek, and Jerry quickly seized on it, telling his mother that we had learned through a news report that his father was hospitalized and that was why we had showed up. Though dubious, his mother accepted the explanation then arranged for us to visit Jerry's father in the hospital. Fortunately he wasn't that seriously injured and was on the mend.

The next day Jerry had a long talk with his mother. In the meantime, I arranged to make a call to my messenger, George Jendyk. He told me that my mother was furious. She had told him to tell me to get back home as soon as possible. I didn't know this at the time, but my mother was panicking. She simply didn't know what to do and had consulted her friends.

They suggested that she report her car as being stolen and tell the police I was the culprit. In this way, her friends suggested, the police would find us and bring us home. Before doing this, however, my mother went to see Father Kowalsky at St. Josaphat's Ukrainian Catholic Cathedral.

Although he didn't flaunt it, Father Kowalsky was no ordinary priest. For one thing, he had a PhD. For another, he was a survivor of Auschwitz. His friends John Lahola and Stefan Petelycky, whom I later came to know, told me they attributed their survival in Auschwitz to the deep and profound prayers Father Kowalsky had offered up to God on their behalf. Thankfully, Father Kowalsky demurred at the suggestion that my mother contact the police.

Instead he advised her to be patient, to pray, and to await her son's return. Because I had contacted her twice, and based on the fact that George had conveyed my mother's anguish to me, the priest concluded that I would return home soon and safely. In hindsight I believe his prayers had an influence on what happened next.

Meanwhile, in Winnipeg, our planning and discussions continued. The biggest obstacle for me was to admit that this had been a big mistake. I dreaded the thought of what I would have to deal with when I returned home, particularly facing the pain that my mother had endured through this whole debacle. Jerry's parents started to talk some sense into him and convinced him that he needed to return to Edmonton. He, in turn, convinced us. In particular he reminded me that since I didn't have a driver's license, and he was the only one who did, it would be impossible for me to legally continue on without him. He added definitively that he was going back to Edmonton. Mike agreed, and that was it. We decided to return home.

The ride home was a seventeen-hour trip through blowing snow that made it difficult to see. I arrived late in the evening. Now it was time to face the firestorm I had created. While I was apprehensive and hesitant, I also felt my mother would forgive my actions because I knew she loved me. I just didn't know how vehemently she would react to my arrival and to what extent I would be punished.

My mother was cooking and had a wooden spoon in her hand. As I entered the doorway and closed the door behind me, she saw me and shouted out, "Where have you been?" While saying that over and over again, she hit me with the wooden spoon. I raised my hands to protect myself. She hit me until the spoon broke.

When it did, we both looked down at the broken piece on the floor. With that my mother's anger seemed to subside. She pointed to my bedroom and told me to get in there. I closed the door and went to sleep.

The next morning my mother made me breakfast and never mentioned the experience again. To this day I marvel at how she handled the matter. It was clear to her that I had learned my lesson, so she didn't need to add anything more on top of that realization.

Lessons Learned

In the days that followed, Jerry, Mike, and I returned to school, and our story was the talk of the town. It was hard for us to live it down. We had to earn the money necessary to reimburse the two priests, and we did. Slowly things returned to normal.

What I learned from this experience was how kind people could be. The Kozaks, the two priests, Jerry's parents, and even Father Kowalsky played important parts in the safe conclusion of this odyssey. Thankfully they were wise enough and helpful enough to get us through it. I was thankful to my mother for not making a federal case out of this incident and for following Father Kowalsky's advice.

I also realized that you have to beware of wayward friends, because they really can have an influence on your life. Finally, if I were to reduce the whole incident into one moral, it would be this—there's a medicine for almost everything these days, but there's no medicine for stupidity.

Life in Canada

I didn't want to see my uncle again, I told my mother.

By 1965 we hadn't visited Helen or Emil in four years, and my mother had proposed we travel to Los Angeles. She reasoned with me, suggesting that we could stay in a hotel in Los Angeles and that we would travel there not to see uncle Emil but to see Aunt Helen. With that plan in mind we flew to L.A.

We slept in a downtown hotel, and the next morning my mother caught a bus to Helen's house. An hour or two later, my aunt and mother arrived at the hotel. My aunt insisted that we stay at her house. She wouldn't hear of us staying at the hotel another minute and reasoned with me that it was senseless for us to stay at a hotel when she had a big house that easily could accommodate everyone. I didn't like it, but the two sisters prevailed, and Helen drove us to her home.

Our arrival opened up a new era in our relationship with Emil. As soon as he saw us enter the house, he got up from the living room sofa, marched to his room, and slammed the door behind him. He obviously wasn't happy about our return. For the next decade, he would give us this cold-shoulder treatment whenever we showed up. Meanwhile Helen reassured us, took our luggage, and made room for us to stay in one of the bedrooms in the house. From then on my aunt lived a double life whenever we visited. She served two meals at each mealtime. First she would serve Emil while we waited in our bedroom or outside. Then, once he was finished and had gone back to his bedroom, she would serve us. Fortunately they had a large house to accommodate us all.

Moving to Vancouver

On December 4, 1966, my mother married Stefan Zmurkevych in Vancouver, where his employer had transferred him. Over the years my mother's relationship with him had grown closer, and in time I could see that he was good for her. Initially he and I struggled for my mother's attention, and she was divided regarding looking after my needs while attending to her own in the context of her relationship with him.

Since I was living at home, he tried to see her at times when I wasn't present—such as during school hours, or on weekend evenings when I was out with my friends, or later when I was at work during the summer. He tried to warm up to me by arranging "family outings," where we traveled to Vegreville to visit the farms, to Jasper, and to Banff and Radium Hot Springs in the Rocky Mountains. Since neither my mother nor Stefan were that good at driving, these trips brought us close together in a perverse way but not as he intended. We grew together by sharing a sense of dread and then relief as they each took turns driving the car and maneuvering through the hairpin twists and turns, ups and downs, and highway hazards at high speed, very often barely making it through them. There's nothing like a brush with death to make you rejoice in your life and those who survived with you.

When Sherritt Gordon, the company Stefan worked for, transferred him to Vancouver, he and my mother made plans to marry so they could be together. By then I had matured enough that I was more accepting of their relationship. So after catching up on a few science courses, I finished high school in Edmonton in the summer of 1967, and my mother and I then moved to Vancouver, where I would enter the Faculty of Commerce at the University of British Columbia.

After they married and took a brief honeymoon in Vancouver, Stefan moved in with us into our apartment on West 10th Avenue. He worked as a chemist while my mother looked after the household. He was a solid man and intelligent, and he tried hard. He was especially good to me, offering me support, occasionally giving me money, and being understanding of my need for freedom and flexibility. Stefan tried to be "cool," and meaning to say something like, "So then we'll go, hey?" instead he'd say, "Den vee go, yah?"—not understanding that this made no sense at all. ("Den vee go, yah?" became my mantra, and to this day, my wife and I say it when we're leaving the house.)

Unfortunately my mother's relationship with Stefan soured, and within a couple of years, they broke up. Neither one would bend sufficiently or be flexible enough to make the marriage work. Neither one was happy with the breakup, but neither of them could continue in the relationship, as it had passed the point of no return. This was the second time my mother was breaking her ties in a relationship. Again she turned to face a state of loneliness and lack of intimacy.

Hello, I'm Your Father

A few years later, while my mother was riding the bus in Vancouver, she looked out the window at a bus stop and saw my father, Jake Holonko, standing there. She was stunned.

Later, when she was looking at some condos for sale in North Vancouver, she inadvertently met up with some of my father's children. Word must have gotten back to him, and it was around this time that he initiated a campaign to contact me. After looking up the name "Andrew Semotiuk," in the phonebook, he went to the home address next to the name. When the owner answered the door, my father declared, "Hello, I'm your father!"

The man replied, "Oh, no, you're not!"

My father responded, "Oh, yes, I am!"

That's how the conversation went until my father finally gave up. Wrong Andrew Semotiuk!

My father Jake Holonko in his later life in Vancouver circa 1970.

Love, Despair, and Those You Leave Behind

One day, in the summer of 1968, while we were in Edmonton, visiting from Vancouver, my mother told me to get in the car. We had to go out to Vegreville to comfort a friend, she said. We drove to William's farm. A neighboring farmer's wife had been found dead. Apparently she had committed suicide by hanging herself from a beam in the barn. My mother wanted to console her husband. When we arrived, the farmer was beside himself, alone on the farm, with three small children.

I remember listening to how my mother spoke with the farmer. She reviewed the facts in an objective, gentle way while helping him gain some emotional distance from the very immediate tragedy. Initially the police considered him to be the prime suspect of what could have been a major crime, but he was able to show that he hadn't been at the scene at the time of her death.

He was certain someone had murdered his wife. The police investigation concluded it was indeed a suicide. Apparently the woman was pregnant with another man's child. As painful as this event was, I watched with considerable admiration as my mother put the neighbor at ease, calming him in the midst of the disturbing allegations and his sorrow.

No stranger to hardships, she was very capable of dealing with tragic circumstances. She had, after all, lived through many of her own tragedies. We were quiet when we drove home that night, each of us reflecting on how the lives of that family had changed irrevocably.

Graduation in Vancouver

During my studies my mother lived what seemed like a peaceful life that contented her. She learned to paint—particularly landscapes and still lifes. Since we were by then traveling regularly to Los Angeles, Helen introduced my mother to the world of art. It was one of the few pleasures she was able to enjoy.

She often traveled on the Nanaimo ferry and walked the Vancouver beaches when the tide went out to sea. She enjoyed good company with friends from church who often visited and also invited her to their homes. Even though she had to return to Edmonton from time to time to clean up apartments when they needed to be rented, she was able to live in Vancouver while a caretaker looked after the day-to-day business of maintaining the building in Edmonton.

As my graduation from the law school of the University of British Columbia approached in 1972, however, it became clear that I soon would have to leave the family home to make my way in the world. This was a big transition for both of us. With the exception of my year in Los Angeles, my mother and I always had lived together. As the realization dawned upon me, I feared I might not be able to break free from my mother to go my own way; after all she depended on me heavily. I also sensed she was bracing for the coming moment and, without saying so, was anxious about it. I searched for a way to tell her what I was about to do so she would understand and accept my decision.

In the spring of 1972, Aunt Helen and Uncle Emil traveled to Vancouver to attend my graduation. It was a remarkable time, as I watched Uncle Emil come full circle. Over time, during our visits to Los Angeles, his attitude toward me softened.

Evidently he began to realize that his life was winding down (he was ten years older than Helen and was by then in his eighties), and Helen would need someone to look after her when he was gone. I was the only real option for that assignment.

Now my mother would have to adapt to living on her own. This was hard for both of us, since she had a handicap that made her a vulnerable target for anyone who wanted to take advantage of her poor hearing. In addition there were considerable security risks. She couldn't hear fire alarms or people shouting instructions or cries for assistance and could be especially vulnerable at night. Nonetheless leaving my mother's side was a part of my passage into adulthood; I needed to do it.

My mother questioned my need to leave Vancouver. For her it made no sense that I wanted to move to Toronto. After all there was no one there with whom I could live, and how could I afford it? "At least here you have a roof over your head and food to eat," she added. We had been living off the income from an apartment house she owned in Edmonton. This was an asset but also a burden. "We are limited in what we can afford," she said. "There is the apartment in Edmonton that I need help with."

I explained why I needed to leave by drawing on an example from nature. I said, "Just like every bird that grows up has to leave its nest one day, so must I leave our home to spread my own wings and to take on life by myself." This was an analogy my mother could relate to, and even if it was emotionally hard, she accepted the logic. To make it easier on her, I added, "I'm not leaving for good, but only for a while, until I complete my articles as a lawyer in training." I left it open that I could return to Vancouver afterward. There was a moment of silence after our exchange, but there was no crying or any recriminations.

She accepted what had to be done without complaint; it was just part of the life cycle.

In the summer of 1972, I packed my bags and moved to Toronto. Difficult though it may have been, my mother managed to adapt and continued to develop friendships with women her own age in the community. This resulted in a few years of very rewarding experiences for her. These women gathered weekly, had tea, gossiped, discussed their problems, and generally enriched one another's lives.

Articling in Toronto

The day I was called to the Ontario Bar, my mother flew in to observe the auspicious occasion; she was quite proud of her only child's achievement. Seeing her pride in me, I recalled that to get me where I was now, for many years my mother had to wash floors and clean washrooms in her Edmonton rental building to prepare units for rent in order to make a living for us both. Verily my mother had put me through law school by washing floors on her hands and knees. That is why, from the moment of my call to the bar, whenever I met up with her again, I made it a point to kiss each one of those overworked hands in honor of what they had contributed to what I had become.

Traveling

Lourdes, France, is renowned because miracles are purported to occur there from time to time. It's a Catholic holy place, where, it is said, the Virgin Mother appeared to three children.

In September 1973, my mother traveled to Europe, and during the trip, she visited Lourdes. Although she never said it, I'm sure she secretly hoped by going there she might encounter a miracle that would restore her hearing. It did not happen.

No doubt she was somewhat disappointed. In later life she rationalized her trip by saying it was impossible for the Virgin Mother to heal everyone, and there were thousands upon thousands who came to Lourdes with similar intentions but with greater needs. At least she was traveling a bit and seeing the world.

In spring 1974 I took a trip with my mother back to Europe, where we traced her journey from Ukraine as a refugee to Canada. We traveled to Paris, a city she had never seen before and which she loved for its colorful cafés and nice hotels. We stayed there overnight; then we took the train to Salzburg, Austria, to visit the Lehener Kaserne refugee camp, where she had stayed before coming to Canada.

"*Haben sie ein zimmer?*" she asked the hotel desk clerk when we arrived at our hotel. *Holy smoke*, I thought. *She speaks German!* This was something I didn't know about her but obviously having lived in Vienna and Salzburg for several years towards the end of the war she picked it up.

While the visit to the camp was historically rich in meaning, it wasn't pleasant for my mother to recall her stay there. She recognized the building as we approached it in a taxi. As we entered it and climbed the steps to the second floor where she once lived, she shook her head, acknowledging she had been here before. The memories came back: the uncertainty of what was next, the unpleasant experiences with bed bugs that kept her from sleeping, the dread of having lived through the war.

Despite her discomfort, I was so thankful to her for bringing me here to show me where she had lived back then. It made my understanding of her life and travails so much clearer. While she was glad to have come to show me the building, she also hastened to leave.

She then took me to Fuschl, a small Austrian town a short distance from Salzburg, near Lake Fuschl. We sat on a bench near the lake while my mother reminisced about her life in Austria and how she had come here to escape her troubles. We ate lunch in one of the houses there and were served a delicious meal—cauliflower soup, pork with potatoes, and sauerkraut. There's no doubt about it; Austrian chefs know how to cook! Then we returned to the bench to relax after the meal.

As we sat watching the small waves lap the shoreline, a duck slowly waddled by in front of us. My mother turned to me and, with a devilish grin, blurted out, "Grab the duck, twist its neck, and eat it for supper!"

What made the remark so funny was that it was such a striking departure from her usual self and the somber memories she was recounting. We definitely needed the levity after having dealt with so much difficult history. So we had a good laugh.

We then traveled to Warsaw. Again I was struck by my mother's fluency in Polish, even though I had heard her speak the language in Canada. Where did this linguistic versatility come from? A family friend, Kazik Skiwowolk, picked us up in Warsaw and drove us about two hundred miles to Novy Sacz to visit the grave where my mother's father had been buried during the last months of the war.

Another elderly woman friend of my mother's who lived in Novy Sacz greeted us and took us to the cemetery and the gravesite. There, for the first time in her life, after 30 years my mother saw her father's grave. As we stood there looking at the monument, my mother solemnly recounted her last days with her father and their escape from the invading Red Army during the war. She broke down in tears as her memories of those final moments with him flooded into her consciousness. I was moved by the sense of despair she described because of his serious illness and her choice to escape before the invading army arrived.

We then traveled into the Soviet Union to visit Lviv. She was returning there for the first time in thirty years. We met Ivanka Markovska, a close friend of my mother's. When they first were reunited, they gazed into each other's eyes in silence for a long time. I could see from the glow in their eyes, which were rich with tenderness and meaning, that they understood each other's plight. Then they reminisced and caught up on each other's lives over the last three decades. During that visit under Soviet rule, Ivanka took me into an isolated field, cupped her hand over my ear, and whispered the story of her life under Soviet rule to me. She told me about the death of her husband, who had committed suicide rather than surrender to the Bolsheviks. She told me how she hadn't revealed that story to her son for fear that some day the fact that his father had been in the Ukrainian insurgent army may be used against his son. She told me she attributed her survival to one thing, and one thing only, and then she motioned as if she were closing a zipper across her mouth. That was just the way it was. I later shared the conversation with my mother the next day while we ate breakfast. She peered into my eyes and nodded to signify she understood.

When we visited the building where my mother once lived, we learned that one of the apartments on the second floor had been turned into a museum to honor the life of Solomea Krushelnytska. So we dropped in on the museum staff. They were delighted to have us visit. As part of the visit, we were allowed to view the apartment where my mother once lived. There she took me to the bedroom where some thirty years earlier she had approached her brother Alex's bed, pulled on his blanket to get his attention, and asked him to flee with her to Warsaw. She then bowed her head in sorrow while saying he would not leave without his fiancé and then perished. I put my arm around her shoulder to comfort her and said we should leave.

Later we walked near Brygitky Prison, where Alex had died, so she could show me the place where they had searched through bodies to find his. While we could look on only

Brygitky Prison in Lviv where my mother's brother Alex perished in 1941.

at a distance, since authorities would not let us approach the structure, her face reflected the intense regret and the lingering terror evoked by the building. I felt revulsion for the place as well.

We returned home in a thoughtful and pensive mood. How fortunate we were to have been able to return there to see her friends and family and also to come back to Canada, where we now lived.

Fractured Bones

In February 1977, when I was in New York working as a journalist at the United Nations, I slipped and fell on a frozen street corner and broke my left leg. When my mother found out while she was living in Vancouver, she packed her bags and immediately flew to see me.

She arrived late in the evening; she had taken a taxi from the airport straight to my address in Manhattan on Second Avenue and Ninth Street. I lived right across the street from a drug rehabilitation center in one of the seediest parts of town. In fact the Martin Scorsese movie *Taxi Driver*, which depicts a young prostitute working the streets, was filmed at that time in my neighborhood. It was a troubled, rundown neighborhood. Because of this, as a precaution, my apartment building was locked up at night.

I still don't know how, but my mother—not able to speak English very well, new to New York, and standing on the street alone at ten p.m. in the dark—was somehow able to locate the building's owner. She talked him into letting her into the building, unlocking the door to my third-floor apartment, and letting her in without any permission.

I was a young bachelor, and my flat was stark and disorganized. My friends used to bring girlfriends to the apartment whenever I was away or when I wasn't using it. I had a pile of *Playboy* magazines strewn across the floor of my bedroom. This wasn't the kind of place I wanted my mother to see or to ever stay in. But I had no choice.

As it turned out, none of this bothered her, although later on, after I confessed to others having used my place as a bachelor's den, she did protest about how dirty my sheets were and how many times she had to wash them to get them clean.

The following morning my mother was at my hospital bedside. My left leg was in a huge cast up to my waist and elevated as I sat in bed. It was a bad fracture of both major bones in my leg. The doctor called it a "tib-fib" fracture. My mother was mortified. From that day on, she stayed with me through my recovery over the next few weeks.

When I was finally told I could go home, my friends arranged for me to stay at Dr. Alex Danylewych's place for a couple of weeks. He was going to be away. This was a great help, since his apartment was nice, clean, and on the main floor of a building right across the street from the hospital.

My mother pushed me in my wheelchair as we crossed the street and helped me back and forth as I returned to the hospital for checkups. When Alex came back, we returned to my apartment, and my mother helped me hop up and down three flights, one step at a time, since there was no elevator there.

The Long Road Back to Health

While being laid up and no longer able to fulfill my functions at the UN, I studied for the New York State Bar exams. I attended lectures and studied while my mother looked after the cooking and cleaning. Then on March 15 and 16, 1977, I took the required tests.

By this time I was walking around on crutches and was fairly mobile. My mother and I agreed that it would be best for me to return to Vancouver until my leg healed. But my friend Bohdan Sirant called me from Toronto to tell me he also had broken his leg and was in a cast like mine. I managed to persuade my mother to return to Vancouver a few days ahead of me so that I could have Bohdan come down for a visit before I left. She reluctantly agreed.

Bohdan visited me in April. We rented a car and traveled all over New York City together, both of us with crutches. At Times Square we hobbled around, checking out all the stores and looking in on all the seedy joints. We were fascinated by the decadence and the city's willingness to put up with it all. Every depravity known to mankind was on display. As we made our way around on crutches, we were as much a curiosity to those we observed as they were to us. Visiting various New York restaurants and bars, as well as Grand Central Park, we bared our souls to each other, expressing the disappointment of our setbacks. Sharing our experiences this way, while taking in the vibrancy of this bustling city together, helped our recovery.

When Bohdan returned to Toronto, I flew to Vancouver. My goal was to rest and recover from my injury and then return to New York. Although I was able to withdraw from my active life for a while, I felt that my life was in crisis. Debt ridden, unable to work, totally dependent on my mother, experiencing complications with my leg, and feeling friendless, emotionally down, and physically degenerated due to a complete lack of exercise, I felt like my life was heading toward an abyss.

I also was smoking heavily—two packs-a-day. When I wasn't smoking, I was sleeping. I slept for twelve to sixteen hours a day and still felt exhausted in my waking hours. I could hardly breathe, at times having to consciously force myself to inhale. I wondered if this was it. Was I on the way out? Was this how I was to end my life? Who would care for my mother if I died? How would she cope?

Some nights, as I lay down to sleep, I felt myself blacking out. I had to suddenly jolt myself up and consciously breathe deeply. My lungs tickled, but I was hooked on those cigarettes. I tried to quit a hundred times without success. I likened my condition to Elvis Presley's (who also was born January 8), who was in terrible shape, overweight, and eating five banana splits a day. He would die only a few months later.

I started to read a book about exercising called *Aerobics*. My cousin, Alex Tyshovnytsky, had recommended it. I couldn't run, walk, or cycle, but I could swim, which is what I decided to do. I started to swim every day at the Vancouver Aquatic Center. In time I began to feel better and eventually pulled myself together.

Which Way Are You Going?

Your life can change with a glance.

In June 1978, after a brief stint practicing law in New York City, I found myself back in Toronto, heading into a Swiss Chalet restaurant on Bloor Street near St. George. I had just bought a *Globe and Mail* and was planning on reading it while having dinner.

Inside the restaurant, I looked up and saw two young women sitting together and recognized one of them—Helen (Halya) Lozynsky, who had been a friend of mine for some time. I was disappointed because I realized I'd have to sit with them and wouldn't be able to read my newspaper. Helen introduced me to her friend, a blonde woman named Ann Tworynsky. Ann was attractive and friendly, had beautiful blue eyes, and was very earnest and sincere. Toward the end of dinner, I started to hope I could split these two women up so I could talk with Ann some more on my own.

As we left the restaurant, I used my best strategy in such circumstances, asking them both, "Which way are you going?" Luckily the two were splitting up into opposite directions. I said I was going in the same direction Ann was heading. As we walked down Bloor Street, I told Ann I was going to see a movie and asked her if she would like to join me. She answered that she couldn't because she had to go to a university class. I managed to get her phone number and told her I would call.

I didn't call.

At least I didn't call until early July. Meanwhile I bumped into Helen again. I asked Helen if she thought Ann would be a good match for me. Helen enthusiastically answered, "Yes." I brazenly wondered out loud whether I'd be better off with a brunette or a blonde, and Helen answered, "Definitely a blonde!" Admittedly it was a shallow question—as shallow as my knowledge of women's hair coloring back then. Ann, a natural brunette, had died her hair blond. Regardless she was my perfect match. See how these things work?

I started to phone Ann regularly. She was never home, and her phone was busier than Grand Central Station. Whenever I did get through, her mother would tell me she wasn't home. I'd leave a message, but it never seemed to get to her. Finally, after about a half-dozen messages, I managed to reach her and set up a dinner for a couple of days later, at a Mexican restaurant on Bloor Street near Yonge.

The One!

The morning of our date, some Eastern European students announced they were going on a hunger strike downtown, in front of Toronto City Hall, to demand the release of political prisoners in the Baltic States. I decided to go on a sympathy hunger strike with them. But first I called Ann to confirm our date and told her about my hunger strike with them. That must have seemed more than a bit contradictory to Ann. But then there are long hunger strikes and short ones. I promised to break my fast in time for dinner. So that was how we had our first date.

The attraction was undeniable, but there was only one problem about starting up a new relationship with Ann at this time. I had decided to move out West again. In fact I was already packing for the move.

Since we had just started up a relationship, I found it odd that Ann wasn't fazed by my desire to move. I would have thought she would at least raise the issue of why I was leaving if we were together now. Yet she didn't, even though it was on my mind. We continued to see each other. I bought an old Chevy car, and we emptied all my books from my law office into the trunk then packed away my clothing. Ann volunteered to help me pack and send me on my way.

Now that I had packed everything in Toronto, I needed to travel to New York to empty my apartment there. I was headed to Winnipeg for a conference, where I had been invited to speak. I asked Ann if she would like to drive down with me—first to New York and then to Winnipeg. She was planning to attend the same conference anyway, so she agreed.

This was getting serious!

I decided I should arrange for my mother to meet Ann, who, like me, was the child of Ukrainian immigrants. It wouldn't be a big deal; I'd just have them meet so I could get my mother's opinion. I arranged for my mother to fly to Winnipeg while we made our way in my Chevy across the northern United States on our way to Winnipeg.

The meeting turned out well. My mother liked Ann immediately but played her cards very smoothly, not fussing or in any way encouraging me to choose Ann. She knew that any such effort would backfire. Ann was subdued and didn't seem that nervous about the encounter, although that's what I would have expected. One of her strengths is the ability to deal with any kind of person on that person's level. That came in handy in dealing with my mother, who was not as gifted in that area.

My mother was able to relate to her, since Ann spoke her language and shared a similar background; Ann's parents were refugees who had come from Galicia after the war. Ann was a good communicator and very accommodating, so she ended up taking my mother to visit one of my mother's old friends in Winnipeg. They had a good time together having tea at the friend's house.

Ann and I parted in Winnipeg but agreed that I would return to Toronto in November, since I would be on my way to another conference, this time in New York.

After our meeting in Winnipeg, my mother and I drove across the rest of Canada to Vancouver. We stopped in Edmonton on the way home, and I was persuaded by friends that, given the boom in Edmonton at the time, due to high world oil prices, it would be wise for us to return there instead of moving to Vancouver. Besides, my mother had her apartment house in Edmonton, and because of this we had a place to live. Right there and then my mother and I decided to move back to the city we had left more than ten years earlier. We had some lingering attachments to Edmonton, since many of our friends were still there, and we would feel right at home the moment we arrived.

My mother and I continued on to Vancouver, packed all of our things, and made our way back to Edmonton. In the course of a few months, after years of living in various cities, I would be consolidating my life in Edmonton. There was only one thing missing.

In the midst of doing my work, I'd find my attention drifting off as I wondered what Ann was doing right then. This was happening quite often.

Earlier, while I was still in Vancouver, I received a letter from Toronto. I didn't recognize the handwriting and thought it was from one of my male friends. He wrote about how he was up "at the cottage." *What cottage?* I thought. I didn't even know he had a cottage. He talked about "the beauty of the leaves falling to the ground." *Strange*, I thought. We never talked about nature to one another like this. He mentioned "how very much" he missed me. OK, we were apart. But what was the big deal? I never thought he would miss me that much. It seemed like a pretty sentimental thing for a guy to write. What was the deal? Was he losing it? Maybe he was gay, and all this time I had no idea.

I finally came to the end of the letter. Then I realized it wasn't from my male friend at all. It was from Ann! So she was missing me as much as I was missing her.

Actually, it was more than that. I was looking to find more meaning in my life, and Ann was the meaning I was looking for. I was a ship hopelessly lost at sea. I was looking for a beacon, and Ann was that guiding light for me.

Proposal from a Phone Booth

One night that summer, I pulled together all the change I had and went to the phone booth in front of the A&W restaurant on 118th Avenue near my mother's home in Edmonton. I called Ann and suggested, "Maybe we should get married." Ann hesitated, asking whether I was sure and recommended that I come back to Toronto in November so that we could talk about it further. That's how the matter was left. I told my mother what I was planning to do then waited for the upcoming trip.

In November, as promised, I showed up in Toronto. At first we just spent some time together and talked, but I didn't pop the question. That night, after I had checked into my hotel room, Ann came up to see me. At what I thought was an appropriate moment, I turned to her and asked, "So will you marry me?" She hesitated for a moment and then asked whether I was sure about this. I said yes, and she agreed.

We made plans for a small wedding to take place early in the New Year. The next day we had dinner with Ann's parents, whom I'd never met before. Then, in the middle of dinner, I asked them what they were doing on January 14, 1979. They said they weren't planning anything. I said, "Good, because that's when I would like to marry Ann." They were surprised, to say the least.

Ann's father was fine with it. Ann's mother, on the other hand, got up and walked out of the room to cry. She was thinking this was not the way it was supposed to happen. She was most upset about the fact that we were moving to Edmonton, and in the process, she would lose close contact with her daughter. She had her doubts. Who was this guy anyway? Who comes for dinner for the first time and then announces he wants to marry your daughter? Ultimately, however, Ann's mother gave in, and she and I had an excellent relationship for the rest of her life.

Ann and I marry in January 1979 in Toronto

New Stages of Life

One day in 1980 a Rottweiler attacked my mother, knocking her to the ground. While she cried out for help, the dog kept biting her and took a big chunk out of her left thigh. Fortunately someone was walking down a nearby alley and managed to get the dog to back off long enough for my mother to get up and limp away.

She had been bitten in several places and was badly hurt. Someone came running over to our yard and called to me for help. I arrived to see my mother bent over, crying, her pants ripped, and teeth marks on her arms. Her thigh was bleeding badly.

Immediately I drove her to the Charles Camsell Hospital, where she was given a sedative and her wound was patched with about a dozen stitches. As we drove home, my mother related her sheer terror of being attacked repeatedly by the vicious animal. The dog was removed from the neighborhood shortly thereafter, but the memory lingered. She was almost seventy at the time. The incident was a turning point in my mother's life. She was entering old age.

Ann and I lived in my mother's building next door to her. Ann had gotten a job as a social worker at the veteran's hospital and adapted to Alberta quickly, to the point where she had become more of a loyal Westerner than I was. Ultimately I became a partner at Biamonte, Cairo & Shortreed, where I stayed for five years.

In 1982 Ann informed us that she was pregnant and would be delivering in October. While I was pleasantly surprised, I calmly reflected on how this development would change our lives. I also was completely disoriented, as I had no idea what to expect.

Remember the classic *I Love Lucy* episode where Lucy is picking up pastries as they're coming down a conveyer belt, but she's having trouble with the increasing speed of the flow of the pastries? Well, I had a bit of a sense that our lives were heading into that kind of territory. Could we handle the increased pace that would be demanded?

My mother, on the other hand, was ecstatic. We shared the news with Ann's parents and my aunt and uncle, who were all very pleased to hear it.

Following Mark's birth, my mother became an indispensable asset by looking after him, particularly when we needed to go out in the evenings. She would cook for him, play with him, read to him, or tell him stories from her life. She had a painted wooden apple that could be opened to find smaller wooden apples inside in the same way as a stacking doll. They would play with the apples together.

We traveled down to Los Angeles with Mark so that my aunt and uncle would get to know him. As grumpy as my uncle still was, he couldn't help but like Mark. My uncle kept warning Mark not to bump his head on the edge of the table as Mark kept walking into it as he tried to hide. To see Mark was to see the future and to gain a sense of perspective on our own lives—how fulfilling the coming years could be and how they were rushing by.

Relentless Rain

In the summer of 1985, Edmonton experienced a series of heavy downpours that flooded the basements of many houses including the duplex where my mother and Ann and I were living. Both of our basements were full of water, and we had to work hard, with buckets in hand. Eventually we installed a pump to clear out the water.

While we were able to take this in stride, my mother was very alarmed. At one point she falsely accused our neighbor of purposefully redirecting water from her yard into ours. She was exhibiting the first signs of a decline in her mental ability to process information objectively. It became clear that a chapter in our lives was closing. She could no longer cope with all the responsibilities of a life in a house with a yard.

Eventually my mother moved into a condo on 116th Street, while Ann and I bought a house in the west end of Edmonton. While this helped distance us from her day-to-day problems somewhat, it was also a source of worry for me. My mother was living by herself in a condo. If there were ever any problem, such as a fire, given her hearing impairment, she would not possibly know of it until it would be too late.

She couldn't answer the door when someone knocked. On the other hand, it was unsafe to leave the door unlocked for someone to be able to enter to alert her, particularly at night. Even though we spoke to her neighbors about the problem, we couldn't expect them to completely assume responsibility for her well-being.

Time and again I'd show up on her doorstep only to realize I had forgotten to take the key to her condo. Because she couldn't hear me knocking, I'd have to return home to retrieve the key.

I hired an electrician to install flashing lights to alert her that someone was at the door as well as special telephone equipment so she could see when it was ringing and could better hear what was said, but none of this seemed to work for her. She was so finicky that even slight hardships with any device would result in her refusal to use it. For example once she tried a hearing aid that was embedded into a pair of glasses she would don when visitors came to see her. The hearing aid emitted a high-pitched screeching sound when she turned up the volume too high. Just how badly her hearing was impaired was revealed by the fact that her guests often could hear the sound even if she didn't. Soon she moved on, always in search of another device that would open up the world of sound to her, but never with any success. The one item that worked for us was a fax machine I installed at her place so that I could fax messages to her that she could read. Otherwise, however, I realized that we simply couldn't protect her from every hazard; I often sat up at night thinking about her, wondering how she was coping.

A Malady Even a Million Dollars Couldn't Cure

Whenever my mother did have trouble, she would phone us to let us know. Sometimes it would be just to complain about the pain of arthritis in her knees. Other times we'd have to rush over to deal with some other challenge. To alleviate her loneliness and to help bring some happiness into her life, we'd bring her to our house on festive occasions such as Christmas or Easter. Sometimes she'd make supper for us. Occasionally we went on picnics and to other social gatherings with her. She was able to keep up with the latest news by reading newspapers or watching television with the captioned headlines streaming across the screen.

It was around this time that my mother began to especially suffer from tinnitus, an illness involving a roaring in the ears.

The symptom is something like the unbearably loud sound of an incoming tide on a seashore; the relentless surf never subsides.

Tinnitus is the same illness that plagued the famous painter Vincent van Gogh to the point where he chopped off one of his ears. Barbra Streisand, the famous singer, also was troubled by the illness to the point where she offered a million dollars to anyone who could come up with a cure for her. My mother's tinnitus was particularly nasty. She had suffered from it all of her life, but now the roaring was getting louder. And it was incurable.

My mother would call us and complain that the neighbor below was playing his stereo so loudly in the middle of the night that it was waking her up. At first we took her complaints at face value and knocked on the neighbor's door to ask him to turn down the volume. The neighbor insisted he wasn't playing his stereo at all. After numerous and repeated complaints from my mother, I tried to investigate further and ultimately reported that the neighbor downstairs hadn't been responsible since he wasn't even home when the complaints arose. We then investigated other neighbors in the building and reached the same conclusion again and again. No matter what we did, my mother refused to accept that it was her tinnitus and not some neighbor causing the problem. One night it got so bad that when we arrived at the condo we found my mother sleeping outside, under the concrete steps at the front of the building, in order to avoid the noise she had complained about.

While we attended tinnitus meetings at the Glenrose Hospital and tried various natural homeopathic remedies, the problem never really went away. One small insight was that it seemed to be worse when her blood pressure was high. Avoiding salt and anything else affecting high blood pressure was a must. Meanwhile we all just had to learn to live with the problem.

Natalie

On July 29, 1986, Ann was hooked up to a fetal monitor at the University of Alberta Hospital. Our second baby, several days past her expected birth date, had decided today was the day. The first evidence of birth came in the form of a heartbeat and a red dot on the monitor that kept going on and off as the child's heart beat.

Ann was wheeled into the OR, and I was dressed with surgical clothing so I could join her. Ann didn't suffer from any hemorrhaging this time and managed the birth mostly on her own. Still there were a few delicate moments during the process.

I guess fathers naturally identify with daughters more closely than with sons, as Natalie's birth had more of an impact on me than Mark's. I guess it was simply different; I now had a baby daughter! Ann said to me from the delivery table, "It's a girl, Andriy!"

As I held my newborn daughter in my arms, she looked at me with her beautiful dark eyes. Like all newborns she came out a whitish-blue color until the oxygen in her lungs could turn the blood red.

I noticed Natalie had some birthmarks on her leg and some peach fuzz on her head and forehead. The doctor told me not to worry; fuzz was natural and would disappear in a day or so. As for the birthmarks, even though they would remain, I was happy that they were only the size of a couple of quarters and were on her legs and not elsewhere. No problem. God had blessed us with a second healthy baby! We had a "million-dollar family"—first a boy, then a baby girl. Everyone was healthy. What more could we ask for?

Me with my wife Ann, son Mark, and daughter Natalie in Edmonton in 1988

Recovering from Whatever Came Her Way

One early morning my mother called me in distress, saying she was dizzy and needed my help. I rushed over. She had been sick most of the night, vomiting every five or ten minutes. She waited as long as she could before calling me, hoping to spare me any lack of sleep. I rushed her to the hospital, where she underwent a battery of tests and was given Gravol to settle her stomach. This seemed to calm her enough that I could leave her side to go to work.

When I returned that evening, the doctors told me she had suffered a mini stroke. She would be fine but had to spend about a week in the hospital. Miraculously there were no significant side effects, and she seemed to recover completely. She was a remarkably resilient woman.

On other occasions she broke, respectively, her knee, some ribs and later a shoulder bone. With each mishap somehow she recovered without much trouble or much of an enduring setback.

In April 1988, however, we encountered another troubling symptom. My mother delicately complained to me that her urine was coming out blue in color. When I visited her shortly thereafter, she further confided in me, took me to the washroom, and then showed me the toilet bowl. Alarmed and perplexed, I took her to visit her doctor. After a cursory examination, he asked her for a urine sample. Two hours went by. Finally, when she produced a sample, the color was, well, the normal color of urine. That's when the doctor asked my mother whether she used a toilet bowl cleaner with a blue dye. We left totally embarrassed!

My mother sometimes asked me to take her shopping. On one occasion, while we were at her local Safeway store, she asked a saleswoman where she could find the "peeted prooness." I thought, *Peeted prooness? Peeted prooness? What the heck are peeted prooness?* Then she added, "Sunshine peeted prooness." *Ah,* I thought, *Sunshine Pitted Prunes!*

During these years my mother established a remarkable record as a donor to various charitable causes. Apart from the church and various Ukrainian community causes, she regularly donated to the Red Cross, the Heart and Lung Foundation, and the Canadian Cancer Society, to name just a few. A particularly notable event was a prominent story about her that was published in the University of Alberta Hospital's Annual Report that recognized her for her financial support.

Meanwhile, by 1990 my aunt, on the other hand, was preoccupied with only one cause, namely, serving as my uncle's dedicated caregiver. By now she had lost all but Emil's physical companionship to Alzheimer's. Food, clothing, and toiletry—she did it all. I felt she was too dedicated or too stubborn to allow me to get her extra help. She did all of this while my uncle's life hung by a thread.

Crisis Management

My mother was both a source of great stress in my life and some happiness. She was suffering from two acute problems: her ongoing tinnitus in her ears and her arthritis pain in her legs. By this time she was so unstable and so dependent on me that I found it nearly impossible to plan my life from day to day.

I never knew when I could take a vacation or when she would need me. Her health was always so variable. I would see her about twice a week, usually taking her on an outing. We'd go shopping to Safeway on Saturdays. Despite these short trips, my attention, and my visits, I still worried every time the phone rang. I wondered whether it was her calling about a crisis. Ann and I had to lead our lives as best we could, taking risks as they came, trying to live as normal lives as possible under the circumstances.

Ukraine Is Free

While on a trip to Radium Hot Springs and Banff in the Rocky Mountains of Alberta on August 24, 1991, Ann and I turned on the television at our hotel to learn that the Verchovna Rada, Ukraine's parliament, had declared independence. It was the most anti-climactic and surreal moment in our lives. On the one hand, I wanted to leap for joy. After all this was the moment my family and I had been waiting for. On the other hand, I couldn't understand how this had happened and why leaders of the communist party of Ukraine suddenly wanted a free Ukrainian state. It certainly wasn't the way I imagined the Soviet Union would dissolve.

In the weeks that followed, matters clarified themselves.

The result was a "free and independent Ukraine," but one in which the leadership hadn't yet been freely elected by its people. That would come several years later. As my mother pointed out many times, "Ukraine is not some country out there," Pointing to her heart, she continued, "Ukraine is here." But now I could tell her it was also out there, for the world to see.

A Real Playhouse

On the eve of Natalie's sixth birthday, August 4, 1992, I told my mother I would be building our daughter a playhouse. She nearly went into a frenzy about it, arguing that it wasn't needed, that it would cost too much, and that a swing would do just as well. I held my ground, and despite her ranting, the next morning I went to pick my mother up so she could participate in our daughter's big day.

Initially she was somewhat standoffish. Building the play-house took a lot of work, and through the whole process, as my mother looked on, she criticized each step, reminding me that I wasn't much of a house builder. I shouldn't be wasting good wood on such things, she said. After a while she decided to leave me alone to finish the job.

About five feet tall, the playhouse had a shiny red roof, white walls, and even a door and windows that a child could climb through. When my mother returned to the backyard and saw my construction, she seemed genuinely impressed and actually gushed with delight, complimenting me on how nice it looked. The whole experience was personally very rewarding for me. Even when my mother was protesting, she remained engaged in the process and in her own way helped me here and there. Then her enchantment with the playhouse at the end became warm. Most important she spent the day with us.

That evening we had friends over, and we watched with great pleasure as all the children played inside and around the house—going in through the door and crawling out through the windows. Later they opened presents, ate supper, and demol-ished a birthday cake, while the adults sat by, looking on, talk-ing, eating, and listening to music.

Tickets on the Piano

Friday, October 2, 1992 is a day I doubt I will ever forget. It started out innocently enough. I went to the office and completed some last-minute duties before leaving at 2:00 p.m. to pick up my mother and travel to the airport. The plan was that I would attend my twenty year law class reunion in Vancouver while she would visit some friends she hadn't seen for ten years after moving to Edmonton.

My mother was waiting at the entrance to her apartment building as I pulled up shortly after 2:00 p.m. As we were driving to the airport, she reminded me of our standard joke, which we told whenever we traveled anywhere; it's about a family of five at the airport, with the children running around. The wife is trying to calm them down, and the husband is lamenting the fact that they didn't bring the piano with them. The wife, overhearing him talking about the piano, turns to him and asks, "What are you, crazy? Here we are trying to catch this flight, the kids are out of control, and you're talking about our piano?" He says, "Yes, because I forgot our tickets on the piano."

Just as my mother told me that joke, a sinking feeling overwhelmed me. I frantically looked for my binder with our tickets. I like to think of myself as being very disciplined and organized, so it came as a real shock that I had forgotten our tickets at the office. We were going to miss our flight, and I was about to miss an event that happens just once every twenty years.

We debated what to do next. My mother encouraged me to call the office to check whether the tickets were there. I felt too embarrassed to call and said I would just drive there, grab the binder, and then see what could be done about finding another flight.

Over my mother's protests, we headed back to Edmonton. I tested my minivan's reliability to the maximum in a frantic attempt to get back to the airport in time for another flight, which, hopefully, if available, would get us there in time for the big event. As any self-respecting mother who is eighty-one years old would do, my mother reminded me of my shortcomings and concluded that my forgetfulness was directly related to my failure to listen to her over the years.

If it were anyone else, I wouldn't have taken such a berating. But my mother? Hey, she was entitled. I would have to grin and bear it!

Back at the office, my staff leapt into action. They noticed I had left my tickets behind. Panic! They contacted taxis, couriers, and the airline, and through a superb effort, they managed to get our courier service to deliver my tickets to the airline ticket counter in time for me to catch my original flight. That's when I showed up at the office!

Again a discussion ensued. I instructed my staff to get on the phone, tell the airline that I was on my way, and make arrangements for us to catch the next flight. Meanwhile I hopped back into my van and, remembering to take my mother with me, once again headed for the airport.

Guess what we talked about along the way? If it had been anyone else, I wouldn't have taken the comments as kindly. But it was my mother, and she was eighty-one. Hey, she was entitled! Besides, it was true! If I had just listened to her back at the airport, we wouldn't have had this problem.

We were speeding to the airport. I was going as fast as I could safely go, but we needed gas. I pulled in to a station and bought $10 worth. I felt my blood pressure rising as I kept looking at my watch. I could hardly wait for the gas to get into the tank. We headed out while the service station attendant was still wiping our windows and wondering, *Why the hurry?*

While we were driving down the highway, a huge transparent plastic bag, about ten feet high and twenty feet wide (no kidding!), came out of nowhere, drifted across the road as it was blown by the wind, and came to rest immediately in front of us. I made an instant strategic decision to drive right through it. As I did, the bag collapsed but then latched on to my back fender. It trailed us for about five miles, flittering wildly in the wind behind the van. There was simply no time to stop.

We pulled into the airport. The tickets were there. A new reservation got us into Vancouver with plenty of time to spare. I attended my reunion. My mother saw her friends. Praise God! But I hope I don't ever have to relive an experience like that again.

Memory Loss

A few weeks later, my mother telephoned. It was clear that she had been crying, so I went over to comfort her. I could see that loneliness was wearing her down. Now I noticed a new, more serious problem—memory loss. She showed me some letters she had started to write that didn't make sense. In one she mistakenly addressed the letter to herself. "Dear Salomea," she wrote.

All the while her tinnitus was worsening. It seemed related to her loneliness; the longer she was alone, the more her suffering intensified. She renewed her complaint that the people downstairs were playing their "videos," saying she could hear them "even right now." "It is so loud," she said. Again I went downstairs and listened at the tenant's door. There was nothing but silence. I assured her the problem wasn't the neighbors but rather her tinnitus. She said she would be willing to move to a senior's lodge, but she'd only go if she could be guaranteed that there was no noise there. In good conscience I could not promise her that.

Conflict Between Sisters

My mother's relationship with Helen also had changed over the years. They had grown up together, and clearly she loved her sister. Traveling to Los Angeles to visit Helen provided my mother a nice break, and because there was a kind of majesty in air travel back then, it also provided a feeling of dignity and stature. As such it was one of the few luxuries my mother fondly enjoyed.

On the other hand, their rivalry had graduated to upper levels. My mother was convinced that her role in L.A. was to clean her sister's house. Her worthiness as a guest, and indeed as a decent person, depended in her eyes on cleaning and organizing my aunt's house. This subservience often irritated my aunt, who was almost oblivious to the state and appearance of the abode.

"Stop cleaning," Aunt Helen would shout out. "Leave everything the way it is and come over here." She would then seize on anything she could think of as a way to preoccupy my mother. "Here, sit down beside me, and let's watch some television."

My mother would ignore her and keep cleaning. "How can you live in a barn like this?" she'd respond. It was true that increasingly my aunt's house was descending into anarchy as she aged. Yet my mother's fixation on cleanliness in her sister's house was over the top. As the years passed, regretfully, more conflict like this arose between them.

Three Generations Visit Europe

Early in spring 1994, my mother announced her desire to travel back to Eastern Europe. It had been twenty years since she had been there, and she wanted to visit her father's grave and see Ukraine, the land of her birth, once more. The problem was that I had already set my vacation plans with Ann. We were looking forward to a trip to the East Coast of the United States and a visit to Washington, DC.

Now, anyone who has been to my office knows that although I have a fair amount of independence as a lawyer, that doesn't mean I can close down my practice whenever I feel like it. On the other hand, my mother was now eighty-three years old, and there weren't that many years left for us to make such a significant trip together.

As we talked about it, I thought that if I were to go on this trip with her, I also should take my eleven-year-old son Mark with us. It would be a fantastic experience for him as well. In the end I decided that even though it would take a crowbar to pry me away from my law practice for that long, I would do it. My mother, my son, and I would go immediately after our family returned from our American journey.

So on Friday, August 12, 1994, shortly after our family returned from a beautiful vacation to the East Coast, my mother, my son, and I boarded an airplane headed for Europe. Our first stop was Paris.

What a phenomenal impact Paris made on us. For my son it was the first time he was visiting a non-English-speaking country. The culture shock hit him on the Metro. Suddenly we were immersed in the French language; children with their parents singing songs especially caught our attention. At St. Michel Station, we enjoyed a café au lait at one of the outside venues. We had a crepe then went on to see the Eiffel Tower.

As we approached the tower, we discussed going to the very top. My mother objected about the cost. "We can just as easily see it from down here," she said. I countered that since we already had traveled some five thousand miles to see the tower, whatever the cost we had to go to the top! Reluctantly she agreed.

As we traveled up the elevator, the majesty of the Eiffel Tower began to make its impact on us. The silence, peacefulness, beauty, and the aerial view of this great European city is an experience you don't want to miss. Happily we all agreed it was one of the highlights of our entire trip.

Visiting Back Home

In Cracow we drove to a cemetery at Novy Sacz, where, at the end of World War II, my mother's father was buried. We couldn't remember the exact spot of the grave, and an eerie feeling descended upon us as we searched for the site. There was a silence and a stillness within the cemetery. In the background we heard the faint cawing of crows. We had only an old photograph of my grandfather's gravesite to guide us. It included a birch tree and a cross as well as the tomb itself. A friend of my mother's who had been there once before had given it to her.

We searched for a birch tree, then we spotted the cross, and then we found the tombstone.

We sat by the grave for some time while my mother once again related how her entire family had escaped war-torn Ukraine as refugees, initially thinking this would be a temporary relocation but eventually realizing they never would return to their native lands. She recounted how the NKVD, the Soviet secret police, had killed her brother and how she and her sister had fled. She related how her father had caught tuberculosis and how she and Helen had to leave their father and mother behind—here in Novy Sacz. The hope was he would get better and then follow to join his daughters.

She talked about how she had passed a train in the station where freight cars full of prisoners—mostly Jews—awaited further transportation to the death camps. She said she was afraid to look because she knew that one glance in the wrong direction could result in her own arrest. She said her father had died because the doctors did not have penicillin and that her mother had to bury him here, in this grave. The silent backdrop and stillness seemed almost purposefully arranged for this occasion. My son videotaped everything.

Me, my mother, and my son Mark in Novy Sacz, Poland, next to the gravesite of Salomea's father, Julian Drozdowsky, in 1994

In Ukraine we visited with old friends and relatives. We stayed at a sanatorium and drank mineral waters that were supposedly good for internal ailments of all sorts. We visited Drohobych, my mother's hometown, and she showed us where she had lived. "This is the way I walked to school. Here is where we went on sleigh rides, and here is where we promenaded when a boy asked me out," she said.

She showed us her church, where the parish priest had come out of the confessional to scold her for not properly preparing her first confession. And she described how that experience had marred her spiritual life from that day forward.

We met eighty-year-old Ivanka Markovska again, and my son and I watched as they shared fond sweet memories of their youth. Words cannot describe the impact this voyage made on my son and me. We were deeply moved.

I was able to spend about six weeks that summer with my family. Yes, it was expensive, and at times I thought my law practice would completely fall apart. On the other hand, that was a critical time both in Mark's life and my mother's. I knew that these days, once past, would be gone forever. When I came back to my office, I did face some tough times, but somehow I survived. The doom I feared never quite materialized, but the memories we shared that summer will last a lifetime.

Family Setbacks and Advances

On October 26, 1994, at three o'clock in the afternoon, my uncle Emil, then ninety-five years old, died at his home in the arms of his wife. Later that day Aunt Helen called to request that we come down to help make the funeral arrangements.

When we buried Emil, I gave the eulogy. I wept at his grave, as did we all. As much as he made my life difficult when I was young, I was happy to have been able to overcome those experiences with him and to have our relationship mature into a tender and satisfying one.

I can't say I always loved him, but I'm so grateful to him for his sharing his life story with me during our breakfasts together and whenever I asked him about historical events, for the care and comfort he provided Aunt Helen, for setting an example of how to be organized, for showing me etiquette and manners at the dinner table, for sharing an occasional funny anecdote while entertaining company, and most significantly, for being big enough to open up his heart to me in his later years. I realize now that no matter how bad certain moments in our lives together may have been, he was part of my family, and it was part of the divine plan for me to make the best of what I had with him.

Sharing Songs

Sometime during this period, I started to write out the words to songs. I played the songs at full blast on my audiocassette player and got my mother to listen to them through earphones while I pointed to the words. These were moments of great bliss for her, as for the first time, she understood what was being sung as well as how it sounded, albeit barely. But much to my disappointment, she would soon become finicky and then refuse to participate any longer.

If I had to venture a guess as to why she turned away, it was that the momentary revelation of the world of sound only served to remind her of how much her life was missing; having experienced heaven, one does not wish to leave it.

The Lure of Los Angeles

Los Angeles seems to be the only city in North America where you can get up in the middle of the night and find a place to shop for groceries or obtain other services and see people parading around in their pajamas. In Los Angeles there's always somewhere to go. So despite my dreary earlier experiences in Los Angeles, over time I developed a liking for the city.

Since our family discussions raised the prospect of moving everyone there, I began to dream about practicing law in California. I decided to try to qualify, and in July 1996, I took the state bar examinations. They took three days to complete; it was murder. Trying to keep on top of all the events in my life—my family in Canada, the law practice in Edmonton, my Aunt Helen in Los Angeles, and studying for the exams—was a particularly nerve-racking combination of challenges. I had to take a three-month refresher course to prepare for the exams while shuttling back and forth to Edmonton to keep up with things there. For three months my schedule was planned out by the hour. But my determination, as well as my understanding family, helped me to get across that finish line.

Chapter 6
Voices from the Past

6

Unfinished Portraits

ON THE NIGHT of March 29, 1995, my mother phoned me in a rage. She hurled a pile of insults at me for publishing aspects of her personal life. Earlier that evening, I had gone with Natalie to proudly present her with a copy of my newly published book, *A Source of Inspiration: Portraits of Courage, Triumph, and Achievement.* The book included some inspirational material about other people but also details about our lives as outlined in this book up to this point. A few years earlier, I had shown my mother a draft and had asked her to read it. She seemed to be fine with my portrayal of her life and mine.

But now in her rage, she claimed these were private matters that no one needed to know except her. She was furious that I would share with the world the story of her hardships about first coming to Canada, saying I could talk about my life but had no right to talk about hers.

The following evening I went to see her. She was still livid about what I had done. She demanded that I destroy all the books and offered to pay for the whole batch to be shredded. In her anger she recounted some of the early events of her arrival to Canada. She spoke of the invitation from my father (whom she referred to only as "that man who sponsored me" without mentioning him by name). The offer had come to her because a lawyer named Lazarowich in Edmonton earned his living by getting Ukrainian Canadians to fill out support affidavits like the one she had received. It was Lazarowich who had helped my father send her the affidavit.

She recounted that when she received permission to leave for Canada others in the camp warned her that she had to con- duct herself "properly" in Canada and told her to be compliant and not do anything that would jeopardize the prospects for others who also aspired to immigrate there.

She recalled how my father had followed her to Edmonton after she had fled from him and that a widow who had met her at Lazarowich's office found her a place to stay; that a man named Zhmurko, who later became a lifelong friend, paid for her stay in a hotel; that the widow arranged for her to stay at the Beulah Home for unwed mothers; that the widow had faced violence herself from her husband when he would come home, and she had to hide under her bed to escape his attacks while worrying about her children, particularly her older daughter, who was going out with boys the widow didn't like and so on.

The book had stirred all of these deep and sad emotions in my mother again after having long been forgotten. She also was concerned about how this book would be received by the public. She was worried in particular what her close friends— Reverend Tarnawsky, Adolf Hladylovych, and Maria Keyvan as well as others—would think about her life. She perceived what I wrote about her not as being heroic, but as demeaning, even if I had characterized it as heroic. Most important, although she had read the very same lines two years earlier without major objections, now she could not bear them. She felt betrayed.

I could see that the book was causing her such unrelenting pain that I agreed to retract it. It never had been my aim to harm or disturb my mother in this way. And although I recognized that this story was as much my story as it was hers, I owed her the decency of protecting her feelings and her dignity—at least for as long as she lived.

I believe history will judge her to have been a heroine, one who endured great hardships with courage, even style. She had been physically beaten but remained silent so as not to jeopardize chances for others to immigrate. For the time being, I realized I must respect her wishes to keep these matters private.

As a result I had a book that I couldn't distribute. I had an audiotape that was already selling and that I would have to retract. I would later learn that there were chapters in my mother's life that I had still to learn about and that there would be a time someday when I could share them so that others could learn. That night, while driving home I wept because she didn't see that in my eyes she was so sacred. She didn't see that my attempt to share our joint story was the highest compliment I could pay her. Instead she reacted to my book with shame and guilt about what had happened. I didn't realize at that moment that I was far from knowing the whole story. I also made a silent promise to her that night that, as long as she was alive, her story—and therefore also mine—would remain private and not to be shared with anyone.

Searching for My Father

I already mentioned that for fifty years my mother refused to allow my father's name to even cross her lips. Despite the discomfort she felt about the topic, as she aged before my eyes, bit by bit I pushed on, asking her about him before it was too late. Finally one night she blurted out my father's given name, Jakym. A day or two later, again after my urging, she offered up his surname, Holowka.[37] Then came the fact that her first home with him had been in Park Court, Alberta. I tried to find his name in the phonebook but without success. I then pestered her to go with me to Park Court to see where she had lived.

One evening I simply sent her a fax saying I would come by in the morning to pick her up. We would be going to Park Court. On March 31, 1997, very early in the morning, I picked up my mother. Surprisingly she was dressed and ready for our trip when I arrived.

Natalie came along, and we traveled to Evansburg, past Seba Beach, on Highway 16, west of Edmonton, for about sixty miles. There we asked for directions and made our way some nine miles north to the Park Court community hall. We passed a house on our right, and my mother suggested we go back to ask for instructions.

When we drove into the yard, no one came out. I went up to the house to knock on the door, and a lady answered it. Her name was Nina Stepaniuk, and she spoke Ukrainian. I asked her whether she knew where a man named Holowka had lived many years ago. She said no, she did not, but that we could go to the general store just to the east to ask there. I thanked her and made my way back to the van when she noticed my mother. She said she wanted to talk to her.

When my mother came out, she asked Nina how long she had lived there. Nina said they had bought the house in 1953 from a man named Jake Holonko. "Jake Holonko" and "Jakym Holowka" were so close that it had to be the same person! Years later I finally figured out the difference in the names. I believe that Jake's Ukrainian name was Holowka but that he Anglicized it when he came to Canada, turning it into Holonko. At any rate, back then the name Jake tipped me off. I asked more about him, and she said he had six children. She added that he had sold the farm and moved to Vancouver.

I sensed this had been my father's place once, but my mother had her doubts. I asked Nina about the old house, and Nina pointed to an old structure in back. My mother didn't recognize it. However, we took a walk out back, and once we entered the old house, she knew it to be the house where she once had lived. A look of sudden recognition crossed over her face. "Yes," she said. "This is it. This is where we lived." She soberly looked through the house then left. Whatever emotions the place elicited were still frozen deep inside her.

Nina said my father and some of the children had visited after the sale of the farm in 1953. The price had been $6,500 for the quarter section. She named the children:

My mother and me in Park Court, Alberta in the early 2000s standing in front of the farm house where she first lived in Canada back in 1948.

Paul, Walter, Lydia, Mary, Jean, and one other whose name eluded her. She mentioned that the mother had died suddenly and that the youngest child had been sent to Barrhead to relatives who looked after her. Nina said Paul lived in Edmonton, but she had lost track of the others. Meanwhile, after all of Jake's children had left him for the city, he finally decided to sell off the farm in Park Court and move to Vancouver himself in 1953. He bought a rooming house, and from that time forward, his life changed for the better. He often lamented that he hadn't left the farm earlier and commented on the easier life in the city. Remarkably, there he could find fruit hanging freely on his trees.

When we returned home, I called the operator to get the phone number for Paul Holonko. Obviously my previous attempts to search out my father were unsuccessful because I had been looking for the wrong surname. There was no listing in Edmonton. I then called Vancouver information.

They had two Holonkos. One was Walter Holonko; the other was J. Holonko. I called the latter and asked the woman who answered if she knew how I could get in touch with Jake Holonko. She said there was no one by that name there. I asked if she might know someone who could help me track him down. She said she didn't know any Jake Holonko, except for Grandpa, who had died in 1992 at age ninety-two. That was him. She gave me a phone number for a woman named Lydia, who was Jake Holonko's daughter.

I called there, but the line was busy. Meanwhile I had Walter Holonko's number. I called Walter and asked if he was related to Jake Holonko. Walter said yes. I told him I would like to know where Jake was buried, and he said the grave was at Forest

Lawn Cemetery in Burnaby. I told Walter I believed I was Jake's son. He said if I ever came to Vancouver to call him, and he would show me the gravesite himself. He added that two of the children had died the previous year, Jean and Paul. The other children were still alive.

Accusations of Betrayal

That September I traveled with my mother to Vancouver for a weekend visit. As Walter Holonko and I had agreed over the phone on the evening before our meeting, I had arranged to meet him at my father's grave that Saturday.

I didn't know what to say to my mother about the cemetery meeting. I told her that evening I would need a few hours in the morning to meet with someone named Walter, but she didn't realize I was meeting with Jake's son. Still she knew that a part of our visit would touch on my biological father. She asked if I intended to visit his gravesite, and I said I did.

Finally, after some reflection, I resolved to let her know the night before what I planned to do. She didn't take it well. As a matter of fact, she denounced me for what I was about to do. For a few moments, she seethed in her emotional turbulence. But when she calmed down, she said she would go with me because she wanted to pay her respects to the man who had brought her to Canada.

She warned me, however, that she would have nothing to do with Walter and would not speak to him. But she softened her position on this matter soon after.

When I had arranged to meet Walter Holonko over the phone, I didn't tell him that my mother would be coming. We agreed to meet at the cemetery after Walter gave me directions. While my mother waited in the car, she sent me to the cemetery's office to inquire about the grave of a friend of hers named Maria Huculak, who recently had passed away in Vancouver.

Fortuitously the woman who greeted me in the office had made all of the arrangements for the deceased buried there and was able to tell me where the new grave was located. I was on my way back to the car when Walter pulled up in his half-ton pickup truck. I walked over to greet him, and as I did, his two sisters arrived. They all greeted me warmly while my mother watched through the car window. We spoke briefly about our meeting and agreed to take our vehicles to the gravesite, since it was too far to walk.

As I got into our car, my mother again burst into a fit of rage, denouncing me for "setting her up." How dare I reunite her with those whom she had long ago blocked from her life! Why was I tormenting her, pouring salt into wounds freshly opened in this way? She called me "stupid" and vented at me as we drove the short distance to the grave. I sought to console her and pointed out that what had happened was now fifty-year-old history. I made it clear that I didn't know that the sisters were coming. I fully expected her to lash out at them, but she managed to calm herself.

I couldn't believe the turbulence of emotions this incident was eliciting. It was as if emotions that had been frozen for decades were suddenly emerging as the barriers my mother had erected all those years ago were coming down.

When we arrived she did speak to them through the open window of the car, saying that their father had not treated her well and that this was very painful for her. Mary and Anne, the two sisters, tried to console her. I got out of the car, and my mother remained. We stood there, at the gravesite, where Jake Holonko, my natural father, and Jean Holonko, his daughter, and Paul Holonko, his son, were buried. We talked about his family, which was large, both here and in Ukraine. Now the family had found one more member, and I related the story of how I had come to know of them.

We hugged and expressed familial sentiments. I learned that my father had more than forty grandchildren and great grandchildren. Today I am "Uncle Andy" to many Holonko kids.

Raw Emotions Explode

My mother sat in the car, her emotions raw. I explained to the Holonkos how difficult a moment this was for her, and when once again they spoke through the window, my mother said she would approach the grave on her own once they were gone.

We exchanged addresses. I gave them a copy of Mark's book (my son had written a joke book called *401 Goofy Jokes for Kids*) and some newsletters. We agreed we would meet again as a family, and then they drove away.

Wave after wave of uncontrollable emotions overcame my mother. She even cursed me. And for the first time in our life together, she declared that she would be leaving to go live on her own, even if she had to go on welfare. She said she wanted nothing more to do with me.

Why did I persist in opening wounds long since healed? Had she not given me a good education and a great start in life?

Was there something wrong with concluding our lives as they were? Why dredge up all of these painful experiences? She felt ashamed, full of guilt about what had happened. She walked off, leaving me alone, and I sensed the need to let her go off by herself for a while.

As she got out of the car and walked off, I tried to make sense of her emotional reactions. As best as I could make out, my father had gotten her pregnant, perhaps only with her reluctant consent. He desperately needed a wife to help him look after his six children. He may have thought that by getting her pregnant she would have to stay.

My mother also may have felt a profound sense of guilt. The guilt would have come from the fact that although my father had paid for her to come to Canada and to marry him, she had refused to complete the implied bargain. Since money was very scarce and my father's first wife had died suddenly, my mother felt guilty that he had spent money on her instead of feeding and clothing his six children. She also felt guilty for having me in these circumstances. As far as she was concerned, she had cut these people out of our lives forever, and they now symbolized bygone pain for her.

For me to contact them was to cross over into a zone forever sealed off from her life, bringing back to her all of the remorse, guilt, and pain that period had evoked. More than this, she spoke of her conscience and her deeds—of which she was not proud but which she did not define explicitly. She spoke in clipped, staccato, abbreviated sentences of her darkest moments, when life had been far from easy. I sensed I had reached a wall between us. Suddenly I broke from my thoughts to realize I had lost her. She had left me, wandering off, distraught in this cemetery, of all places.

In Search of My Mother

I drove around in the cemetery; I thought I might never find her again. Then I saw her sitting on some steps. I approached her, and she sank into dejection. "All I need is a bullet through my head," she screamed. "How could you do this to me? How could you embrace these people?" Her words rang with disgust and humiliation. She saw my embraces and conversation with these individuals as the ultimate insult. She called me a Judas. I had betrayed her, and she declared she was disowning me and signing her estate over to someone else.

After some time I managed to calm her down enough to get her back into the car. Until that moment I sincerely thought I had passed the point of no return with her. I thought I had completely severed my ties to her forever. Had I unleashed emotions so strong that they threatened to upend my mother's mental health?

Thankfully she regained her composure. We then went on to find the grave of her friend, Maria Huculak. There we prayed. Remarkably we meandered back to Jake Holonko's grave, where we prayed. I even took her picture next to it. Despite all the pain, the day also brought a little bit of closure.

Me kneeling next to the grave of my father, Jake Holonko, in Vancouver in 1997

I had a "new" family and was elated by the journey that was about to unfold. All the while, I was also aware of my mother's sentiments—aware of her warnings to stay away from them. "You don't need them," she chastised. "You have a name. You have a legacy. William Semotiuk was a good man. He is your father. They are not like us. I warn you—stay clear of them." To her they only served as reminders of a painful past and her own previous shortcomings.

My newfound family members at Jake Holonko's gravesite in Vancouver, BC. Present are his children from his first wife, Evdokia—Walter Holonko, Mary Smith, and Anne Prokopchuk—in September 1997.

What's Next?

The turbulent emotional storm seemed to die down, as if a wicked wizard had suddenly lost control over our lives and let go of his spell over us. That evening we went to Chinatown for soup and to look at the shops. I felt very close to my mother.

In reflection it seemed that I was the black sheep of the Holonko family. I still felt some apprehension about getting to know them, and it was strange walking around thinking at any moment someone could walk up to me and introduce themselves as my sister or brother. *What do you call someone born of the same parent but of another spouse, anyway?* I thought. *Is it your half-brother? Your half-sister?* Strangely I felt no overwhelming emotion for my father at his gravesite. It was my dealings with my brother and sisters that would have emotional meaning for me.

Later that evening I met up with some friends, and my mother displayed an almost childlike impatience waiting for me—a side of her I never had encountered before. When she finally saw me walking toward her, she almost broke down and cried.

When it was time to return to Edmonton and we traveled to the airport, she quietly reiterated her hopes that I would not follow up on these new contacts with my brother and sisters. But I didn't believe she herself had yet entirely settled in her mind what should happen next.

Sticky Times and Family Ties

In November 1997 I learned that I didn't pass the exam for the State Bar of California. I resolved to write them again in the summer of 1998. I was determined to make California a part of our lives, and to do so, I felt I needed to pass the exam. Passing it would make it possible for us to move to Los Angeles and keep our family close by. My plan was for all of us to move close to Aunt Helen, and thus I would be able to care for both her and my mother while pursuing my career goals.

Both my wife Ann and I have care giving as a natural part of our characters. Philosophically, therefore, we were ready to take on the roles of looking after my mother in Edmonton and my aunt in Los Angeles as they aged. From Ann's point of view, my mother had helped raise our children and had lived by our side for many years. My aunt had helped us financially by contributing to our children's education, and there was some pleasure in escaping from the cold winter nights of Edmonton by traveling to Los Angeles to see her from time to time. Besides, neither my mother nor Helen was a financial burden. So Ann naturally worked at my side to attend to our care-giving roles, and we tried not to significantly compromise our own lives and our roles as parents to our children. I was the primary caregiver, and Ann helped out when I couldn't be there.

As for the children, they felt a natural affection for both their grandmother and their great aunt. To them these women were part of our larger family.

Calling Aunt Helen

In January 1998, as Natalie recovered from a broken right knee, I made weekly telephone calls to Aunt Helen during this period to stay up to date with her. I never looked forward to these calls because they usually involved a verbal berating. She would scrutinize my actions, my lack of financial success, and my inability to move my family immediately to Los Angeles. Still these calls were my only contribution to my aunt's life apart from visits, and it was through these calls that I tried to focus her on a brighter future. I tried to bring her hope that her life and our lives would improve when we made our move to Los Angeles once everything was ready.

A Fading Dream

At the end of one Saturday, while I was with my mother on our regular weekly shopping trip, she hysterically asked me why she was still alive. She had exhibited similar bouts of depression from time to time, particularly when she got tired. I quickly drove her home. I felt that she too needed some hope in her future, and I tried to provide it. I sensed that I needed to play a positive role in my mother's life and needed to be patient to allow her to settle. While I was concerned about her hysteria, I felt confident that it would pass and that she would regain control over her emotions.

While earlier in her life she had supported the idea, now she categorically rejected any suggestion of her moving to Los Angeles to be with her sister. However, I still believed that if we were able to set up the right circumstances and to find a house near Aunt Helen's home in L.A., my mother could be persuaded.

Achievements Under Stress

On June 2, 1998, Aunt Helen attended the State Bar of California admission ceremony with me in Pasadena. We were both very proud and rightly considered this to be our joint achievement.

The following weekend in Edmonton, after celebrating Mark's graduation from Saturday morning Ukrainian school classes, Ann and I took a walk in the river valley and had a heartfelt discussion about the strain of the large debt we were carrying.

The discussion became emotional and Ann insisted that I stop embracing any new projects and that I stick to practicing law. She felt overwhelmed by our financial hardships. I acknowledged I had put her through a lot and felt guilty for doing so. She expressed regrets about our being so dependent on her work for our economic livelihood. I had to admit it was a point well taken. She said we weren't paying off our debts and not even paying them down. As we talked we felt as if we had painted ourselves into a corner by our lack of foresight and the consequent absence of financial alternatives. It was a tortured discussion, but it helped me to better face the economic realities, and even more important, it helped me better understand the toll our situation was taking on Ann and her happiness.

My thinking was that there was no need to despair and that what was needed was a position of defiance. We must not allow our debt or economic disappointments cripple our lives. We could not—and must not—succumb to a sense of hopelessness or defeat. The mere belief in our ability to overcome these challenges was in itself a victory. Although mere belief wasn't enough, however, I also promised to take actions to ensure our survival. The conversation helped to soothe some of Ann's grief and helped me to better understand the strains that she was facing and that I needed to better address.

Sticky Business

Before my mother and I left her place for our regular Saturday shopping trip in July 1998, she opened her fridge, pulled out the half-full bottle of grapefruit juice I had recommended to her the week before, and said, "Here, you take this home because I'm not going to drink it."

I thought, *What am I, some kind of garbage disposal?* But knowing how she didn't like to waste anything, I agreed to put the bottle in a plastic shopping bag and take it home. We got into the car, and I put the plastic bag on the floor on the front passenger's side where my mother was sitting. My wife had just taken my car to the carwash after complaining about how dirty it was and how I had been neglecting it.

As we were driving along, I looked down at the bag and noticed that the floor of the car was wet. I mentioned this to my mother, thinking that the car hadn't dried adequately from its cleaning. Now my mother's shoes were getting wet. As I picked up the bag, I realized it was soaked. The cap to the bottle was loose, and grapefruit juice had leaked into the bag and then on to the floor. My mother complained that I hadn't made sure the top of the bottle had been fastened properly when I removed it from the fridge. Now I had grapefruit juice all over my hands, her shoes, and the floor of my car. Everything was getting sticky.

Since the juice was partly caught in the plastic bag, I pulled my car over, got out, and emptied it out of the bag onto the road. However, as the bag crossed over my lap it dribbled juice on to my pants and all over my steering wheel. By now there was sticky juice all over the front of the car. I managed to dispose of the bulk of the leakage on the roadside. But now my mother was complaining that the car was wet. I told her we would soon be pulling over at a service station.

When we stopped I went into the men's room to clean up. I looked for some paper towels to take out to the car but found only a hand-drying machine. OK. I decided to take out some toilet paper. My mother complained about the sight of my unrolling toilet paper that everyone could see.

Normally I wouldn't take that kind of abuse, but hey, she was older and she was my mother. She didn't get much done the way she wanted it done. Her only way to change things was to complain until someone around her listened and did what she wanted. Then she was happy. This was one of those times.

I cleaned up the mess as best as I could. I soaked up the juice from the floor then threw the toilet paper away. We drove on.

Now my mother noticed that while the juice was gone, the floor was sticky. She took the bottle and said she would hold it on her lap. "No, give it to me, and I'll put it in the trunk," I replied. She said, "No. I want to hold it." We tussled over the bottle, and she finally let go. I put the bottle in the trunk, but now we both had sticky hands.

I left the bottle in the trunk and sat down to drive away again. She complained that her hands were sticky. "Fine," I said, and turned around to head back to the gas pumps. I stopped there, reached out for some paper towels, and gave her a few. Have you ever tried to wipe sticky juice off your hands with a dry paper towel?

"It's not working," she said, stating the obvious. I got out and, using a process that was probably a first in service station history, took the squeegee and washed the steering wheel with it. Unfortunately the water in the pail was filthy. I was desperate. I felt that at least I could get the juice off the steering wheel.

We finally found a McDonald's, where we cleaned up in the washrooms, and I made a mental note to take the car to a carwash for an interior cleaning before offering to drive Ann anywhere.

My Newly Discovered Family

It was impossible for me to tell my mother that I was flying to Vancouver to celebrate the sixty-fifth birthday of Alex Prokopchuk, the husband of my newly discovered sister, Anne. My mother never would have accepted this. But the fact that I also would attend a Canada Ukraine Foundation (CUF) meeting was an acceptable cover. I brought along Natalie to meet up with some of my family.

While there I met another sister for the first time, Lydia. I was deeply moved, as was Lydia, by our meeting. A wave of emotion swept through me. Meeting a sister fifty years into my life for the first time was deeply significant. The emotion of the moment was so touching that it brought Mary and Anne, my other sisters, to tears. Lydia and I also cried, punctuating the joy of it all.

Sadly I realized that I was the youngest of my siblings; time moved relentlessly forward, and there wouldn't be much time left to enjoy our newfound family ties. We resolved to make of it what we could.

Me with my newfound surviving Holonko family members in Vancouver—Lydia, Anne, Mary, and Walter—in 1998

My father with his children, from left to right: Walter, Paul standing, Jean, Lydia, Mary, and Anne sitting circa 1965

Meeting my extended family (on the Holonko side) for the first time in Vancouver, BC, in 1998

Chapter 7
The Declining Years

7

Just Coping

URING THE NEXT five years I traveled back and forth from Edmonton to Los Angeles, staying in each city for three-week intervals, to provide care and support for both my mother and my aunt while also looking after my own family and doing my work as a lawyer. Initially both seniors lived by themselves, but in time they had to be moved to nursing homes. Since I stayed with my wife and children in Edmonton, and later in an apartment near my aunt's house when I was in Los Angeles, my main interactions with my mother and aunt took place on weekends, primarily Saturdays, when we went shopping, or to the park, or to the beach. We celebrated important holidays together as best we could. Though the events in our lives moved forward like a motion picture, my memories from these five years are more like snapshots taken here and there of memorable moments we shared.

During a Christmas visit to our house in Edmonton, on January 6, 1999, my mother, who was eighty-eight years old, tripped on our stairs. We thought she would be fine and that whatever bruises she had would heal in a few days. Nothing really came of it for about a week. Then we realized we were wrong when she continued to complain.

When I got to her condo to take her to the doctor, she was unable even to stand up. I got her into the wheelchair I had brought, rolled her out to the car, then drove her to Dr. Boyko's. He concluded that she had suffered a hip fracture.

Within hours she was checked into the emergency ward at Royal Alex Hospital. The only reason I was still in town was because I had missed my flight to Los Angeles the day before. I felt grateful for that. God works in strange ways!

Eldercare on Steroids

I was fifty years old and starting from scratch in Los Angeles. In late January 1999, the law firm of Manning & Marder had hired me to work with them as an immigration attorney. The job didn't pay a salary; rather it involved sharing the revenues I generated with the law firm. My aunt was skeptical about this arrangement at first, but she agreed that at least it was a start in the direction of a family move to Los Angeles.

Staying with my eccentric aunt who was eighty-nine years old and played the TV at full volume at strange hours of the day and night was not easy. Her house resembled a bomb blast site; it was entirely in disarray, reflecting, probably, the psychological state of her inner being. Nearly every day a series of cross-examinations took place. Helen interrogated me about where I had been, whom I saw, and what I ate. My life in Los Angeles consisted of work and wrestling with my aunt over every moment of free time I had. In the morning there was a confrontation about food and about what she needed me to do immediately. In the evening it was also about food, why I had to come home so late, and what I was doing at the office that kept me there so long. She viewed me as a source of social comfort from her extreme privation that had resulted from her insistence on living in her house on her own and managing her own business affairs. Her senility was becoming more evident daily.

Meanwhile, back in Edmonton, my mother had been diagnosed with a hairline fracture of her pelvic bone as well as a broken right rib. She was moved from Royal Alexandra Hospital to the Glenrose Hospital. Fortunately, when I couldn't be there, Ann was with her. My mother ended up there for several weeks. Then, just when she got out and back to her home, she tripped and fell and injured herself again. By then, however, I was back in Edmonton.

Unfortunately, between my aunt and my mother, I had problems attending to my law practice, which was having an impact on my income and my family. I truly found my life challenging; the responsibility of taking care of two elderly people was overwhelming at times. How was I to lead my own life, care for my own family, keep my marriage intact, look after my career, and also devote myself to helping two elderly women on opposite sides of the continent? This was what you would call providing "continental care."

Sometimes I reflected on the fact that I hadn't brought in any significant income for more than a year and was debt ridden, which built a sense of guilt in me. My wife worked in a pressure-intense environment, which certainly didn't help her own state of health. It seemed as if my two kids were growing up without me. And my mother was now in her fifth week of in-hospital care with a fracture to her pelvic bone. I felt disappointed with my life and exhausted. There were times when I felt I was at the end of my rope. I scrambled as best I could, but even then there were times when I was barely able to cope with all of it. *There's only so much I can do,* I thought. *This is overwhelming. What can I do?* Yet every day I just got up and continued.

A Major Move

My mother had a hard time adapting to the move from her apartment to St. Michael's Millenium Lodge, a Ukrainian-Canadian senior's facility in Edmonton. When the move occurred in March 1999, I was in Los Angeles looking after my aunt, so Ann helped my mother through the transition. When Ann let my mother speak to me on the phone, my mother was in tears. In my conversations with her previously, I had noticed over the previous few years an emotional deterioration in her. She would complain that life hadn't treated her well. Whether during her years at home during their childhood, when compared to Aunt Helen; or in her early Canadian days with my father; or now wondering why she was living so long, sadness permeated her thinking.

On my part I was feeling the stress and the guilt associated with caring for two seniors in two cities a continent apart, both in need of my presence and my attentiveness at the same time. These feelings were particularly acute when I was in Los Angeles at a time when my mother was going through the trauma of a change in her living conditions with the help of my wife.

Although the situation wasn't perfect, by April 1999, my wife reported that my mother's life at St. Michael's Lodge was a

100-percent improvement over what she had experienced living alone in her condo. In a sense her fall and pelvic-bone fracture had been a blessing in disguise, since it forced her to move into St. Michael's. Despite the initial heartache we all felt over the move, at least life was stabilizing for my mother.

Earlier that year, my mother had realized she was beginning to lose her memory and her ability to look after her own finances. Over the course of about two months, she began to turn everything over to me. Now my wife and I were taking care of her financial affairs. I felt my mother displayed a great deal of wisdom and grace in the way she handled this transfer of her affairs. It was fortunate she had looked after this when she did, as it now made our lives much easier in terms of looking after the costs of her care.

Eldercare in Two Countries

One night in April 1999 while I was staying with her in Los Angeles, Aunt Helen woke me up at 1:30 a.m. by turning on the television full blast again. Helen, whom I had taken to the chiropractor's office at noon, slept all afternoon and evening. Now she was awake with a vengeance. As a result, when I came out to ask her to turn down the TV, she said she had finished sleeping and was totally oblivious to the fact that it was the middle of the night and that others were sleeping. It was becoming clear that she also was suffering from mental deterioration.

As incredible as it may seem, we had a neighbor directly to the back of our lot with the same sleeping and television habits. Sometimes their TVs would keep me up at night. Also, the neighbor next door to the north sometimes exhibited similar tendencies; in short we lived in a community of insomniacs, and had they ever set their television sets to the same channel, I would have heard the resulting stereo of unwanted programs in surround sound.

In late April 1999, after arriving in Edmonton and catching up with Ann, I went to visit my mother at St. Michael's Lodge. I expected a highly emotional scene, but oddly she seemed calm and accepting of her new environment. My mother was having supper in the cafeteria when I arrived.

At first we didn't recognize each other—she had aged terribly in the short time I had been away—but then our eyes met, and we greeted each other happily. My mother seemed quite set-tled in, and she had a comfortable room. While the first week of adjustment, according to Ann, had been very challenging, she now seemed to have found a home, one where she would receive around-the-clock care.

New Challenges

One of my biggest challenges occurred in the spring of 1999, when, at the same time, I got two phone calls at work in Edmonton. Line one was from the emergency ward at the Royal Alexandra Hospital, informing me that my eighty-nine-year-old mother had just been hospitalized in Edmonton. Line two was from the Kaiser Permanente emergency ward in Los Angeles, informing me that my ninety-one-year-old Aunt Helen was also hospitalized. I attended to my mother first. She had been diagnosed with a fractured pelvis from a fall; she would now need rehabilitation at Glenrose Hospital. My wife would help out with that.

Meanwhile I flew off to L.A. to attend to my aunt. Peter and Teresa Fairbrother, our next-door neighbors, related how Helen had fallen and had been too weak and helpless to get up. They had gotten her up, cleaned her up, and then asked her what she wanted to do. She said she wanted to go to the hospital. So Peter called 911.

When I got to the Kaiser emergency ward, Aunt Helen was lying in a weakened state on one of the beds. She looked up and moved her hand as a sign of recognition, but she didn't appear specially relieved or happy to see me.

I spoke to the social worker, Lee Jackson. He was a tall man who didn't strike me as particularly concerned about us and immediately asked where I was going to take Aunt Helen. Indeed, everyone in the hospital who spoke to me spoke in terms of where Helen would be going from here. The social worker gave me a list of convalescent homes and transportation facilities. The rest, he said, was up to me. He tried to be reassuring, adding that God never gives you more hardships than you can shoulder. This last comment has stayed with me ever since.

I spent the next day looking at nursing homes and decided on Elms Convalescent Home in Glendale, which seemed like both a good place and within financial reach. The transfer occurred without a hitch. I managed to get Aunt Helen's cooperation by having the hospital staff portray the move as an "investment" toward her return home. They told her she was too weak to be on her own and that since she couldn't stand up she was at risk if anything were to happen. If she would stay for a while at Elms, she would build up her strength. She accepted this.

Meanwhile I arranged for a cleaner to attend to Aunt Helen's house. The place looked like a hurricane had just blown through it. Although it was just the home of one senior and a few cats, there was a lot to do.

Each time I saw Aunt Helen at the Elms Convalescent Home, she told me she wanted to go home. Each time I in turn told her she couldn't go home because she was too weak. That was the message I left with her again the morning when I went in to tell her I had to return to Canada for a while.

My departure was awkward; I really couldn't properly prepare her for my leaving Los Angeles. I was in a rush, and she hadn't slept well because the patient in the bed next to her was suffering from discomfort. Aunt Helen called Elms a "mental ward" ("*dim varyatiw*"). But that's just the way things had to be. It meant doing what I knew was best for my loved one, even though she didn't want it and would prefer to be somewhere else. As I was leaving, she asked me what her home address was, obviously wanting to get up, take a taxi, and go there. I told her but knew she was too far gone to make it home on her own. Her neighbors, Peter and Teresa, agreed to look after the cats until I returned in a week. I told myself that this was tough love, but I also knew it was about simply coping.

Normal Lives Again?

On July 22, 2000, my mother and I were walking down the hall at St. Michael's nursing home. She fussed and refused my attempt to hold on to her arm. Waving me off instead, she held on to the back right pocket of my pants. It felt awkward, but I complied.

As we moved along, I felt a sharp tug. At first I thought she had stumbled. But in fact she fell. She cried out in pain and said she couldn't move. We brought over a wheelchair and took her to her room. The nurse couldn't tell whether she had broken any bones.

Later X-rays at Royal Alexandra Hospital revealed that my mother had broken her pelvic bone for the third time. The clean break, clearly visible on the x-ray, required surgery.

I was thankful this had happened while I was in Edmonton so I could be present. All went well, and my mother was able to return to St. Michael's in a few days. She was now eighty-nine, while my aunt was ninety-one.

That summer I arranged for Aunt Helen to return to her home from Elms Convalescent Home, but with the help of several professional caregivers. Eventually Maria Minjares, a pleasant woman originally from Peru who lived in the neighborhood and her family became Aunt Helen's twenty-four-hour caregivers. For the time being, this seemed to work. I had kept my promise. My aunt's time away from the house had been an investment in her stability and well-being.

I finally took an apartment nearby so I could cope with the challenges of looking after Aunt Helen but also be able to sleep at night and have some time to myself. Our lives seemed to return to a regular routine when I was in Los Angeles. I would look in on her a couple of times a week and take her out on various expeditions on weekends such as to Santa Monica beach or to Hollywood. This was working.

That summer our son Mark, who was eighteen years old, graduated from Archbishop MacDonald High School. We attended a big celebration. Then, after he learned he had been accepted at UCLA in Los Angeles, Ann, our daughter Natalie and I traveled by car down the West Coast to accompany him there and to set him up in the dormitory. Mark was now in college; it was hard to believe how fast time had flown by.

Transcontinental Care

Each time I left my mother at St. Micahel's Nursing Home I found it harder to bear. I didn't know which conversation would be our last. I knew that maybe this time, maybe next, she would pass on and take her legacy with her to her grave. My mother's life, my aunt's, and those of others like them were the concluding chapters of a story that would be lost to all of us.

In February 2001, while visiting my mother, I asked her to reflect back on her life and tell me something about it. She replied that it had been a life not worth living due to her hearing impairment. She said her poor hearing had affected everything. She flashed back to the time when she was with me as an infant, with no place to go and no roof over our heads. She cried out in anguish. She said I was too little to understand back then. I asked her if she cried a lot back then. She replied that she had, and now she was obviously distraught again.

I asked her what she was happiest about in her life, knowing on previous occasions that when I posed that same question to her she had answered that it was me and my birth. But this time she backed off the question, dodging it instead with a noncommittal "Nothing."

Both of us knew she had a lot in her life to be grateful for. She was, after all, in Canada. She was living in a safe and pleasant home. She had a good family and had lived a long, healthy life despite her childhood illness and hearing impairment.

When I returned to L.A. in June 2000, I went to see Aunt Helen at her home. She was frail and spoke with a weak voice. It was shocking how she was degenerating before my eyes. Her signature was a dead giveaway. Over the last couple of months, her handwriting had so deteriorated that now she could barely write. In fact she could no longer sign her name, not even to endorse a check. Also, she was unable to stand on her feet. She had to be fed because she couldn't lift her arm to feed herself.

Maria Minjares, our caregiver, said Aunt Helen was afraid of dying. She fretted from time to time, thinking she was on the edge of death. She often called out to Maria, wondering if she was about to slip away and seeking Maria's assurances that everything would be all right. Aunt Helen's estate and financial planning were as shaky as her health. I was doing what I could to set things up properly, but she would not always cooperate.

By now I was thinking she would soon need to go into a nursing home. I hoped St. John of God Retirement and Care Center, an excellent facility in the downtown Los Angeles area run by Roman Catholic Brothers, would soon come through with a place for Aunt Helen. I was glad I had taken the time to locate them a few weeks earlier. Maybe she would soon have a nice room there.

In July 2001 I went to see her around suppertime. I found her lying restlessly on her bed, nude. Maria had left her there a few hours earlier. She called me "*Mychashku*" (Emil's nickname – based on his middle name of Michael) when I called out to her as I entered the house. Clearly her care giving was not working as well as it should.

I helped her dress and wheeled her into the kitchen. I warmed some food up for her then helped feed her since she didn't have the strength to feed herself.

That week I took Aunt Helen to see Dr. James, a psychiatrist with Kaiser Permanente on Sunset Boulevard for an assessment of her healthcare needs. We arrived on time but had gone to the wrong building. By the time we found the right office, we were a half-hour late. Dr. James insisted there wasn't enough time to do a proper interview. After admonishing us for our tardiness, she agreed to see us for a few minutes but indicated we would have to return another time. Since we had waited three-and-a-half months for the appointment, I felt she could wait twenty minutes. I pointed out we were late because we hadn't been told which building to go to and that my aunt was ninety-two years old. I also said I was from Canada. Well, at least she saw us and gave us a quickly scheduled appointment the very next day.

An Uneasy Feeling

Toward the end of that first visit with Dr. James, Aunt Helen softly announced, "I need to go pooh pooh!" We said goodbye, and I quickly wheeled Aunt Helen into the woman's washroom. I didn't expect it then, but we were about to be put into a situation that would test our human dignity in the face of a terrible challenge. The worst imaginable scenario ensued.

The women's washroom was empty. I wheeled Aunt Helen to the toilet quickly, but it was too late. As I pulled her pants down with all the efficiency and decency I could muster, I tried to move her into a sitting position over the toilet seat. Before we could successfully arrive at this destination, she let go. Feces flew all over the place—on my shoes, on the floor, and all over the toilet bowl. In short, it was everywhere.

It was quite the cleanup job, and at the same time, other women were trying to enter the washroom. I waved them away, telling them it was out of order. As I worked at the cleanup, I caught myself smiling and asked myself what exactly God was trying to teach me. Was it humility, patience, maturity, or love? Maybe it was that I needed a bit of all of these and also a tiny stash of human kindness. Besides all that, I also was learning another competency in eldercare—Bathroom 101.

The biggest etiquette question was where to put the towels after the cleanup. I couldn't flush them down the toilet, so my only option was the wastebasket. No doubt our remnants were quite a surprise for the cleanup staff that evening.

While I cleaned everything up, Aunt Helen scolded me, saying I should leave it for the staff to clean. Despite her protestations I finally managed to clean up the place. Fortunately Aunt Helen didn't soil herself too badly. We were actually able to exit the washroom with some remaining dignity.

Our rest stop behind us, we decided to go to McDonald's for hamburgers before returning home.

Dr. James had told us to come back the next day, this time with Maria. So we did. This interview went much better. Dr. James spoke Spanish with Maria. She prescribed some medicine and recommended we move in the direction of a nursing home and full-time care.

Those were the words I wanted to hear, the validation I needed. We would coordinate the move with the St. John of God nursing home as soon as a spot opened up.

Ann at Fifty

In October 2001 when I came to visit, I found Aunt Helen in a wheelchair in front of the house with Maria pushing her. I came up to them and bent over to say goodbye, as I usually did before leaving for Canada. Aunt Helen cried out in anguish as she reached out to me. I hugged her tightly for a long time. We both wept, but we knew there was nothing we could do; I had to leave her behind. My wife was turning fifty, and I was needed at my home in Canada to celebrate her birthday with our children. I also needed to look in on my mother in Canada. All I could do was thank God for Maria and her family for taking care of my aunt for the three weeks I would be gone, even if their care giving was not perfect.

When I returned to Edmonton, we celebrated Ann's fiftieth birthday in November. We had about two dozen people over. The biggest and best surprise was our son Mark's arrival from Los Angeles, which Ann never expected. She burst into tears upon seeing him. She was just so happy.

Meanwhile when I went to see her I noticed that my mother was losing her memory but otherwise in excellent health for her age. She hardly ever mentioned her tinnitus or her arthritis now, which once had been sources of daily complaints.

The Good Ol' Days

When I returned to Los Angeles three weeks later, Aunt Helen was even less coherent in her speech. Now she mixed up dreams, hallucinations, and reality. Even so, she was still "with us" about half the time.

Aunt Helen's lifestyle had stabilized considerably after her previous hospitalization. I was lucky to have Maria, who helped clean up Helen's house for her arrival from Elms Convalescent Home and then eventually assumed the full responsibility for her day-and-night care. It seemed to me that this would be a temporary arrangement—maybe a few months, perhaps a half a year.

Aunt Helen was becoming increasingly more difficult to deal with. Transfers from her wheelchair to the bed or washroom now required two people. Her care was becoming more demanding as well. There was potential for more belligerence, upset, and discord. She would need more medical and nursing care. Any crisis involving Aunt Helen would embroil me at times when it was not easy for me to respond, since I was often up in Canada. I would have to manage schedules, accounting, and related matters, such as filling in with Aunt Helen's care in a pinch, to a degree that I wasn't always able to handle. And of course there was the significant issue of the cost of the extra care.

The result was, as I mentioned, that I believed a move for Aunt Helen to the St. John of God Retirement and Care Center would be the best alternative to address her long-term needs. We waited more than six months for an opening.

I had become so used to the strains of the existing situation that, when it became clear to me that Aunt Helen would be moving, I became stressed out rather than relieved. I knew just how hard the move would be based on my previous attempts to move her to other assisted living facilities we looked at. The day finally came on April 8, 2002, a Monday. It was one of the hardest things I've ever had to do.

It was difficult for several reasons. First, Aunt Helen didn't want to go, although surprisingly she didn't put up much of a battle on the way there. As I anticipated, though, within a half-hour of our arrival, she told me to get her out of there. I quietly, respectfully, and firmly refused.

What I hadn't counted on were Maria's objections. She and her family made it clear that they preferred Aunt Helen to stay at home. Again, surprisingly, after reading a letter I wrote to them explaining what I was doing, they didn't put up much resistance, despite the significant drop in income it caused them.

The day I checked Aunt Helen into St. John of God, I made sure that Maria would remain with her throughout the day. I personally visited Aunt Helen three times that first day. Somehow she made it through her first night in the residence. I visited her twice the next day. On Wednesday I visited her around 6:00 p.m. After three days she still wanted to go straight home.

By now I had to return to Edmonton. As I pondered what might transpire over the next few days, I considered the fact that Aunt Helen had lost five pounds in less than four days. Could she adapt? I had to believe she would. I took the risk and flew out.

Let's Go!

Back in Edmonton my mother, while increasingly forget-ful, still she remembered who I was. She sat in her wheelchair in the dining room on her floor at her table for hours at a time. That was her favorite spot. On my visits to St. Michael's, after having been away in Los Angeles usually for three weeks, I would come up behind her. Then I would gently lean for-ward and into her line of sight and smile while looking into her eyes. I would say, "Ha!" while spreading my hands out to present myself. She would look up, pause to search her mem-ory, then hesitatingly ask, "Andriy?" I would nod my head yes. Then she would smile.

I would then try to bring her joy just by spending time with her taking her outside while wheeling her in her wheelchair to the nearby park, or more often, by sharing a quiet pleasure—such as going to a shopping mall together.

I'd say, "Let's go!" ("*Chodim!*") She'd ask, "Where?" I'd answer, "Shopping." Then I'd wheel her wheelchair out to the front door of the nursing home, and we'd wait for the Disabled Adults Transit (DATS) bus to come to pick us up to go to the mall. One day I took her to a beauty salon to get a perm at Kingsway Garden Mall. I left her with the hairstylist. Initially it looked like she was enjoying the visit, but suddenly she burst out angrily and stopped the perm. When I returned I found her alone, waiting for me in her wheelchair in the reception area. She was seething. I believe she was tired, and sitting patiently in a chair while the stylist worked on her hair was too taxing for her. I took her back to St. Michael's and settled her down before I left.

An Expired Dream

As I headed back down to Los Angeles on April 24, 2002, I was apprehensive about how things were going for Helen at St. John of God nursing home. I had to fulfill my responsibilities to my mother and now couldn't pull up stakes to move full-time to Los Angeles, which is what my aunt wanted.

When I saw Aunt Helen the next day on her birthday, she had lost another ten pounds. I had arranged for Maria to be with her three six-hour days a week—Monday, Wednesday, and Friday. Basically I was paying for Aunt Helen to have company. While it was worth doing, it clearly wasn't enough for her.

Aunt Helen asked me to take her home as soon as she saw me. I told her she was at St. John of God because she could no longer be by herself at home. As good as Maria was, I said, we couldn't arrange a satisfactory situation in the home environment for her. I told Aunt Helen we couldn't allow her to end up alone in her home in the dark, stuck somewhere with no one to help.

Aunt Helen repeated her offer to provide the money for the purchase of a house for us in Los Angeles. I explained to her that I hadn't been able to move my family down to L.A. because my mother was at St. Michael's nursing home and I wasn't making the kind of money that moving would require. I explained that I wouldn't feel comfortable relying solely on her resources since I could easily foresee how this could lead to exhausting those resources. There would be nothing left with which to pay for her care.

Despite these conflicts, I managed to take her out on a few expeditions to Santa Monica beach. We sat on the pier looking down and listening as the waves crashed down on to the beach below. We watched the seagulls fly around swooping down for a morsel of food here and there. We observed the other people walking by us. This was great therapy for her.

I found that a good way to better relate to her was to take her in my car and play some songs for her. It was amazing how songs united us in spirit and cut across the generational divide. I particularly sought out love ballads that I liked and played them to her, explaining along the way what the lyrics were saying and the emotional import they had. She responded well to these shared moments together. I did this with increasing frequency over the next while.

My stay in Los angeles this time was far from satisfying. Mark had been in a minor crisis with parking tickets, a minor legal problem dealing with a failure to appear, and a communication breakdown between us—all behavior uncharacteristic of his normal self. I was hopeful he would return to a more normal state of affairs, which he eventually did. Meanwhile Helen was in crisis; every day in the nursing home was a struggle. And my cases at work were less than satisfying; I had a string of rejections and complications. I battled with all this and did my best. Long, hard days sapped me of my enthusiasm for life, and I grew weary by the end of the day.

As unhappy as Aunt Helen was about her living circumstances, she was even unhappier when I was away. Even visits from Mark did little to cheer her up. While I wasn't her savior, my presence there did seem to make it easier for her.

Law Class Reunion

I had an opportunity to pay tribute to my mother in my speech at my thirty year law class reunion in Vancouver in September 2002. I said,

"I still remember nights when I would come home and find my mother cleaning one of the apartments." These were the apartments my mother rented out in the building she owned.

"It would be late at night, but she would be washing floors on her hands and knees. This is how she provided the income we needed, and this is how she put me through school. I am eternally grateful to her for doing that. I'm willing to bet that if you reflect on it you'll find that there is someone who has made a similar contribution to your life or career.

"I imagined that I could become a kind of Henry Kissinger, a political leader who could employ his knowledge of the law to solve international political problems. This was the vision that propelled me into law school, and that was the vision that guided me when I went into the profession in 1972.

"In looking back over my thirty year career, I am grateful to the legal profession for the many opportunities it has provided me. I can't say that everything in my career has worked out without disappointment. I am disappointed, for example, by the low esteem in which our profession is held in the community. I have had my fair share of failures, setbacks, heartaches, and frustration. In those darkest moments, I have often said to myself, *I don't want to lead this life.* I have said, *I don't want to be Andy Semotiuk. I want to be Henry Kissinger, or Bill Gates, or Stephen Spielberg...anyone except Andy Semotiuk.*

"But I've learned over the years that the best I could be is an imitation Henry Kissinger, an imitation Bill Gates, et cetera. But I can be a unique Andy Semotiuk. I've come to understand that the gods up in the heavens decided to assign me way down here the task of leading the life of Andy Semotiuk—to find the purpose and meaning in his life and to squeeze out every ounce of happiness, joy and fulfillment out of his life.

"Finally, I've come to understand that the biggest contribution I can make to the world and myself is to be the best that I can be."

If that meant contributing to the well-being and care of my mother and my aunt as part of my life journey, so be it.

Honoring Emil's Memory

On my next visit to Los Angeles, I picked up my Aunt Helen to go to visit Uncle Emil's grave. As we drove into the cemetery, a security guard sitting in his car near the fence stopped us. He said the cemetery had closed at 5:00 p.m. It was five thirty.

I explained that my Aunt Helen and I just needed to go in a couple of hundred yards. He said he was sorry but he couldn't help us. I said it was the eighth anniversary of my Uncle Emil's death (October 26, 2002) and that my aunt would like to pay her respects. He said he really shouldn't do this, but took down the chain to let us drive through. He asked us to turn off our headlights, so his boss, who was in the office nearby, wouldn't see what we were doing. We drove in the dark.

I found the grave quickly, remembering roughly where it was from previous visits. I took Aunt Helen out of the car, helped her into her wheelchair, and pushed her over on the grass to the gravesite. She asked about the graves—whose they were. I pointed out Emil's grave and her mother's. She was surprised to learn her mother was also buried there.

275

Then we prayed. First we recited the Our Father (*Otshe Nash*), then we said a Hail Mary (*Bohorodytse*). My aunt, who was ninety-three and an atheist most of her life, objected that I wasn't praying loudly enough; she said she wanted to pray along. I spoke louder, and she joined me in prayer.

We then went to McDonald's before I returned Aunt Helen to St. John of God.

When I returned to Edmonton, our family celebrated Christmas Eve together, though it was a time of mixed emotions for me. I was feeling somewhat down because the Norwalk virus, a gastrointestinal illness had hit St. Michael's nursing home and made it impossible for my mother to join us. She had been sick with diarrhea the previous day, and the folks at the nursing home called us to let us know we couldn't visit. So it was quiet—Ann, Mark, and Natalie around the table with me. It was the first Christmas in Edmonton where my mother was not in our home with us. Meanwhile Aunt Helen was on her own at St. John of God. I was no Henry Kissinger, and the shuttle diplomacy and attention to two elders at two ends of our continent had taken its toll. On this night I understood more than ever how important family really is. The people in my family, all of them, provided me with reasons for living and a meaningful purpose, and for this I was grateful.

Shuttle Diplomacy

The greatest gift my mother gave me and, to some extent, also my aunt, was to teach me how to read between the lines in all social settings—to be sensitive to how people really feel. This skill came in handy in the days that followed.

On January 7, Ukrainian Christmas Day, I took Aunt Helen to Junior's Restaurant for a turkey dinner. While we drove back from the restaurant that evening, she joined me in singing some Ukrainian Christmas carols. Her weak voice weaved in and out with mine as we sang along. It was dusk. There was a note of sadness as the two of us drove along, each of us thinking about how life could be better, but each aware of how lucky we were to be together here nonetheless. We felt a simple, unspoken joy.

The next weekend, while my aunt and I were on an outing, she turned to me in the car and said, "Kill me." (*"Zabej mene."*) Stunned, for a moment I paused to collect my thoughts and then I replied, "Oh no, you think we're going to let you go that easily? No way. You have to suffer here with the rest of us. Besides, what's your big hurry? You don't know what's waiting for you there. Maybe hell."

Aunt Helen's question stunned me.

Why Can't I Die?

Aunt Helen would return to this theme on a following visit with her. We were returning from lunch at the Farmer's Market on June 21, 2003, in Los Angeles. I had played her some music while we drove there and back. Once home, I was lifting her out of the car and into her wheelchair when she turned to me and said in Ukrainian, "Is it hard for you?" I replied, "Why are you asking me that?" She answered, "Why can't I die?" I turned to her and said, "That's not your business!" I told her it wasn't for us to decide how long we should live. Where I found such answers to those profound questions I'll never know. But I did.

As her health continued to deteriorate, Aunt Helen was put under observation in a room right across from the nurse's station. It had been a long wait, and I was very happy about these recent developments.

My biggest challenge was not to run out of money while looking after her care, not to mention my mother's. Long ago I had arranged to become a cosigner on Helen's bank accounts so I would have access to funds to look after her without having to go for conservatorship.

Because Aunt Helen's funds were slowly dwindling to nothing, I estimated that between a year to two years from now, possibly sooner, I would be forced to apply for conservatorship in order to sell off her property or to mortgage it to continue to pay for her care.

I was also concerned that I wouldn't have sufficient income for myself from my law practice and that I would have to dip into her funds to pay for personal costs unrelated to her. No one knew how long she would live. I could only pray to God that I was managing her affairs well enough and that my practice would bring me enough income to make it.

A Birthday to Remember

I had invited Aunt Helen to celebrate Mark's twenty-first birthday, which took place on October 30, 2003. The three of us were sitting at a table at Junior's Restaurant in Westwood in the back room. She seemed unsettled, impatient to be served. She was hungry. The way I saw it, she was entitled to her occasional outburst, such as banging on the table with a spoon to attract the attention of a waiter. After all, she was now ninety-four years old. As if to underscore her upset, we felt the jolt of a mild earthquake.

After lunch I gave Mark a birthday card in which I wished him well in Ukrainian, and then added, "The purpose of life is to find your unique God-given abilities, to put them in the service of others, and to become everything you can be."

Then it was time to sing "*Mnohaya Lita.*" As we began to sing softly and looked into each another's glistening eyes, a poignant moment came over us. After a few bars, we stopped as we realized we were singing for Mark's twenty-first birthday. We knew that at any time Aunt Helen could drift off into another world, but she was intent on being "with us" at this moment, to carry the song for Mark. Toward the end we began to tear up a bit. I leaned in to say to him, "You couldn't buy this at any price." Mark nodded in agreement.

I returned to Edmonton shortly after that.

Trouble with Aunt Helen

In early December 2003 the nurse on Aunt Helen's floor in Los Angeles called me at my office in Edmonton to say that Helen was having trouble breathing. They had put her on oxygen, taken chest x-rays, and discovered she had pneumonia in both lungs.

I remembered on several of my previous visits Aunt Helen was coughing and wheezing while trying to breathe. I thought she was just getting over a cold. I didn't have the presence of mind to think the condition could develop into pneumonia. In a rash of follow-up phone calls over the next few days, I learned she seemed to be recovering, although Dr. Bucher suspected she might have suffered a stroke. There were signs of weakness in her left hand.

Some days later I had a discussion with Dr. Ripey about whether heroic measures should be taken in the event of a crisis. I answered that all we wanted was to minimize any suffering. I told him Aunt Helen had wanted to die for some time now, but I had hoped it would be for something more sudden or gentle, rather than fighting for her every breath. He agreed to monitor her progress and have the staff keep me posted.

The next morning her nurse called again. Aunt Helen had eaten about half of her breakfast, but now she wasn't responding to the nurses; she apparently was sleeping. Mark, who was in Los Angeles, visited her that Saturday and reported that she was OK but added that he couldn't summon her to consciousness. That phone call troubled us because Aunt Helen usually responded to stimuli. It seemed that she indeed had suffered a stroke and was unable to swallow liquids. I decided I needed to be with her.

Fretting about Circumstances

Before leaving Edmonton, I went to visit my mother and take her to West Edmonton Mall, then the largest indoor shopping mall in the world. The Christmas rush was in full swing, and she loved the stimulating environment. On the way home, she started to sob. She felt she was a burden on me and wished she wasn't. She thanked me sincerely for everything I had done. As usual, when I was leaving she said this could be the last time we would see each other. I reassured her that I would be back.

At that moment I was more worried about Aunt Helen's health. I was afraid of the future; since I had been caring for my aunt for so long, particularly on Saturdays, I wouldn't even know what to do with myself in Los Angeles when she was gone. It was a selfish fear to be sure, but undeniable nevertheless.

Death, Death

When I returned to Los Angeles and went to see her, as Aunt Helen breathed into her mask, she repeated one word again and again—"*Smert.*" She was saying, "Death, death." I couldn't determine, however, whether this was an expression of her wish or an evaluation of her state. Over the next few days, her condition became more precarious. She took oxygen and antibiotics and had an IV hooked up to her arm. When I visited her again, her pallor seemed better; her face wasn't as ashen as it had been the day before.

Over the next several days, Aunt Helen was able to recognize me once in a while when I visited, but she barely responded. We now knew she definitely had suffered a stroke, but the therapists thought that she could recover to her pre-stroke condition with some work. She was being taught how to drink again, but her state had to be monitored very closely. Her breathing was impaired, and she had pneumonia.

On December 20, 2003, with great trepidation I returned to Edmonton for Christmas, knowing that my cell phone could ring at any moment and that I might have to return to Los Angeles. It was hard to leave L.A. not knowing what would happen to Aunt Helen, but I couldn't put all our lives on hold either.

Aunt Helen's Final Sprint

By January 6, 2004, Ukrainian Christmas Eve, Aunt Helen's condition had seriously deteriorated. I found myself at the Seattle airport awaiting a connecting flight to Los Angeles. The day before I had spoken with Dr. Bucher. She said she would like to put Aunt Helen on "life-ending" medications to treat pain and keep her comfortable, and didn't think it prudent to maintain her current medication regime.

I asked if I should fly back. She said it was hard to say, but she agreed that it was a reasonable idea. Aunt Helen was still on oxygen, not eating much, not responding to stimuli, sleeping continually, and had a buildup of fluids in her legs as well as bedsores. Maria said Aunt Helen had told her she wanted to die.

Throughout the Christmas period, I had kept in touch with Los Angeles daily by cell phone. There were moments when my aunt wasn't responding and her oxygen levels were very low, but then she would rally and life went on. One day she ate half her breakfast, and the next day she ate half her lunch. These were improvements on her recent eating patterns. So I had been hopeful.

Now I was anxious to get to L.A. in time. It was snowing hard. A bad storm made it difficult to get a flight down to Los Angeles.

On January 7, 2004, Ukrainian Christmas day, I arrived in Los Angeles at two in the morning. Freezing rain had delayed my flight for seven hours in Seattle. When I finally arrived, I slept for a few hours then went straight to St. John of God.

Aunt Helen was sleeping and, I was told, doing better than the day before. I spoke to her, called her name, and sought to comfort her. She didn't respond but slept and heavily breathed through her oxygen mask. I kissed her hand and put my hand on her forehead to wipe back her hair. After a couple of hours, I left to check out my office; I hadn't been there for two weeks. My plan was to return that evening to stay with her. I immersed myself in my files, working hard to catch up on everything, since I had left them back on December 19 when I had gone to Edmonton for Christmas.

Shortly after 6:00 p.m., I received a call from one of the aides at St. John of God. She said, "I'm sorry to tell you that your aunt is dead." I dropped everything.

Maria greeted me upon my arrival. She had been with my aunt at 6:05 p.m.—her final moment. She was sobbing as she stood by the bed.

I touched Aunt Helen; her body was still warm. Until that moment I hadn't appreciated the connection between warmth and life. I held Aunt Helen's arm for a long time. Waves of emotion came over me; I struggled not to be overwhelmed with grief. One painful thought plagued me—how could I miss Aunt Helen's last moment on earth? Silently I cursed myself. *Damn it! Damn it! Damn it!*

I had called our Ukrainian priest on my cell phone on the way to the nursing home. I left a message on his answering machine. Since I couldn't reach him, I asked for a priest at the nursing home to perform the last rites. Soon Brother Raymond appeared and led us in prayer. He underlined that "Helen has simply changed her address" and was now with God. She was ninety-five years old when she died.

I called Edmonton to let Ann and Natalie know what had happened. I asked Ann to tell my mother, who was then ninety-three years old. Some time later Ann told me how she had gone to St. Michael's nursing home to tell my mother. After settling in with her for a while, my wife turned to the subject. She told my mother, "Olena died." There was a pause. Then Ann repeated the comment. Again there was a pause. Then my mother looked Ann in the eyes and responded, "Ah ha, Olena has died" and nodded in recognition. The realization sank in and was greeted with deep sorrow as her eyes glistened. Then she turned her gaze away into the distance.

My Final Words for Aunt Helen

"I remember one conversation in particular one evening at Helen's house," I said in my eulogy for her at the Ukrainian Catholic Church of the Nativity of the Blessed Virgin Mary in Los Angeles.

"She pulled out a Ukrainian poem and gave it to me to read. She told me how much she loved that poem. While I don't remember the exact wording, I do remember the story in the poem.

"In the first scene we find a young man lying under an apple tree. This guy is so lazy that instead of getting up, he kicks the apple tree in order to have an apple fall so he can eat it. In the second verse, we are introduced to a young girl who is drawing water from a well, baking bread in the oven, and washing the floors of her elderly mother's house. In the third verse, we are told that these two individuals were meant for each other. The young man could not make it in the world without the help of an industrious wife. The young woman needed an outlet for her energy, and he would become that outlet.

"Aunt Helen always wanted to know exactly where we were when we were traveling in the car. Sometimes she would ask me, 'Where exactly are we?' Ribbing her I would answer, 'If you please, we are driving down Fairfax approaching...if you please, Olympic.' She would ask, 'Are you sure you know where you're going?' I would answer, 'I have an outstanding sense of direction.'

"Experts in death say that it is a real honor to be present when someone breathes their last breath. And I had sincerely hoped that I would be present when she passed on. It is one of my greatest regrets that I was not with her at that moment, but I take consolation in the fact that Maria Minjares was present. Maria was someone that our family has grown to love and admire for her efforts at care giving over the course of the last two years with Aunt Helen. It was Maria who ultimately closed Aunt Helen's eyes.

"Let me conclude these reflections by relating a story that I believe well summarizes what I am trying to say. It is a true story. One day the famous French artist Henri Matisse came to visit his friend, Pierre August Renoir. As Matisse sat in Renoir's drawing room, he watched as Renoir painted. With each touch of the brush onto the canvas Renoir recoiled and cringed as arthritic pain shot up his arm. After a while, when Matisse could not stand it any longer, he blurted out, 'If it hurts so much, why do you persist in doing it?' Renoir replied, 'The pain passes, but the beauty remains forever.' And so it is that the pain of Aunt Helen's death will pass over time, but the beauty of her life will remain forever engraved in the hearts and minds of everyone she touched and loved. May she rest in peace."

Even in dying it seemed that my aunt's life would overshadow my mother's. But for me, my aunt's death was a prelude to the upcoming main event. In the meantime, for the next two years my mother and I would share various events in our lives together.

A Breaking

One morning in late April 2004, the nursing home staff at St. Michael's called us to say that they found my mother lying on the floor of her room covered with blankets. They rushed her to Royal Alexander Hospital, where Ann and I went to see her.

My mother, who had turned ninety-three a few weeks earlier, had climbed out of her bed and fallen suffering a "tib-fib" fracture on her right leg below the knee. Her doctors decided to put on a cast. The pain of adjusting the leg to get the cast right was excruciating for her.

Once done, the hospital decided to discharge my mother and send her back to St. Michael's nursing home. I was eating lunch in the hospital cafeteria at the time they made that decision, so Ann rushed over to get me. Before she left she had asked the hospital staff not to move my mother until Ann returned with me. But before we could return they already had started. My mother—feeling worthless, confused, in terrible pain, and not knowing what they were doing or even who they were as they moved her from the bed to the stretcher—screamed.

The nurse was trying to remove my mother's IV, and since my mother was bleeding, the nurse had to press down on my mother's arm to pinch off the blood flow. My mother couldn't bear the pain and kept crying out. While we all watched—Ann, Natalie, the ambulance attendants, the nurse, and I—my mother was moved to a stretcher, then out the door to the waiting vehicle.

The drive back to St. Michael's wasn't pleasant. My mother cried out in pain with each bump along the road. She couldn't be calmed down, no matter what we tried. Then something strange occurred. She cried out to the Blessed Virgin Mary, asking why she had forsaken her, and asked for her divine intervention. Two minutes later my mother was calm again.

In the months that followed my mother pretty much made a full recovery.

My Mother's Final Hour

On my fifty-sixth birthday, on January 8, 2005, I took my mother from St. Michael's to West Edmonton Mall. Taking my mother there reminded her that there was more going on in the world than just the mundane, day-to-day life at St. Michael's. I believe it was good therapy to take her to various shopping malls like this one every Saturday whenever I was in town. I had done it for years.

My mother and late aunt had worried about the same things as they aged. Perhaps their greatest fear was running out of money, since the older they got, the more vulnerable, economically, they were. Strangely, neither was economically impaired.

Neither liked the fact they had become so dependent and incapable of looking after themselves. We all knew that my care of them included taking risks with them by taking them on outings where they could at any time become ill or fall, but we did it anyway. They wouldn't have it any other way.

At the mall with my mother, there wasn't much we could converse about now. She was ninety-four years old, and her deafness had become complete. On top of that, she had lost most of her memory. But we shared sympathy for each other—she for the inconvenience her continued life in this state had caused me, I for her suffering and hardships. We peered into each other's eyes with understanding of each other. As we walked through the mall, we pointed out what we saw of interest to each other, but otherwise we strolled without speaking.

When she spoke, her high-strained voice reflected the many hardships she had endured over the last decade. We stopped for an ice cream cone—always vanilla, her favorite flavor. On other occasions we'd have a coffee and a cookie as a treat.

That was our last visit to West Edmonton Mall.

At Her Side

On August 5, 2006, Ann and I were called at 3:00 a.m. by St. Michael's nursing home to come to my mother's bedside. Due to her age, dementia, and frail health, her condition had deteriorated since her ninety-fifth birthday in April to the point where she had been put on oxygen and had stopped eating.

Several months earlier I had come on a Saturday to take her out and found her in bed in the afternoon. She looked weak and groggy. She wasn't wearing a hat, which was out of character for her. I thought then that her life drama was coming to an end. But she rallied.

Now, as Ann and I stood by her side, I heard her raspy, labored breathing and the sound of bubbles floating through the oxygen machine. The sound was disconcerting. Her mouth was open. Her white fine hair underscored her age. Her flesh was pale; she was skin and bones. *Death awaits behind the curtains, I thought, as her heart beats its final rhythm.*

Over the last couple of months, my mother had remained largely bedridden. Occasionally, when she seemed stronger, I was able to take her to a smaller shopping mall on the Disabled Adults Transit System bus. But I noticed she no longer had the strength to travel farther to her favorite venue, West Edmonton Mall. Each trip we took was more difficult for her.

About a week before we got the call from St. Michael's, the care coordinator had advised me that my mother had developed a wound at the base of her spine. It was probably a bedsore, and later conversations with the staff at St. Michael's pinpointed the cause to likely be a deflated cushion on her wheelchair. Although I was unaware of it at the time, such a sore can bring trouble, because due to advanced age such a person is weak to start with, and her body could be susceptible to infections. In fact the septic aspect of such a wound often leads to death.

I thought about how marginalized and humbled my mother had been and how few people ever had taken the time to relate to her. Wherever she went she always had felt she was at the lower end of the social scale. I reflected on how her hearing impairment marred her life and how helpless she was to change that about herself. Her life and the lives of her contemporaries were caught up in the sweep of history. Ann reminded me that my mother had lived for me—that I was her reason for living, particularly when I was young.

Memorable Moments

Each time I parted with my mother, my heart ached, as I didn't know if I would ever see her again. Her life was so hard that I often prayed to God that he would let me look after her until her death. I prayed that he would make it possible for me to survive her, as I had my aunt. I dreaded any thought of leaving her on this earth alone. In the last few years of her life, my anxiety in this regard subsided as I realized she was being cared for at St. Michael's and that, if I were to die, Ann, Mark, and Natalie would be there for her. Still I prayed to God that he would let me be the one to fulfill that role.

Watching her now I realized she was my last remaining tie to my past. She was the anchor of my life in this world. Although physically we were apart, I still felt a profound emotional tie to her. Anyone who has had a loving mother would understand this.

When my mother was still mentally coherent, we talked about death. I remember asking her whether she was afraid to die. She answered that there was nothing to be afraid of and that she was ready to go.

Ann was resting in the chair in the corner of the room. Her eyes were closed. I wrote a few notes to remember these final moments of my mother's life. I was fully focused on the environment around me; the hum of the oxygen machine was sporadically interrupted by the hiss of the release of oxygen. I supposed that was so it could be carried through the tubes to my mother's nose. My mother's chest jerked with each breath, as if her heart were jumping through it. The sun had come out, and it was the start of a bright summer day. For three days now she'd had little or nothing to eat. Her eyes were sunken in her face, her cheeks drawn with the telltale sign that she had lost much of her weight.

Strangely, I thought, the closer we came to her final moments, the less I felt overwhelmed by the events. Weeks ago, when I had come here, I wept as I watched her sleep. I thought about her life, about how she had been uprooted near the end of the war, how she had ended up in the refugee camp in Salzburg, and how she had come to Canada, swept by events like a leaf fallen into a river. How differently her life had turned out from the life she imagined she would have in Ukraine.

We were so lucky, however. Thankfully my mother could die without concern over war or famine. She was resting on an expensive KinAir III bed to make the sores on her back less painful. Kind and decent nursing home personnel cared for her around the clock. I couldn't imagine a better place for her to spend her final moments than here, in Canada, one of the richest and best countries in the world. We had so much to be thankful for. After all, despite all her hardships, she was able to live true to the pledge she had made to herself as a child not to allow her disability to rob her of a full and meaningful life.

I had been bracing myself for my mother's death because it had been a long time coming. Her memory slowly had dissolved to the point where the week before she barely had recognized me. Such had been the toll of Alzheimer's.

On Call

While my mother's eyes half opened from time to time, it was difficult to say whether she saw anything or whether she was able to identify us. Her mouth was now open, and uncharacteristically, she was breathing through it. A drip was introduced through her IV to keep her fluid levels up.

While we were somber, we were not despondent, since we knew this was the way it must be. I knew my mother's death would have a big impact on me.

I found myself flitting through more self-centered thoughts. Although my mother was a great source of stability and roots for me, she also held me back. I was never able to completely cut myself loose from Edmonton because of her. And it seemed, even in death, since she would be buried here, she would continue to exert an influence over me emotionally by tying me to this city forever.

Long ago, when I first introduced Ann to my mother and told my mother I would marry Ann, she said, "Good. Maybe she will be the one who will be beside me when I die." It seemed her prophecy would come true.

I was mindful of the fact that St. Michael's wasn't a paradise on earth for my mother. When she first came there, she was physically frail but mentally far more alert than other residents. She had to reconcile herself with this placement and accept the fact that her life there was necessary in order not to eclipse my life.

Though she felt she had much more to live for and that to be there would reduce her quality of life, she also knew she would get round-the-clock care and that she would be safe. She reluctantly had agreed to stay.

I tried to brighten her life through regular visits, bringing her home for holiday dinners and celebrations, and generally helped to make her life happier. It was a fact that in time the condition of the other residents and the limited surroundings all exerted a negative influence on her. After all, observing semiconscious patients wandering the hallways all day and moving essentially between her room and the lunchroom from time to time didn't provide her much in the way of stimulation. But she knew and I knew this was the best we could come up with. It just had to be enough.

They say the dying can hear everything to the last moment. But since my mother was hearing impaired, the only way to communicate our love for her was through our touch. We held her hands. I wrote in the palm of her hand the words "I am Andriy. I am your son. All is well. Our Father who art in heaven..." in letters with my finger. *Dear God, take her to you now,* I thought. *Don't make her suffer anymore! Mother of God, help us. Let God take my mother's life if it is his will. It's been a long, long journey.*

Surrender

My mother's death came in a wave of silent moments, followed by gasps for air, her eyes open but unfocused.

I never will forget the titanic struggle I witnessed that day. I never will forget the loud, raspy crackling sound emanating from her chest, where the fluid had built up in her lungs. I never will forget the helpless yet struggling body striving to survive, breath by breath, to fight off the end. I never will forget the moments of silence, as the body appeared to give up, only to draw in one more gasp of air, then again and again, before finally surrendering forever. I cried out in anguish at why her death had to be so difficult, so hard. Just then she closed her mouth, made a defiant gesture with her face, and then she surrendered.

Salomea Drozdowska died on Sunday, August 6, 2006 at 5:30 a.m. as Ann and I wept by her side.

At that moment, my mother's presence vanished from this earth. All that remained was her memory. Ann pointed out to me that I had been her greatest joy, and following me, her grandchildren. She reminded me that I had been with my mother at two transcendental moments in our lives, the moment of my birth and now at the moment of her death.

We sat near the body for a few moments in silence. The staff left us alone to grieve. Though sad that her life was over, we felt relieved that her suffering had ended and that hopefully now she could be at peace with God and the Blessed Virgin Mary and be reunited with other members of her family.

Ann then drew my mother's eyes shut for the last time.

My Final Words About My Mother

At her funeral, I gave the eulogy.

"By sheer coincidence, while we [my mother and I] were in Ukraine, a new museum to honor her aunt, Solomea Krushelnytska, the opera singer, was opening," I said. I was referring to a trip I had taken with her to her beloved Lviv in October 1990, when she was eighty years old.

"Since Ukraine was still under Communist control and travel was somewhat restricted, our attendance at this event was a novelty. When the Ukrainian media heard that the family of Solomea Krushelnytska was there, the visit turned into a national sensation.

"For the first time in her life, my mother became the focus of a national news media and an instant 'public personality.' Some two hundred people lined up to get her autograph. TV cameras juggled through the crowd to get a good view. Reporters noted her every word. The public seemed to hang on to every syllable she uttered. In fact she was so much a star on the occasion that people lined up to get *my* autograph simply because I was traveling with her.

"And that is where I witnessed a most astonishing transformation. My mother was once again energetic, buoyant, and electrifying. The pall of old age lifted from her shoulders, and she walked out of that museum—the home where she once had hid from invading police, both Soviet and German, looking and acting ten years younger.

"Right there I made two resolutions. First I decided to take my mother on more trips abroad. Second I resolved to get my mother's autograph."

Then in my eulogy I talked about another memory.

"In the 1980s, during a particularly bad snowstorm in Edmonton, I was driving to the courthouse when I stopped for a red light. As I looked out my window, I noticed my mother crossing the icy street in front of me. I wanted to pull over, but there was no place to stop. I tried blowing my horn, but she didn't hear me, so all I could do was watch with wonder at how this eighty-five-year-old woman walked with a cane across the icy street. As she came to the curb, there was a three-foot-high snow bank left by the street cleaners from the night before that she had to cross. It was obvious she couldn't make it alone.

So she looked up through the snow-swept flurries and spied some guy leaning against the building where she was going. She lifted her cane to point it at him. With her other hand, she removed any doubt about whom she was recruiting and what she wanted. She motioned for him to come help her. I watched in amazement as the man jumped to attention, leaped over the snow bank and helped her across it."

I concluded with one more thought that could best summarize my feelings that night at the funeral. I borrowed from the libretto of *Madame Butterfly*, the opera that Solomea Krushelnyska had rescued from collapse by playing the lead role of Cio-Cio San when it was restaged by Puccini after a dismal first premier, in view of the significance of the opera star in my mother's life.[38]

"The opera is about a young Japanese geisha who marries an American naval officer. The naval officer then indicates he must return to the United States but promises Cio-Cio San he will return to her, not knowing that she is pregnant with his child. While she waits for him, the naval officer marries in the United States and years later returns to Japan with his American wife. When he learns of the existence of the young boy, the parents must decide what to do. It becomes evident that the child would not have a good future in Japan as the son of a disgraced geisha. Therefore Cio-Cio San agrees to give up the boy to his father so he can be taken to America.

"There is a particularly poignant passage near the end of the opera sung by Cio-Cio San, addressed to her boy, who she knows is about to leave her forever. Holding him in her arms and looking into his eyes, she says, 'Look at this face. It is the face of your mother. Remember it. You will never see it again.' "

Laid to Rest

Occasionally I visit my mother's grave and the graves of other members of my family. I am always struck by the calm and peaceful silence there. I think about how unfair it was to them to have to be laid to rest here in this strange land, thousands of miles away from where they had started their lives. Detached from their ancestors back home, their lives were like windblown leaves scattered far from the trees they once adorned. Looking at their names engraved on their gravestones brings back memories from their days on this earth but also reminds me of how much more they wanted out of their lives, how many dreams they left unfulfilled, and how unpredictable their life journeys were.

Like millions of others from Eastern Europe and elsewhere who, due to world events, left their homeland and faced extraordinary hardships to emigrate, they endured and made new lives for themselves in North America. Along the way the lives of my mother and the other members of my family merged with mine, and I was enriched immeasurably. My life became one of the threads that, intertwined with the threads of their lives, created a family tapestry—a part of the history of that time.

Just as their remains are now buried in Canadian and American soil, their life stories also are now part of the North American experience. The deep sense of gratitude I once felt to Canada and the United States for rescuing my family members from hardships faced overseas remains. But now, as someone born here and whose children were born here, I see our Ukrainian identity as a native part of the North American mosaic. The price of our successful integration into North American society, however, has been high. We struggle to maintain our Ukrainian language, and our North American lifestyles increasingly crowd out what remains of our Ukrainian identity.

As I go on with my life, now that they have all passed on, when I look back over my shoulder at the road we once traveled together, it seems as if that road is fading before my eyes and the memories we once shared are being lost in the process. I hope this book will be a way to preserve whatever memories remain and offers a suitable tribute to their lives and the lives of those they touched along the way.

Selected
Bibliography

Appleman-Jurman, Alicia. *Alicia, My Story.* New York: Bantam Books, 1988.

Armstrong, Diane. *Mosaic: A Chronicle of Five Generations.* New York: St. Martin's Press, 1998.

Armstrong, John. *Ukrainian Nationalism.* New York: Columbia University Press, 1963.

Baker, Nicholson. *Human Smoke: The Beginnings of World War II, the End of Civilization.* Old Saybrook, CT: Tantor Audio, 2008 (print and audio CD).

Bartov, Omar. *Erased Vanished Traces of Jewish Galicia in Present-Day Ukraine.* Princeton, NJ: Princeton University Press, 2007.

Berger, Joseph. *Displaced Persons: Growing up American after the Holocaust.* Prince Frederick, MD: Recorded Books, 2001 (print and audio CD).

Bilas, Lev. *Looking Back, 1922-2002.* Lviv, Ukraine: National Academy of Sciences of Ukraine, Ivan Krypiakevych Institute, 2005 (written and published in Ukrainian).

Bilovus, Anastasia. *My Life Memories.* Greeley, CO: Ukrapress, 1982.

Bilyj, Mychajlo. *Parallel Crimes.* Ternopil, Ukraine: Aston, 2002 (written and published in Ukrainian).

Black, Edwin. *IBM and the Holocaust.* New York: Time Warner/ Random House Audio Books, 2002 (print and audio CD).

Blawacka, Alexandra. *Chronicle of My Life.* Lviv and Kyiv, Ukraine: International Economic Foundation, 2010 (written and published in Ukrainian).

Boshyk, Yury, ed. *Ukraine during World War II: History and Its Aftermath.* Edmonton: Canadian Institute of Ukrainian Studies, 1986.

Bradwin, Edmund. *The Bunkhouse Man.* Toronto/Buffalo: University of Toronto Press, 1972.

Brajchevskyj, M.Y. *Association or Subordination?* Studiom Publishers, Kiev, 1972.

Broadfoot, Barry. *Ten Lost Years, 1929-1939: Memories of the Canadians Who Survived the Depression.* Toronto: McClelland & Stewart, 1997.

Buchanan, Patrick. *Churchill, Hitler, and "The Unnecessary War": How Britain Lost Its Empire and the West Lost the World.* Westminster: Books on Tape, 2008 (print and audio CD).

Cehelsky, Lonhyn. *From Legends to Facts.* New York: Bulava Corp., 1960 (written and published in Ukrainian).

Chajkivskyj, Bohdan. *The Chessboard of My Life.* New York: self-published, 2007.

Childers, Thomas. *World War II: A Military and Social History.* Chantilly, VA: The Teaching Company, 1998 (lecture on audio CD).

Cipko, Serge. Various articles and reports regarding the 1932–1933 famine in the Ukraine. Various Edmonton newspapers, 2006.

De Zayas, Alfred M. *The Wehrmacht War Crimes Bureau, 1939–1945.* Lincoln, NE: University of Nebraska Press, 1989.

Dimont, Max I. *Jews, God, and History.* Ashland, NC: Blackstone Audio Books, 1997 (print and audio CD).

Dragan, Anthony. *Vinnytsia: A Forgotten Holocaust.* Jersey City, NJ: Svoboda, 1986.

Drohomyretskyj, Ivan. *Prisoner under Three Regimes.* Self-published (written and published in Ukrainian, Ivano-Frankivsk, 2003).

Dydyk, Halyna. *The General's Adjutant.* Hadyach, Ukraine: Hadyach Publishers, 2007 (written and published in Ukrainian).

Eberle, Henrik, and Matthias, Uhl. *The Hitler Book: The Secret Dossier Prepared for Stalin from the Interrogations of Otto Guensche and Heinz Linge, Hitler's Closest Personal Aides.* Old Saybrook, CT: Tantor Media, 2006 (print and audio CD).

Eisenhower, Dwight D. *Crusade in Europe.* New York: Books on Tape/Doubleday & Company, 1948.

Eliach, Yaffa. *There Once Was a World: A 900-Year Chronicle of the Shtetl of Eishyshok.* Newport Beach, CA: Books on Tape,1998 (print and audio CD).

Farrell, Robert H. *Harry S. Truman.* New York: Recorded Books, 1995 (print and audio CD).

Fast, Howard. *The Jews: A History of a People.* Charlotte Hall, MD: Dial/Recorded Books, 1968 (print and audio CD).

Finkelstein, Norman G. *The Holocaust Industry,* second ed. New York/London: Verso, 2000.

Fishman, Lala, and Weingartner, Steven. *Lala's Story.* Evanston, IL: Northwestern University Press, 1997.

Gilbert, Martin. *History of the Twentieth Century, Vol. 1–3.* Books on Tape, 1997 New York (audiotapes).

Goldelman, Solomon I. *Jewish National Autonomy in Ukraine 1917–1920.* Chicago:, Ukrainian Research and Information Institute, 1968 Print.

Gotskyj, Volodymyr. *Memoirs of a Son of Peremyshl Lands, Vol. 1.* Lviv, Ukraine: Svichado (written and published in Ukrainian).

Haliy, Mykola. *Organized Famine in Ukraine, 1932–1933.* New York: East Side, 1963.

Holovinskyj, Ivan. *National Consciousness as the Decisive Factor in Statehood.* Kyiv, Ukraine: Akonit, 2004 (written and published in Ukrainian).

Horton, Marc. *Voice of a City: The Edmonton Journal's First Century, 1903 to 2003.*

Edmonton: Edmonton Journal Group, 2003.

Hrytsak, Jaroslaw. *Life, Death, and Other Unpleasantries.* Kyiv, Ukraine: Hrani-T, 2008.

Hunczak, Taras. *Symon Petlyura and the Jews: A Reappraisal.* Lviv, Ukraine: Ukrainian Historical Association, 2008.

Isajevych, Jaroslav. *The History of Lviv, Vol. 3.* Lviv, Ukraine: Tsenter Evropy, 2007 (written and published in Ukrainian).

Ivan Krypiakevych Institute of Ukrainian Studies of the National Academy of Sciences of Ukraine Lviv historical essays. Lviv, Ukraine: National Academy of Sciences of Ukraine, 1996.

Ivshyna, Larysa, ed. *Day and Eternity of James Mace.* Kyiv, Ukraine: Ukrainian Group, 2005.

Jachnenko, Natalia. *From the Office to Brygitky.* Munich: Author's Publication, 1986 (written and published in Ukrainian).

Junge, Traudl. *Until the Final Hour: Hitler's Last Secretary.* New York: Arcade, 2002.

Kahan, Stuart. *The Wolf of the Kremlin: The First Biography of L.M. Kaganovich, the Soviet Union's Architect of Fear.* New York: William Morrow Company, 1987.

Kahane, David. *Lvov Ghetto Diary.* Amherst, MA: University of Massachusetts Press, 1990.

Kalba, Myroslav. *Nachtigal, A Battalion of the Ukrainian Nationalists.* Denver, CO: Ukra, 1984 (written and published in Ukrainian).

Kashuba, Steven. *Once Lived a Village.* Victoria, BC: Trafford, 2007.

Ketchum, Richard M. *The Borrowed Years: 1938-1941.* Newport Beach, CA: Books on Tape, 1999 (print and audio CD).

Keyvan, Maria. *The River Hums and Flows.* Toronto: Kyiv Printers, 1985 (written and published in Ukrainian).

Knysh, Zynovij. *In the Lion's Jaws: A Ukrainian in the Polish Underground.* Toronto: Sribna Surma, 1976 (written and published in Ukrainian).

Knysh, Zinovyj. *Dryzhyt Pidzemnyj Huk.* Winnipeg: self-published, 1953 (written and published in Ukrainian).

Knysh, Zinovyj. *Rozbrat: Memoir and Materials Regarding the Split in the OUN in 1940-1941.* Toronto: Sribna Surma, undated (written and published in Ukrainian).

Komar, Luba. *Scratches on a Prison Wall: A Wartime Memoir* (translated by Christine Prokop). New York: iUniverse, 2009.

Kostach, Myrna. *Bloodlines: A Journey into Eastern Europe.* Vancouver: Douglas & McIntyre, 1993.

Krajkiwskyj, Omelian. *Liberators.* Drohobych: Vidrodzhenya, 1998 (written and published in Ukrainian).

Kramer, Clara. *Clara's War.* Toronto: McClelland & Stewart, 2008.

Kubiovych, Volodymyr. *I Am Eighty-Five.* Munich: Molode Zhytia, 1985 (written and published in Ukrainian).

Kulchytsky, Stanislav. *Ukraine between Two Wars (1921–1939), Vol. 2.* Kyiv: Alterativy, 1999 (written and published in Ukrainian).

Lalka, Mykhayla. *Mykhayla Lalka: Autobiographical Sketch.* Toronto: Basilian, 1999.

Lazarowich, Mykola. *Hey, You, Sich Riflemen.* Ternopil: Dzhura, 2004 (written and published in Ukrainian).

Lazorenko, Tymofij. *Memoirs and Thoughts from the Lessons of the History of Socialism.* Kyiv: Vadym Karpenko, 2006 (written and published in Ukrainian).

Lazurko, Roman. *On Europe's Crossroads: Memoirs.* Chicago: Brotherhood of Former Soldiers of the First Ukrainian Division of the Ukrainian National Army, 1971 (written and published in Ukrainian).

Lenkavsky, Stepan et al. *Murdered by Moscow.* London: Ukrainian Publishers, Ltd., 1962.

Selected Bibliography

Levin, Dov. *The Lesser of Two Evils: Eastern European Jewry under Soviet Rule (1931–1941)*. Philadelphia: Research Publications, 1995.

Luciuk, Lubomyr, and Marco Carynnyk, eds. *Between Two Worlds: The Memoirs of Stanley Frolick*. Toronto: Multicultural History Society of Ontario, 1990.

Luciuk, Lubomyr, ed. *Heroes of Their Day: The Reminiscences of Bohdan Panchuk*. Ontario: Multicultural History Society of Ontario, 1983.

Lupul, Manoly R. *The Politics of Multiculturalism: A Ukrainian-Canadian Memoir*. Edmonton/Toronto: Canadian Institute of Ukrainian Studies, 2005.

Lytvyn, Volodomyr. *Ukraine: The Interwar Era (1921–1938)*. Kyiv, Ukraine: Alternatyva Publishers. 2003 (written and published in Ukrainian).

Macchello, Lorraine P. *The Dowry Legacies to an Italian American Daughter*. Grand Rapids, MI: Tramondi Co., 2004.

MacMillan, Margaret. *Six Months That Changed the World: The Paris Peace Conference of 1919*. Prince Frederick, MD: Recorded Books, 2003 (print and audio CD).

Magocsi, Paul R., ed. *Morality and Reality: The Life and Times of Andrei Sheptyts'kyi*. Edmonton: Canadian Institute of Ukrainian Studies, 1989.

Magocsi, Robert. *Ukraine: A Historical Atlas*. Toronto: University of Toronto Press, 1985.

Manning, Clarence. *Ukrainian Resistance: The Story of the Ukrainian National Liberation Movement in Modern Times.* New York: Ukrainian Congress Committee of America, 1949.

Marshall, Robert. *In the Sewers of Lvov: A Heroic Story of Survival from the Holocaust.* New York: Macmillan Co., 1990.

Mazepa, Isaak. *Ukraine in the Fire and Storm of Revolution (1917–1921), Part 1.* Kyiv, Ukraine: Prometej, 1950 (written and published in Ukrainian).

Melnyk, Andrew. My *Grandfather's Mill: Journey to Freedom.* Bloomington, IN: Xlibris, 2008.

Mirchuk, Petro. *Outline of the History of the OUN, Vol. 1 (1920–1939).* Munich: Ukrainian Publishing, 1968.

Mosley, Leonard. *The Reich Marshall: A Biography of Hermann Goering.* Garden City, NJ: Doubleday & Company, 1974.

Mudry, William, ed. *Lviv: A Symposium on Its 700th Anniversary.* Jersey City, NJ: Svoboda, 1962.

Nakonechnyj, Evhen. *Shoa in Lviv: A Memoir.* Lviv, Ukraine: National Academy of Sciences of Ukraine, Lviv Educational Library, 2004 (written and published in Ukrainian).

Olson, Lynne. *Citizens of London: The Americans Who Stood with Britain in its Darkest, Finest Hour.* New York: Tantor Media, 2010 (audio recording).

Olson, Lynne, and Cloud, Stanley. *A Question of Honor: The Kosciuszko Squadron, Forgotten Heroes of World War II.* New York: Random House, 2003.

Pankivskyj, Kost. *The Years of German Occupation (1941–1944)*. New York: Zhytya I Mycli, 1965 (written and published in Ukrainian).

Piotrowski, Tadeusz. *Poland's Holocaust.* Jefferson, NC: McFarland & Company, 1998.

Piotrowski, Tadeusz. *Vengence of the Swallows: Memoir of a Polish Family's Ordeal.* Jefferson, NC: McFarland & Company, 1995.

Potichnyj, Peter J. *My Journey.* Ancaster, ON: self-published, 2012.

Prymak, Thomas M. *Maple Leaf and Trident: The Ukrainian Canadians during the Second World War.* Toronto: Multicultural History Society of Ontario, 1988.

Pyskir, Maria Savchyn. *Thousands of Roads: A Memoir of a Young Woman's Life in the Ukrainian Underground during and after World War II* (original in Ukrainian, translated by Ania Savage). Jefferson, NC: McFarland & Company, 2001.

Radzinsky, Edward. Stalin: *The First In-Depth Biography Based on Explosive New Documents from Russia's Secret Archives.* New York: Random House, 1996.

Recorded interviews with Salomea Drozdowska and Emil and Helen Tyshovnytsky. Los Angeles: 1980s (twelve hours of recorded interviews).

Redlich, Shimon. *Together and Apart in Brzezany: Poles, Jews, and Ukrainians, 1919–1945.* Bloomington: Indiana University Press, 2002.

Rigg, Bryan M. *Hitler's Jewish Soldiers.* Lawrence, KS: University Press of Kansas, 1984.

Roth, Cecil, and Wigoder, Geoffrey, eds. *Encyclopedia Judaica.* New York: Macmillan Co., 1971–1972.

Rubenstein, Joshua, and Altman, Ilya, eds. *The Unknown Black Book: The Holocaust in the German-Occupied Soviet Territories.* Bloomington, IN: Indiana University Press, 2008.

Rudnycka, Milena. *Western Ukraine under the Bolsheviks, 1939–1941.* New York: Shevchenko Scientific Society, 1958.

Savaryn, Peter. *They Brought Ukraine with Them.* Kyiv, Ukraine: self-published, 2007 (written and published in Ukrainian).

Seleshko, Mychajlo. *Vinnitsia: A Memoir of a Translator of a Commission of Inquiry into the Crimes of the NKVD in 1937–1938.* New York: Olzhych Foundation (written and published in Ukrainian).Undated.

Semotiuk, Andriy. *Journals of Andriy Semotiuk: Personal Recollections, 1972–2005* (unpublished).

Sharyk, Mychajlo. *Thorny Trails across Canada.* Vol. 2. Toronto: Toronto Free Press Publishers, 1971 (written and published in Ukrainian).

Shestopal, Matvij. *Jews in Ukraine: A Historical Exploration.* Kyiv, Ukraine: Oriany, 1999 (written and published in Ukrainian).

Snyder, Timothy. *The Red Prince: The Secret Lives of a Habsburg Archduke.* New York: Basic Books, 2008.

Snyder, Timothy. *Bloodlands*. New York: Basic Books, 2010.

Stefanyk, William. *The Stone Cross*. Kharkiv, Ukraine: Folio, 2006 (written and published in Ukrainian).

Steinberg, Mark. *A History of Russia: From Peter the Great to Gorbachev, Part 3*. Chantilly, VA: The Teaching Co., 2003 (print and audio CD).

Struk, Danylo H., ed. *Encyclopedia of Ukraine*. Toronto: University of Toronto, 1993.

Subtelny, Orest. *Ukraine: A History*, third ed. Toronto: Toronto Press, 2005.

Suchoverskyj, Mykola. *My Memories*. Kyiv, Ukraine: Smoloskyp, 1997 (written and published in Ukrainian).

Szende, Stefan. *The Promise Hitler Kept*. New York: Roy, 1945.

Talpash, Orest S. *Rybalski's Son*. Victoria, BC: Trafford, 2008.

Taubman, William. *Khrushchev: The Man and His Era*. Newport Beach, CA: Books on Tape, 1998 (print and audio CD).

Truemer, Diane King. *Hawrelak: The Story*. Calgary: Script Publishing, 1992.

Tymochko-Kaminska, Iryna. *My Odyssey*. Warsaw: Ukrainian Archive, 2005 (written and published in Ukrainian).

Tyshovnytskyi, Emil. *My Mementos*. Los Angeles: self-published, 1974 (written and published in Ukrainian).

Ukrainian Weekly. *The Most Significant News Stories and Commentaries Published in the Ukrainian Weekly, Vol. 1–3.* Ukrainian Weekly: Parsippany, NY: 2000.

Various authors. Various Canadian newspaper articles dealing with Ukrainian Canadian themes, assembled under the leadership of Jars Balan. Canadian Institute for Ukrainian Studies.

Velmans, Edith. *Edith's Story: Courage, Love, and Survival during World War II.* Auburn: The Audio Partners Pub. Corp., 2000.

Veryha, Wasyl. *The Roads of the Second World War: The Halychyna Division.* Toronto: Shevchenko Scientific Society, 1998 (written and published in Ukrainian).

Volchuk, Roman. *Memoir of Post-War Austria and Germany.* Kyiv, Ukraine: Krytyka, 2004 (written and published in Ukrainian).

Volchuk, Roman. *Memoir of Pre-War Lviv and Vienna during War.* Kyiv, Ukraine: Krytyka, 2002 (written and published in Ukrainian).

Volosevych, Olena. *Solomea Krushel'nytska: Cities and Fame.* Lviv, Ukraine: Apriori, 2009 (written and published in Ukrainian).

Voskobijnyk, Oleska. *The Story of My Life.* Kyiv, Ukraine: Vus, 2004 (written and published in Ukrainian).

Vychrystenko, William. *Special Forces in the Genocide in Ukraine.* Odessa, Ukraine: Mayak, 2002 (written and published in Ukrainian).

Vytryvalenko, Y. *Bloodied Roads: A Chronicle of the Twentieth Century.* Parana: Basilian Fathers Printers and Publishers, 1967 (written and published in Ukrainian).

Williamyk, Teodor and Mychajlo Williamyk. *The Barbed Roads of Life: A Memoir.* Ternopil: The National Association of Writers of Ukraine, 2004 (written and published in Ukrainian).

Wistrich, Robert S. *Hitler and the Holocaust.* Prince Frederick, MD: Recorded Books, 2001–2002 (print and audio CD).

Wytwycky, Bohdan. *Other Holocaust: Many Circles of Hell.* Novak Report: New York 1980.

Yones, Eliyahu. *Smoke in the Sand: The Jews of Lvov in the War Years (1939–1944).* Jerusalem: Gefen Publishing House, 2004.

Significant Articles

Himka, John P. "Ethnicity and the Reporting of Mass Murder: Krakivski Visti, the NKVD Murders of 1941, and the Vinnytsia Exhumation." University of Alberta: 2004 (unpublished paper).

Hunczak, Taras. "Metropolitan Andrey Sheptytsky: Savior of Jews During World War II." *Ukrainian Weekly,* 2006.

Lozynsky, Askold. "An Enlightened Liberation Movement" (shared by the author via the Internet, April 29, 2010).

Pancake, John. "In Ukraine, Movement to Honor Members of WWII Underground Sets off Debate." *Washington Post,* January 6, 2010, page A07.

Rud, Victor. "John Pancake's UPA Article on January 6, 2010" (letter to the *Washington Post*).

Stetzko, Jaroslaw. "The Truth about Events in Lviv, West Ukraine, in June and July, 1941." An Open Letter to the *Rheinischer Merkur*, Cologne. Published in *The Ukrainian Review*, a publication of the Association of Ukrainians in Great Britain, Ltd., London, Vol. X, No. 3, autumn 1963.

Viatrovych, Volodymyr. "The Stand of OUN in Regard to the Jews: Formation of a Position on the Backdrop of a Catastrophe." Kyiv, Ukraine: Ukrainian Center, May 4, 2010 as reported in the *The Ukrainian Weekly*..

Zolotareov, Vadim. "The National Composition of the NKVD in the Ukrainian SSR in the Mid-1930s." Journal article from the Archives of the Cheka-GPU-NKVD-KGB, a collaborative effort of the Security Service of Ukraine (SBU), the National Academy of Education of Ukraine (NAN), Institute of Ukrainian History at NAN, and the Ukrainian Government Archive Committee. Kyiv, Ukraine: 1994.

Films

Chemych, Taras. *Golden September: The Galician Chronicles 1939-1941*. Lviv, Ukraine: Western Ukrainian Center of Historical Research, 2010 (DVD).

Acknowledgments

ITHOUT THE HELP of countless individuals who made suggestions, provided insights, added encouragement, and exhibited goodwill to me, I never would have finished this book. There are, however, certain individuals who made outstanding contributions. I would like to mention those I can recall and express my deepest apologies to any I might omit.

I have been married to Ann Semotiuk for more than thirty years. Without her encouragement, patience, and support through all these years—in particular during the last seven or eight years that I devoted to writing this book—I never would have completed this volume. Indeed my writing this book began with a suggestion from her. While I sat at computers in my office and at various Internet cafés over the years, Ann looked after our household, made sure our kids were fed, paid our mortgage, took care of our cat, and fulfilled a thousand other lackluster obligations that kept our lives running smoothly. For all this I am indebted to her without measure. Her example proves the point that behind every successful man there is a surprised woman. I love her dearly and thank her for every moment she spared me and kept me away from day-to-day household chores and other obligations that she assumed so that I could complete this manuscript. I was able to write this book because she was willing to take on the hard work that I was spared. In this sense this book is as much Ann's achievement as it is mine. She also provided me with innumerable valuable suggestions and editing help to get the project done.

Both of my children, Natalie and Mark, made invaluable contributions to this book as well. Natalie repeatedly provided insightful and helpful feedback regarding where I needed to improve the text and which direction to take to do so. Again and again I was surprised by her wisdom and maturity in commenting on my writing. Her words of encouragement helped me continue in moments of doubt, and her demands that I reach no less than the highest levels spurred me on. Her views were so solid, clearly so correct, and so thoughtful that at times I wondered if she had some kind of magical internal compass that directed her thinking. Mark also offered well-thought-out suggestions and encouragement. Knowing the storyline as he did, he was able to make valuable comments that helped keep me on track and improve what I had written. More so than others, Mark provided me with a sense of mission and energy about my work.

It goes without saying that I owe a profound debt of gratitude to my family members who were the subject matter of the book. Salomea Drozdowska, my mother, who raised me as a single parent at a time when that was not easy, and who put me through law school on her hands and knees washing floors, obviously played a key role in my life. Whenever I even pause momentarily to think my life is getting too hard, all I need to do is recall her example to set myself straight. I was so grateful to her for all she did for me that, whenever I visited her in our latter years together, I made it a point to take her hands in mine and kiss them to honor their great contribution to my life.

William Semotiuk left me a shining example of how one man can make a profound difference in someone's life. His contribution to me can best be described by former UN Secretary General Dag Hammarskjöld's statement that "it is more noble to give yourself completely to one individual than to labor diligently for the salvation of the masses." For this reason I will carry William's surname as a badge of honor for the rest of my life.

I am so thankful to the other family members who contributed to my life and therefore to this book. My Aunt Helen was a second mother to me, so good and so unique. She taught me so much about life, particularly not to take people at face value but to probe with my eyes and ears for the real meaning behind what they say or do. She generously shared her wealth of knowledge with me. Whatever shortcomings my father, Jake Holonko, and my uncle, Emil Tyshovnytsky, may have exhibited, overall I am thankful for the contributions they made to my life as well. Jake Holonko was wise enough to leave my mother and me in the arms of William Semotiuk when he saw we were settled there in my youth. I also am thankful to him for his efforts later in his life to reconnect with me, albeit unsuccessfully. In the case of Uncle Emil, I am thankful that he left behind a published memoir in Ukrainian, as well as detailed résumés for himself and Aunt Helen, from which I was able to liberally draw to reconstruct his life story as well as the story of life events that affected my aunt and other members of my family. In that regard I am thankful to Sergeii Medintsev in Kyiv, who translated my uncle's book into English for me to facilitate my work. I am also deeply grateful to my sisters, Mary Smith and Anne Prokopchuk, who recounted their life stories, as well as my other siblings on my father's side mentioned in the book: Walter, Lydia, Gene, and Paul, even though, in the case of the latter two, I was only able to visit their graves in Vancouver and never met them in person.

Of all my friends, Steve Andrusiak, a former television producer and reporter and friend for more than forty years, contributed most to the success of this venture. I am thankful to him for his taking weeks of time out of his busy life to help me hone this book and shape it into a readable format. All this he provided freely and without remuneration. I am especially thankful to him for understanding why I was writing this manuscript and how much it meant to me to pay tribute to my mother and other family members.

On a professional level, I am immeasurably indebted to George Tabah, who is not only a professional writer but also a dear friend who took it upon himself to help me with the rewriting of this book to focus on the story and to delete extraneous material that detracted from it. His work and the numerous suggestions he passed on to me were most helpful in my honing the book down to what it needed to be.

Bohdan Vitvitsky, a US attorney and also a dear friend, contributed his time and wisdom to help me get the story straight and the historical facts right. He spent innumerable hours reviewing what I wrote and cleaning up the text to ensure the narrative rose to an appropriate level. I admire him for his contributions, for his professionalism in helping me, and for his appreciation of what I was trying to do. I know I taxed his patience to the limit, and I am thankful that he endured with me to get me where I needed to go—all at his expense. One would be hard pressed to find someone more decent and professional in his work.

Will Zuzak, a friend from my student days at the University of British Columbia in the 1960s, and a nuclear physicist, was invaluable in helping me clean up and straighten out the narrative of my book. His patience and depth of knowledge of Ukrainian history is astounding. I am especially thankful to him for going through the rough spots in my text and having the endurance to provide guidance regarding how to best deal with them. In hindsight I am embarrassed that so much of the text I submitted to him had to be edited to reach anywhere near acceptable levels. Again his contributions were made willingly and without remuneration. He is a man with the kindest of hearts and the greatest of intellects.

Karen Kwan Anderson, a lawyer and colleague of mine at Pace Law Firm, took the trouble to wade through my manuscript and edit it long before it was in a manageable state. I am grateful to her for her interest, for taking the time to help me, and for providing me with an outsider's view of the book, including where it needed work. Few people have as noble a spirit as hers. Similarly Toni Marsnik, my UCLA writing seminar classmate, colleague, and member of our Los Angeles writers' group, helped me get my act together and was so accurate in her early comments about my book. I am thankful she persisted in the face of my disregard of her advice about overloading the book with history at the expense of the story. It took me a while to appreciate what she was saying, but I am grateful that she drove the point home with me so I eventually was able to shape the book into the form it took.

Acknowledgments

Similarly Fran Turner, my Humber College summer writers' workshop classmate, colleague, and friend in Toronto,
helped me greatly with her targeted suggestions over months
of exchanges. Her wisdom and Czech background, from which
she was able to identify with my Ukrainian background, helped
to make her points particularly useful to me. Good suggestions
from Ester Zirkind, Dew Williams and Marg Krutow, the other
members of my writer's group, were appreciated.

Antanas Sileika, the program director of Humber College's
School for Writers in Toronto, was particularly helpful in steering me toward writing goals that I needed to attain to make my
book marketable. He helped me understand the importance
of the introduction in a book and how to present this book in
a way that measures up to today's writing standards. On many
occasions Antanas took time from his workday to answer my
e-mail inquiries, even though I was not his student and even
though I was a complete stranger to him. I am not the only person who has benefited from his charitable and giving disposition and his talented insights into what makes for good writing.
All the writers Antanas has helped over many years owe him a
great debt of gratitude. He is one of a kind in this world and is
known widely for his generosity. I am also grateful to Al Pace,
my boss at Pace Law Firm in Toronto, for understanding the
importance of this book to me and for introducing Antanas to
me.

There were several people whose reflections on the history
of Galicia were of enormous help to me in piecing together the
narrative for my book.

Myron Stefaniw of Edmonton, a lifelong friend and a walking encyclopedia of Ukrainian affairs, shared his excellent memory of international political events in the twentieth century,

life in Galicia between the two World Wars as well as during World War II, and the immigrant experience in Canada in order to fill in many details in my book that I otherwise never would have been able to find. He was like a second father to me, and time and time again, at various social meetings over the years, we happily spent hours together discussing those price-less memories he was able to recall. His insights into the life of Ukrainians under Poland, the mistreatment of Ukrainians under the Soviets and Nazis, and his experiences passing by the Jewish ghetto in his hometown of Kolomeya and observing the mistreatment of Jews by the Nazis were particularly relevant and powerful.

Another leading individual in this regard was Oksana Zazulia, another lifelong friend from Los Angeles. She provided me with a firsthand recollection of many events from the World War II period in Galicia that no one else could have provided, such as how she repeatedly was stopped by the NKVD for the sake of invoking terror in her, as well as the insight that her grandfather, who was a judge, probably had been saved by the Jews of Galicia, with whom he had excellent relations before the war. Oksana was such a solid source of historical informa-tion and wisdom that to this day I count her as one of the great-est blessings in my life.

Among other individuals who shared their life stories in World War II in Lviv with me was Alexandra Blawacka, a friend of my mother's who lived in Lviv through the war. She was par-ticularly helpful in recalling the mistreatment of Ukrainians by the Soviets, the Nazis persecution of the Jews, the reasons for the helplessness of the Ukrainian population as a minority in Poland to do much in regard to the German excesses, and the help that the Ukrainian community of Galicia sought to extend to Soviet Ukraine in 1933 when it learned of the great famine there. Ivanka Markovska, another friend of my mother's who lived in Lviv, was also able to recall the Soviet atrocities first-hand. I remember Ivanka taking me out to a barren field in Lviv in 1974 while I visited her with my mother; she cupped her hand over my ear and whispered her life story, in particular the events that had led to the death of her husband in an army bunker. She showed me how she had survived under the Soviets by mimicking a zipper being zipped up across her lips and confessed that she dared not tell her son, who was my age at the time, how his father had died, for fear that her son would be persecuted by the Soviet Union even then, some thirty years after the war, for accidentally admitting that his father had been a Ukrainian patriot. Iryna Polotnianka, a neighbor of ours in Los Angeles, shared her reflections of Lviv and Ukraine with me on her deathbed a few years ago, telling me how appalled she and others in her community were by the events in Ukraine during the famine and by the Soviet mistreatment of Ukrainians in Lviv while it was under occupation during the war. Myroslaw and Larysa Skoryk, my family members living in Kyiv, shared similar stories with me when we visited them in the mid-1970s. While they weren't adults during the war years, they were able to pass on stories from the lives of other members of our family. On this side of the Atlantic, Ernie Semotiuk and Mary Bennett helped me with stories related to our family in Alberta and were people through which I was able to learn more about William's family life.

One other invaluable source of historical information was the Solomea Krushelnytska Museum in Lviv, in particular one of its researchers, Lesia Kyryk. Lesia was able to reconstruct many of the missing facts in my family's life story by virtue of my family's connection to the museum and the building formerly owned by Solomea Krushelnytska. I am immeasurably indebted to her and the museum for their work and support.

Several individuals opened my eyes when it came to the 1932–1933 Ukrainian *Holodomor* (famine) and the impact of Soviet life on Ukrainians. Among the more prominent were author Eugenia Dallas of Los Angeles and Professor Yars Slavutych of Edmonton, both of who lived through the genocide. Others who filled me in on facts include Peter Borisow of Los Angeles, who lost many of his family members in the tragedy, and Andriy Bandera, the son of Ukrainian nationalist leader Stepan Bandera, who was assassinated by a Soviet NKVD secret service agent. In the early 1970s, Andriy first drew my attention to the facts about the artificial famine.

Several sources were critical to my understanding the circumstances of Poles, Ukrainians, and Jews during World War II, as well as the Holocaust as it played out in Galicia. The most helpful were John Lahola of Edmonton and Stefan Petelycky of Vancouver, both Ukrainian survivors of Auschwitz. My extensive conversations with them over the years helped me better understand the conflict between Ukrainians and Jews during World War II. My visits to Yad Veshem in Jerusalem (and especially its video of Brygitky Prison burning during the war), the Auschwitz and Dachau concentration camp museums, the Museum of Tolerance in Los Angeles, and the USC Shoa Foundation also shed light on these issues. I am particularly thankful to Askold Lozynsky, an attorney in New York, who has written extensively on these topics and whose father was in Auschwitz; historian Lubomyr Luciuk, who has written on both the *Holodomor* and the Holocaust on many occasions; Marco Carrynyk, an author and writer in Toronto, who was especially helpful to me by sharing some of his research findings and photographs related to the persecution of Jews by Ukrainians in Galicia during the war; and Professor John Paul Himka of Edmonton, for sharing some of his articles with me and also for lending me his original copies of the newspaper *Krakiwsky*

Visti from the war period. I also am thankful to Juri Darevych, for his contributions on this subject through his work as the head of the Human Rights Commission of the Ukrainian World Congress, and Professor Roman Serbyn of Montreal, for his articles on these themes over the years. I also have consulted with—or discussed materials in this book and obtained guidance from—the following individuals: Dr. Bohdan Klid of Edmonton; Dr. Roman Petryshyn of Edmonton; Lubomyr Markevych, a Canadian lawyer in Kyiv; Bohdan Romaniuk, a Canadian lawyer in Calgary; Roman Kupchinsky, the former head of Radio Liberty and Prolog of Washington, DC; Dory Tovstiuk, a dear friend in Edmonton; Dr. Jaroslaw and Olya Grod of Toronto; Peter Smilsky, a Canadian lawyer in Kyiv; Bohdan Futala of Los Angeles; Bohdan Sirant a lifelong friend from Toronto; and Dr. Jaroslaw Pikolycky of La Jolla, California. I have had the good fortune of engaging in many discussions with all these individuals over the years to clarify my understanding of the events I describe in this book.

Jars Balan at the Canadian Institute of Ukrainian Studies at the University of Alberta was most helpful in providing me access to news stories about the lives of members of the Ukrainian community in Canada. Jas and Amrit Mangat, my soul brother and sister in Canada, were very helpful in listening to my family stories, commenting on them, and providing me encouragement to write the book. A number of people helped me by participating in writing groups in which I was a member. These include Kristin Martin, Terry Schmidt, Teri Graves, and Marcia Feldt Bates. Caroline Megechaen, a Humber College Writing School student, contributed useful editing observations and suggestions. Victor Malarek and Sean Berry helped me locate literary agents, and for this I am also much indebted.

While preparing this book, I employed a number of editors to help me. These include Shreeja Dayand and the Hi-Tech Group in India; Ilona Specht, my former legal secretary and faithful go-to editor for several decades; Evelyn Gabai, whose goodwill I was fortunate to have when asking her to edit rough, raw, materials I needed to clean up; Melissa Fraser, who helped immeasurably with my bibliography; Carolyn Walker from my *Writer's Digest* course, who provided helpful suggestions, corrections, and observations regarding my text; author Myroslaw Petriw, who helped edit early drafts of the manuscript; and Orest Martynovych and Taras Kurylo, historians and experts on various aspects of Ukrainian life in Eastern Europe who helped me get the historical events in the book straight. Create Space was immeasurably helpful in bringing this book to publication and I thank all their editors, designers and staff for their wonderful work.

As much as I appreciated the help and guidance of all these individuals, I alone am responsible for any inaccuracies or errors in this book.

In addition to these individuals and the books I have listed in my bibliography, I also have numerous family letters, documents, and pictures from which I was able to draw a great deal of information. A good friend, Dr. Walter Maksymovych, generously gave me dozens of hours of videotaped television news programs about important historical events, such as the Ukrainian declaration of independence and the opening of the Berlin Wall, which were very helpful. Without a plan to write this book in mind, many years ago I recorded approximately twelve hours of audio and videotapes involving interviews with my family members. This turned out to be an invaluable asset when I found the tapes some twenty years later. In addition, for the last forty years, I have maintained a personal diary in which I've recorded important family events and historical information of our lives together. I was able to use all of these resources to help fill in important details in the narrative.

Notes

1   There was also a son, Yarko, who died in infancy from an unknown illness in Pidhajci.

2   Maryna Drozdowska served as a cook for the Sich Riflemen (*Sochovjy Striltsi*) in Drohobych during the war. They were the most intellectually enlightened and nationally patriotic Ukrainian young men and even women brought together into a military unit to fight for a united and free Ukraine. Drohobych was their center of operations. Initially they fought in the Austrian army until Austria-Hungary fell apart, and then they unsuccessfully sought to establish a Ukrainian state.

3   Chajkivskyj, Bohdan. *The Chessboard of My Life.* New York: self-published, 2007, 73.

4   I am indebted to Alexandra Blawacka, a family member in Lviv, who recounted these family facts to me while I visited there in the 1970s, and also to my Aunt Helen. For more commentary on this, see Voskobijnyk, Oleska. *The Story*

of My Life. Kyiv, Ukraine: Vus, 2004 (written/published in Ukrainian). The deception of the USSR and its refusal to acknowledge that a famine was taking place in Ukraine at the time is now generally recognized by historians, particularly because of revelations in articles by journalists such as Malcolm Muggeridge and Gareth Jones.

5 In 1991, after the breakup of the Soviet Union, more information becamsebecame available about the genocide from the archives of the communist party and the Ukrainian NKVD secret police. These documents provided a clearer picture of what many knew to be true from anecdotal evidence, even back in 1933 in Lviv, namely that millions of people had perished in a manmade famine initiated by Stalin in Soviet Ukraine.

In the fall of 1932, the NKVD consisting of many Russians, Jews (who often held leading positions in the Bolshevik party and the secret police,) and Ukrainians came to Ukrainian villages demanding grain and livestock to meet unrealistic Soviet quotas. Those who resisted were shot. For more details related to the genocide see: Subtelny, Orest. *Ukraine: A History*, Toronto: U of T Press, 3rd Edition, 2000. Pages 363 and 413-424. Snyder, Timothy, *Bloodlands: Europe Between Hitler and Stalin*. New York: Basic Books, 2010. Pages 21–58. Shestopal, Matvij. *Jews in Ukraine - A Historical Exploration*. Kyiv: Oriany, 1999. Print. Written/ Published in Ukrainian. P 124. Ivan Krypiakevych Institute of Ukrainian Studies of the National Academy of Sciences of Ukraine, *Lviv Historical Essays*, Lviv: Published by the Academy, 1996. Page 463. I am also indebted to Proessor Yars Slavutych and Natalia Talanchuk of Edmonton and Eugenia Dallas or Los Angeles, among other survivors of the famine, for their eye witness accounts of events related to me in person.

A subsequent directive from Stalin and Molotov sealed Ukrainian borders to prevent starving peasants from escaping. Armed guards blocked any escape with orders to shoot to kill. Travelers were searched for food. Even a single loaf of bread was seized and the "smugglers" punished. The artificial famine that ensued came to be known as the *Holodomor*—made up of the Ukrainian words *"holod,"* meaning "famine," and *"mor,"* meaning "death."

According to Winston Churchill's *History of the Second World War,* when Churchill visited Stalin in the Kremlin in August 1942, he asked him, "Have the stresses of the war been as bad to you personally as carrying through the policy of the collective farms?" "Oh, no," Stalin said. "The collective farm policy was a terrible struggle.... Ten million," he said, holding up his hands. "It was fearful. Four years it lasted." Stalin went on to say that, apart from a minority of the people that were exiled, the vast majority perished.

While Soviet leaders hid the truth and used sanitized language when talking about their policies, Western journalists, such as Walter Duranty of *The New York Times,* wrote articles that cast doubts on claims that starvation was occurring in Ukraine. Later research in British archives by Western historians uncovered that William Strang, a diplomat at the British embassy in Moscow, had a conversation with Duranty in September 1933 about the famine after Mr. Duranty had returned from Ukraine and the North Caucasus. According to this research, Strang stated, "Mr. Duranty thinks it quite possible that as many as ten million people may have died directly or indirectly from lack of food in the Soviet Union during the past year." See Strang, William; British Embassy, Moscow, to Sir John Simon; Sept. 26, 1933, "Tour by Mr. W. Duranty in North Caucasus and the Ukraine"; *The Foreign Office and the Famine: British Documents on Ukraine and the Great Famine of 1932–1933*; Carynnyk, Marco; Luciuk, Lubomyr; and Kordan, Bohdan S.; Kingston, ON: The Limestone Press, 1988, 313.

Duranty never told the world about those who perished, even though he was a Pulitzer Prize–winning writer in journalism for his stories about Soviet life.

A debate centers on the number of victims of the *Holodomor*. For example see John Paul Himka's "Untruths Tarnish Holodomor Tragedy," an article in the *Kyiv Post*, May 15, 2008, in which the author estimates that between 2.5 and 3.5 million perished. Contrast this to Askold Lozynsky's "Historical Evidence Proves 7 to 10 million Holodomor Casualties," an article in the *Kyiv Post*, May 15, 2008. According to Timothy Snyder's book *Bloodlands* (p. 411), conservatively 3.3 million perished. Other demographers and historians estimate that approximately 3.5 to four million people starved to death in Ukraine. More recent work of Ukrainian-American demographer Dr. Oleh Wolowyna and his research group has established the figure of almost 4 million deaths in Soviet Ukraine which he presented in his 2010 famine lecture at the University of Toronto on November 9th, 2010 and which was reported by Ukrainian Echo newspaper on December 2nd, 2010. This does not include almost one million indirect deaths with the total losses reported by Wolowyna as 4,890,700.

Added to that were some 3.5 million others targeted in the Kuban and Volga regions, which were also heavily

Ukrainian-populated parts of the former Soviet Union. These numbers align with a report of *Izvestia*, the official newspaper of the Soviet Government, which reported in 1935 that "it is likely that seven million have perished." See *Ukrainian Weekly, The Ukrainian Weekly 2000, Vol. 1.* Parsippany NY: Ukrainian Weekly, 2000,

The truth was exposed in the years that followed. Raphael Lemkin, the father of the 1948 United Nations Convention on the Prevention and Punishment of the Crime of Genocide, acknowledged that the artificial famine in Ukraine was genocide. Historians and researchers such as Robert Conquest, James Mace, Stanislaw Kulchytsky, and others dug up evidence to prove that the genocide was real, and in later years the governments of a dozen countries, including the United States and Canada, made public statements to that effect.

If ever there was evidence of a need for Ukrainians to have a free, independent democratic state to protect them from Moscow's malevolence, the *Holodomor* is it.

6 It is important not to overlook the deaths of millions of Ukrainians who lived in areas adjacent to Soviet Ukraine, such as Kuban and the northern Caucasus, that were primarily populated by Ukrainians in calculating the numbers who died. When these people are added in, the numbers mentioned in this passage stand up to scrutiny.

7 I am indebted to many authors whose books helped me reconstruct the events of the war. Among these were Martin Gilbert's *A History of the Twentieth Century*, Richard Ketchum's *The Borrowed Years*, Norman Davies's *No Simple Victory: World War II in Europe 1939–1945*, Patrick Buchanan's *Churchill,*

Hitler, and the Unnecessary War: How Britain Lost Its Empire and the West Lost the World, Robert Farrell's *Harry S. Truman,* Evhen Nakonechnyj's *Shoa in Lviv: A Memoir,* and Orest Subtelny's *Ukraine: A History.*

8   Fishman, Lala, and Weingartner, Steven. *Lala's Story.* Evanston, IL: Northwestern University Press, 1997, 84. Blawacka, Alexandra. *Chronicle of My Life.* Lviv, Ukraine, and Kyiv, Ukraine: International Economic Foundation, 2010 (written and published in Ukrainian), 89-96.

9   Ibid. I am indebted to the descriptions of Lviv found in Lala's Story and Chronicle of My Life as well as to conversations with my Aunt Helen in her later life for the details provided in this passage.

10 Jachnenko, Natalia. *From the Office to Brygitky.* Munich: Author's Publication, 1986 (written and published in Ukrainian). I am deeply indebted to Jachnenko, not only for her insights into the discussions that took place during the Soviet occupation, but also for her observations regarding the conduct of the various nationalities during the transitions involving Soviet and then later Nazi troops invading Lviv.

11 Nakonechnyj, Evhen. *Shoa in Lviv: A Memoir.* Lviv, Ukraine: National Academy of Sciences of Ukraine, Lviv Educational Library, 2004 (written and published in Ukrainian) 70-71.

12 Ibid., 62.

13 Isajevych, Jaroslav. *The History of Lviv, Vol. 3.* Lviv, Ukraine: Tsenter Evropy, 2007 (written and published in Ukrainian), 201-202. According to statistics kept by the

National Memorial Museum of Victims of the Occupation Regimes (*Tyurma na Lonskoho*) in Lviv, approximately four thousand prisoners perished in the prisons of Lviv at the hands of the NKVD in June 1941 and approximately twenty thousand throughout Western Ukraine.

14 Jachnenko, ibid., 229. In fact the NKVD was waiting for final orders regarding what to do with their captives. Earlier, on Monday, June 23, 1941, Lavrenti Beria, head of the NKVD, issued an order to evacuate all of the prisoners to the East. In view of the lack of suitable transportation and the approaching front, however, two commissars from Kyiv, T. Strokach and I. Tkachenko, proposed to change the order and sought agreement from Moscow to set the criminal prisoners free while shooting all the political prisoners. The response was a telegram from Moscow directing them to do just that, signed by Nikita Khrushchev. This was the same man who later became the leader of the USSR and drew world attention in 1960 by pounding his shoe on a desk at a meeting of the Security Council at the United Nations in New York. He would go on to challenge President John F. Kennedy in the Cuban Missile Crisis in 1962. See Isajevych, Jaroslav. *The History of Lviv, Vol. 3.* Lviv, Ukraine: Tsenter Evropy, 2007 (written and published in Ukrainian), 172, 202.

15 Ivan Krypiakevych Institute of Ukrainian Studies of the National Academy of Sciences of Ukraine. *Lviv Historical Essays.* Lviv, Ukraine: National Academy of Sciences of Ukraine, 1996 (written and published in Ukrainian), 460–463.

16 Isajevych, ibid., 202. On the evening of June 26, 1941, the Soviet Commander of the Thirteenth Convoy Division, Colonel Zavjalov, reported to Commissar V. Serhijenko, and

the head of the prison administration NKVD agent of the Ukrainian Soviet Socialist Republic A. Filipov in Moscow, that the order to liquidate the prisoners had been fulfilled.

17 Isajevych, ibid., 202.

20 Nakonechnyj, ibid, 102–103.

19 Jachnenko, ibid., 242–243.

20 Nakonechnyj, ibid., 106.

21 Yones, Eliyahu. *Smoke in the Sand: The Jews of Lvov in the War Years 1939–1944.* Jerusalem: Gefen Publishing House, 2004, 79–80.

22 Yones, ibid., 81. According to Jachnenko, however, the pogrom did not reach full swing and was inspired by the Germans, who allowed hoodlums to cause mayhem to the Jews. See Jachnenko, ibid., 246.

23 Isajevych, ibid., 203.

24 Similar atrocities took place in other parts of Galicia. According to Soviet documents, the NKVD shot approximately 9,700 political prisoners in prisons in Galicia just before the Soviets retreated. Other reports place the number at close to nineteen thousand. It is now clear that the Soviet information bureau in the beginning of August 1941 issued a special communiqué in which it "informed" the world that in Lviv jails that were under German occupation thousands of prisoners and Soviet citizens had been shot without cause. The same communiqué also contended that the Soviet shooting of some twenty thousand Polish officers

in the Katyn forest, as well as Soviet atrocities in Vinnitsa, were all to be blamed on the Germans.

In actuality dead bodies were found in twenty-two cities, towns, and villages throughout Western Ukraine. Throughout Western Ukraine more than forty thousand people were killed. Coming on the heels of mass deportations and growing Soviet terror, these executions greatly exacerbated Western Ukrainian abhorrence of the Soviets. As Germany occupied more and more of the Soviet Union, and Ukraine in particular, more Soviet atrocities, particularly in jails, became apparent.

25 Yones, ibid., 128. See the reprint of the decree in the picture pages with the date July 8, 1941.

26 Jachnenko, ibid., 244.

27 I was able to clarify this point by corresponding with the staff of the Solomea Krushelnytska Museum in Lviv. In particular I was reassured of my conclusion on this matter by Lesia Kyryk, a key staff member who has worked in the museum for more than thirty years, who researched it for me.

28 Pankivskyj, Kost. *The Years of German Occupation* (1941–1944). New York: Zhytya I Mycli, 1965 (written and published in Ukrainian), 406.

29 Isajevych, ibid., 213.

30 Yones, ibid., 215.

31 No German employer could use Jewish workers without the *Arbeitsamt* acting as an intermediary. Failure to report was ruthlessly punished. Furthermore, the police published the following warning on June 3, 1943.

Warning!

In regard to the event that occurred, our previous notices concerning the injunction against bringing Jews into the homes and apartments of non-Jews are presented here for the public's attention. Anyone who shelters a Jew, provides him with food, or conceals him outside the quarter designated for Jews' residence will be subject to the death penalty, as stipulated in paragraph 3 of the Higher SS and Police Leader General Government ordinance, concerning the establishment of residential quarters for Jews, of November 10, 1942. In accordance with this provision, anyone who has knowledge of such an event, such as a landlord, building manager, apartment owner, or sub-lessor, must inform the police thereabout. All of them are tasked with assuring that no Jew find shelter in any houses or apartments whatsoever. Knowledge of the illegal presence of Jews must be reported to the nearby police station. However, those who give information about the concealment of a Jew will be rewarded. The size of the reward will be determined by the Higher SS and Police Leader. Lviv, June 3, 1943

Governor of Galicia District

Commander of Police and SS

Signed: Katzmann

SS-Gruppenführer

and Police Lieutenant-General

Yones, ibid., 233–234.

32 Kahane, David. *Lvov Ghetto Diary*. Amherst: University of Massachusetts Press, 49, 72. Note that according to Hrytsak, the Nazi reaction for helping Jews in the East was more severe and included punishing entire families, unlike in the West, where the Nazis were more lenient with transgressors. (See page 132.)

33 Yones. ibid., 88. For Jews to have a job meant the difference between life and death at this time.

34 Bilas, Lev. *Looking Back: 1922–2002*. Lviv, Ukraine: National Academy of Sciences of Ukraine, Ivan Krypiakevych Institute, 2005 (written and published in Ukrainian), 151.

35 Karliv, later renamed Prutivka by Soviet authorities because it lay on the bank of the Prut River, was a village of 1,500 inhabitants who together owned 1,000 acres of land in the south-eastern corner of Galicia.

36 Before my mother came on the scene, William had made two other efforts to help him with his needs.

His first effort to find someone who could help him involved Olya Korolchuk, a young nurse stationed in Liberetz, Czechoslovakia, following the war. She came to Canada in 1948 but only stayed with William a few months before she decided to seek work as a nurse. Since she was not a strong English speaker, when William took her to the Association of Alberta Nurses, they said she would need to move to a Ukrainian-speaking area. That is how she ended up in Smoky Lake, Alberta, where she ultimately married Petro Kurylo, a local veterinarian.

Later, in telling me her story, Olya expressed her gratitude for William's sponsorship, for his help, and for his understanding of her circumstances.

Following Olya's departure, William resolved to sponsor someone else to help him. He responded to an ad in the Canadian press placed by Ivan Keyvan, who was looking for a sponsor to bring his family to Canada. William had come from Karliw, the same village as Keyvan, and at one time had served in the Austrian army with Keyvan's father. William therefore agreed to file the sponsorship papers for the Keyvans and to pay for their voyage.

The Keyvans arrived in Edmonton on December 5, 1949. The first days after their arrival were filled with lengthy conversations. William wanted to hear everything about his native village. He inquired at length about everyone in Karliw and anything Keyvan could remember. William had left his wife behind in Karliw and of course wanted to hear about her, as well as his friends and neighbors.

The Keyvans spent one winter with William. After that a disagreement broke out between them about what Keyvan should do in terms of work. Soon afterward the Keyvans moved out on their own.

After the Keyvans left William's household, a letter came for Keyvan's wife, Maria. William personally delivered it to her. Maria invited him to stay for supper, and the previous conflict that had arisen between William and the family subsided. They reestablished a friendship until William's death. Later Ivan Keyvan wrote a touching obituary of the life of William Semotiuk, for which we were very thankful.

37 Many people in North America who come from non-English backgrounds struggle with the problem of their name and their ethnic identity. Jake Holonko is an example.

I believe that his name in Ukrainian was Jakym Holowka but that he Anglicized it to Jake Holonko. This belief stems from the first revelation of his name to me from my mother. In the passage I describe here, the woman at the farm mentioned Jake Holonko. Clearly this is the name he used in Canada and was known by there. For the longest time, I could not reconcile why my mother would call him "Holowka," which is a more typical name in Ukrainian than "Holonko." After all one would think my mother would know the name of the man she slept with and whose child she bore. Was it a matter of her deafness and her not registering his proper name? While that might have been a plausible answer, it didn't make sense to me, knowing my mother as I did. She was not easily mistaken or fooled, nor was she gullible.

The quandary was made even more confusing when I saw graves in Ukraine with the name "Holon'ko" on them. I noted that the letter "n" was softened, and thus the apostrophe was included. This appeared to confirm that my father had used the name "Holon'ko" (with a soft "n" unlike in Canada) even back in Ukraine. More recently however, an explanation came to me.

These graves had English names on their gravestones. Why would Ukrainian graves have English names? They were obviously placed there by someone who spoke English.

Could it be that the names had been Anglicized? Is it possible that his surname really was "Holowka" in the past, and this is why my mother used that name? This is the best answer I could come up with to solve this question. It is a question I still need to study.

As I return to the matter of names and identity in North America in general, however, there are a variety of ways immigrants and their offspring deal with the issue. Some stay true to the names they used in their former homeland and accept this daily challenge as part of being true to their past. Some change their names completely, adopting Anglo names, and pretty much abandon their past identity or perhaps only acknowledge it when asked or challenged about it.

Many Anglicize their names or try to find a happy medium that does not abandon their name or identity but softens the day-to-day abrasiveness of using their name in a North American cultural environment that is not overly receptive to "foreign-sounding" names. This was the case, for example, with Ray Hnatyshyn, Canada's first Ukrainian-Canadian governor general. His actual name was Ramon Hnatyshyn, but he used "Ray" for the sake of expedience. It was Hnatyshyn who persuaded me to adopt the name Andy as my nickname in the working world. This is also the route I have chosen in writing this book; I adopted the Anglicized names the various individuals used in their lives in North America. In the case of my family members, however, I hasten to add that despite this accommodation to the country to which they immigrated, or in which their children were raised, they strongly identified with their cultural background, which heavily influenced their identities as individuals. I believe this is a problem common to Chinese, Indian, Filipino, African, and Latin American immigrants to North

America, and that the options I describe are true for them as well.

38 Volosevych, Olena. *Solomea Krushel'nytska: Cities and Fame.* Lviv, Ukraine: Apriori, 2009 (written and published in Ukrainian) 103–105.

Index

Index

Made in the USA
Charleston, SC
15 March 2014